UNPAPERED

UNPAPERED

Writers Consider Native American
Identity and Cultural Belonging

Edited by Diane Glancy
and Linda Rodriguez

UNIVERSITY OF NEBRASKA PRESS   LINCOLN

Acknowledgments for the use of copyrighted material appear on
page 229, which constitutes an extension of the copyright page.

The University of Nebraska Press is part of a land-grant institution
with campuses and programs on the past, present, and future
homelands of the Pawnee, Ponca, Otoe-Missouria, Omaha, Dakota,
Lakota, Kaw, Cheyenne, and Arapaho Peoples, as well as those
of the relocated Ho-Chunk, Sac and Fox, and Iowa Peoples.

Library of Congress Cataloging-in-Publication Data
Names: Glancy, Diane, editor. | Rodriguez, Linda, editor.
Title: Unpapered: writers consider Native American identity and
cultural belonging / edited by Diane Glancy and Linda Rodriguez.
Other titles: Writers consider Native American
identity and cultural belonging
Description: Lincoln: University of Nebraska Press,
[2023] | Includes bibliographical references.
Identifiers: LCCN 2022045684
ISBN 9781496235008 (paperback)
ISBN 9781496236388 (epub)
ISBN 9781496236395 (pdf)
Subjects: LCSH: Indians of North America—Ethnic identity. | Indians
of North America—Tribal citizenship. | Cherokee Indians—Ethnic
identity. | Cherokee Indians—Tribal citizenship. | United States—Race
relations. | BISAC: SOCIAL SCIENCE / Ethnic Studies / American
/ Native American Studies | SOCIAL SCIENCE / Demography
Classification: LCC E98.E85 U57 2023 | DDC 305.897—dc23/eng/20221007
LC record available at https://lccn.loc.gov/2022045684

Set in Adobe Text by Mikala R. Kolander.
Designed by N. Putens.

We dedicate this collection of voices discussing Native identity to Margaret Noodin and all of the many unpapered Native people who have made major contributions to their tribes and to the larger Native community through the years.

INAWENDIWIN / GENEALOGY

In Ojibwe the word for relative is "inawemaagan," literally "one who speaks a similar way." I have come to know who I am through both oral and written histories shared with respect within and beyond our own families and communities. I am not a member of an indigenous nation, but I am a keeper of several languages and can share stories of the relatives who spoke those languages before me.

Nimbaswewe ezhi-inawewaad
gakina indinawemaaganibaniig
indaanikoobijiganibaniig, ingitiziimag
niniijaanisag, indaanikoobijiganag
mazina'iganing, mazinaaziganing
mikwenimagwaa izhisemigag.

Indebweyendaan iidog
anama'aawinan, zibiingwaanan
gii-nibwaakaawaad zoongang
ji-dagotood ziinzibaakwad
ji-dabazitood zaka'igewin
bagidendang gaye ziigwebinang.

Aanind gegoon gidonji-gikendaamin
gii-ozhibii'amowaad mazina'iganing
bakaan gegoon wenji-nisidotamang
gii-dibaajimowaad maawanji'iding.
Aabideg ina daa-bimaadiziyang akiing ge
gii-wiindamaagwag gaye waabanjigaadeg?

I echo the voices
of all my relations
ancestors, parents
children, descendants
on paper, in pictures
and in memories across time.

I believe in their
prayers and tears
their enduring wisdom about
when to add sweetness and
when to escape from the fire
when to make offerings or pour things away.

Some things we know
through documentation
other things we understand
through shared narration.
We must shape our lives based on both
what has been said and what can be seen.
—Margaret Noodin

CONTENTS

Diane Glancy

Introduction

You know, the animals had a ball game. They had no ball or bat or uniforms. How could they play with nothing? The day was dusty. The wind blew. They picked up dirt clods they hit with long sticks. They ran bases. There was the clamor of voices. All the noise and motion of a game. Their stories came together on a windy day. These words they claim as part of the game.

"What do we do with them?" the government leaders asked. Those Indians-in-the-way when they came. The fierce tribes that had opposed them for three centuries. The forces that had defeated England were having trouble moving into the new land they claimed as their own. A place of disruption, defeat. The Indian was making progress more difficult than it should have been. Through the seventeenth, eighteenth, and nineteenth centuries, the Indian impeded. They withstood the advances of the European. Crossing open land in wagon trains under harsh elements and hardships should have been enough. But Indian attacks were too much. The Indian had to be exterminated. In one way or another. The government began to remove them to make room for settlers. They sent the Indian on long marches. If the Plains Indian depended on the buffalo for survival, the soldiers murdered the herds. If a tribe depended on and honored their sheep, the soldiers killed the sheep. They destroyed crops. They put the Indian children in boarding schools to educate and evangelize. As of late 2021, the bones of over seven thousand children have been recovered from the grounds of boarding schools in the United States and Canada. The government stamped them as undesirable. Took their land. Broke treaties. Left them rations with weevils. Withheld annuities for ceded land. Four hundred Chippewa died at Sandy Lake, Minnesota, in the winter of 1850–51 waiting for provisions that corrupt officials withheld. Let the winter kill them.

Later the government set up tables with sign-up sheets. Took a census. Arbitrary and yet somewhat thorough, for those who agreed to sign up. It was a way to distribute homesteads to the Cherokee, Creek, Choctaw, Chickasaw, and Seminole in Indian Territory. It was also a game of manipulation. To confuse. Divide. To incite infighting. To separate Native tribes. To separate those within tribes. Turn them against one another. Set up the bases and let them keep score. Let them fight it out among themselves. Leave loopholes that could be taken advantage of. Leave them in poverty and imposed shame. To skid across the lap of the nation. To skim. To be made mascots. The Atlanta Braves, for instance, in 2021 *tomahawk-chopped* their way to the World Series without knowing that the last of the Plains Indian warriors, sent to Fort Marion Prison in St. Augustine, Florida, between 1875 and 1878, passed through Atlanta. Neither do the Kansas City Chiefs know those same warriors passed through Kansas City on their way to prison in St. Augustine.

That is part of the story, anyway. But the Indian was not eradicated. They survived the decimation. They began again with nothing—and the power of their stories.

These essays in *Unpapered* look at stories of Native identity. There are many voices. Many styles of writing. From academic to narrative to the use of traditional story. The writers share their oralities of indeterminacy. Quandary. Resistance. They speak of experience and memory, sharing a commonality in the different pieces that address the complexity of issues. To extend the baseball metaphor, tribal enrollment is a close call. Those signed up who were. Those signed up who weren't. There were those who did not sign up at all. Enrollment was a government program after all—to account for the Native population. To register into tribal groups. Yet many writers who identify culturally and, to some degree, are recognized as Native Americans do not hold tribal citizenship for many reasons.

In *Real Indians, Identity and the Survival of Native America*, Eva Marie Garroutte writes of the changing rules that determine racial identity. She says that more heated debates are ahead.

This collection resembles a sandlot game, without referee or formality. It addresses unclear issues—who is in, who is out. The dust still rises around family mix-ups. Convoluted stories of bloodlines. Everyone on their different bases. Everyone with their different explanation tales. There are the self-identified. There is also the controversy of the Pretendian who takes academic positions and awards belonging to those enrolled in Indian nations. Dr. Circe Sturm's *Blood Politics* and *Becoming Indian: The Struggle over Cherokee Identity in the Twenty-first Century* describes the threat of the "race shifter" to Native sovereignty.

Citizenship is a legal and political matter of sovereign nations, usually dependent on blood quantum, or a list of names such as the Dawes Rolls, instituted by the U.S. government in the late nineteenth century. For some, only matrilineal lines are considered. For others, the most common determinate of acceptance is being claimed by one's community, including involvement with the community and language. Dr. Kim TallBear suggests the term "identity" should be replaced with "kinship" or "relations" because self-identification is not the same as interaction with the Native community to which one claims to belong. In *God Is Red: A Native View of Religion*, the Dakota scholar Vine Deloria Jr. writes that tribal identity is a spiritual heritage with a specific understanding of how to live in the world.

Those who claim cultural identity often tell family stories of tenuous ties several generations back. There was much turbulence, skirmish, disagreement, exclusion, and expulsion during the upheaval following the European conquest. In all tribes, there have been intermarriage, itinerancy, and families not claiming Native heritage and/or claiming to be something other than what they are. There were, and still are, mixed-blood issues, causing blurred boundaries and erasures. Both documented and undocumented explore the meaning and limits of Native American identity beyond its legal margins.

Native ball games were more than a game. The Mayan games that began 3,500 years ago were a fight between life and death. Light and darkness. There were references to decapitation. To be fair, there were Indian wars and infighting before the European came to this continent. Native tribes removed one another, wanting hunting grounds, horses, the space that another inhabited. The history of the Cherokee ball game also was dangerous and violent. In 1848 restrictions against breaking limbs and heads were placed on the older form of the game.

These are lasting issues. These are the writers who agreed to be up at bat.

UNPAPERED

SHOW YOUR PAPERS

In this initial section of the book, you will find creative nonfiction dealing with the constant demands for all kinds of external documentation of belonging, from tribal citizenship cards to federal CDIB cards to expected physical appearance. The editors felt, in dealing with such an emotional subject, that creative nonfiction allows the widest range of perspectives and attitudes on this topic.

Kim Shuck

Paperwork

YOU ARE NOT REAL.

I have papers. I'm a citizen of the Cherokee Nation of Oklahoma. Many of my unpapered friends seem to think that being a citizen of a federally recognized tribe ends the identity conversation. This conversation isn't about who anyone "really is"; it's not about identity. This conversation is about someone else's idea, and I don't pass either.

Pulling the bones around me in this new
Moon of gathering tucking in the
Poppy seeds the
Borage new
Wild strawberries holding close as
Much of this orange sky as I can and
Every ribbon and magnet and
Bead that I have is
Singing strange
Colors today singing quietly
Just now but
Who knows where this impulse is
Going?

In high school, my boyfriend's father was told that I was Cherokee. "There was clearly an Irishman in the woodpile," he sneered. What did you just say about my mom?

THEY'VE MISTAKEN MY BONES AGAIN.

I was born and raised in Ramaytush territory. The Ramaytush are not eligible for the kind of dual citizenship that I hold because they are not a recognized tribe. Federal recognition is not, as you might imagine, an issue of admitting that a group of people is indigenous to a specific place. Maybe it should be, but it isn't. It's not about historical truth; it's about the story that is told now. Many California Native groups have neither federal nor state recognition because they never had ratified treaties. This leaves many culturally and genetically Indigenous people without a legal basis for their actual identities. There are people who insist that although the papering system isn't perfect we "have to start somewhere." I disagree. I disagree but lack power, so instead of fixing the system, what I do is to not contribute to art shows or books that require enrollment information. I can't make it right, but I won't make it worse. Other people can do as their conscience dictates.

> Buckeyes
> Monument plants
> Tumbled hillside
> Bear grass comes white after the fire
> Waxy dogbane coming up through the
> Cinder cones
> Fireweed
> Scribble oaks
> Write poems to the ghosts and the
> Boulders

In 2018 the Native communities of San Francisco and their allies worked very hard to get a statue removed from the SF Civic Center. The statue was part of a monument to California history. It is called *Early Days*. It consists of three figures: a standing Franciscan, a vaquero, and a Native man lying on his back before the other two. It was meant to be an image of conquering the local Native people. Statues in civic centers represent the cities' current political values and perspectives. We didn't feel that this particular statue did, so we asked that it be removed. It took awhile and the backlash included death threats for at least three of the people involved, but it has been removed and rests comfortably in storage. During the process the Native community was repeatedly told that there weren't enough of us to matter, that individuals among us "didn't look Indian," that everyone knew that all "Indians" are dead already. For three hours I sat in a hearing room in San Francisco's city hall while a man next to me told me, in aggressive whispers, that we were all dead, that I was dead, and that he was going to tear my eyes out. "You don't exist."

> Impossible to write blood without
> Weight of
> Gender of
> Potential feminism of
> Let's face it
> Melodrama

It is rare for me to do a poetry reading without having some strange identity-related moment attached to it. I get random questions. I get asked for help putting together genealogies. I'm not a genealogy expert. I get told people's family stories about being this or that tribe, often with commentary about cheekbones and straight hair. I get told flatly that I can't be Cherokee. In a recent variation of that last scenario, a woman came up to me and told me she was one-third Cherokee. Two parents, four grandparents, eight great grandparents—I'm not getting to a third but I'm also not the identity police, so we'll put that down with mystery lights and spectral ships and move on with the comment that I want to believe. Then she asked me how much Cherokee I am. I told her that I'm a citizen, and she asked me if I was on the rolls. A better human than I would spend time explaining. I'm a bad person, or at least a very tired one, and I pretty much excused myself as politely as possible and walked away. She is either Cherokee or she isn't. That's not up to me. Manners and respect are another thing, and I'm getting old and cranky and prefer to be treated like a person who deserves some consideration. If she's mistaken about any part of her story, there are reasons. There are family reasons, there are social reasons, and there are mythological reasons. I want to empathize. The United States has created some fairly baroque notions about Indigenous people, and the strange laws associated with this identity can create some special stresses. One common one makes people who are not recognized as Native feel anger at people who are and don't look Native to them. (My hand goes up. I get it, don't like it but I get it.) If I believed in overarching evil genius, I would believe that the reason for the laws and divisions was to create just these conflicts. Alas, I don't believe that people are this organized. I think that it's more like the metastatic damage from racism.

> Take hold of your stubborn
> Twine fingers in your defiant
> Dig in
> Breathe deep into your
> Creative
> Make space for your heartbreak but let it start healing

At one point, hanging out, eating, having a great identity conversation, someone asked me when I found out that I was Cherokee. I have to say that the question threw me. I grew up in a house with a Cherokee dad—I've always known. When I ran this question past him, we were both flummoxed. I suppose that the question comes from so many people finding a connection later in life, for whatever reason. Not me. I've always known: Mom is Polish American and Dad is Cherokee. Dad and I had a chat about it the other day. Oklahoma is a very particular place. Not that long ago it was known as Indian Territory. My great grandma, who was someone I knew and hung out with, was born in Indian Territory and was grown by the time it became Oklahoma. Her grandfather held various roles in the Cherokee Nation. My dad, who grew up a military brat and left Oklahoma to join the U.S. Navy, never did his citizenship paperwork until later. I found out, talking to him about it just the other day, that he did it because my work and politics made him want to participate more. As you review this bit of writing, you will notice that I did not say that I'd grown up in a family where my dad could be Cherokee, or that we were of Cherokee descent. There will be people who take exception, because legally Dad wasn't Cherokee because he wasn't papered. I will contrast that with this: when the various members of my mother's family came to the United States, they did not come from a place called Poland. Grandma's family immigration documents said that they were from Galicia. Her family spoke Polish, ate Polish food, hung out at the Polish Hall in the Mission District of San Francisco, and danced polkas. They were not legally Polish. Identity is complicated. By most measures my dad was not less Cherokee without paperwork and yet . . .

People finding their way back to a Cherokee identity often tell me their genealogy to see if we're related. Let me spare you the suspense. If you are Cherokee, we are related.

I get challenged all the time. I was once challenged about my identity on Facebook, by a fairly closely related cousin. She'd never met me. Well, darling, you never met me because you are descended from the second to youngest brother of five and I am descended from the oldest. My dad was his oldest. I am my dad's oldest. The challenge happened very publicly on social media, and the apology—and there was one—happened in a private message. I love my family, but this is part of the problem. If people find that they are wrong, they don't apologize with the gusto of the initial assault. That situation was awkward, and people in interviews still ask me about it, because that can happen in an interview. As sad as that episode was, it was not the worst time it's happened. The worst time I was challenged publicly, and with great sound and fury, was on a book review site. Someone reviewed my first book of poetry, and a guy read the review and scoffed and announced that he would "look me up" to see if I was really Cherokee. I know that he looked me up because the argument changed from "you aren't Cherokee" to "you don't live in Cherokee Territory." We are all, papered or not, subject to this kind of questioning, and we can all be disqualified in the eyes of someone: not brown enough, too brown, not living in the Nation, blood quantum questions, cultural competency questions, clan questions. The Cherokee Nation's TV show did a short documentary about me, and I'm still not Cherokee enough for some people. The bad news is that even if you get papers at some point, even if you have made it your sole job in the world to be Super Indian, you could still not satisfy everyone. You need to find your strength in your identity within yourself. I know, my California-in-the-sixties upbringing is showing, but it's true.

> Implication an
> Innuendo I knew something about this but
> Can't remember what that was like either
> Morning of tracing regional maps that have
> Been moved these star charts from
> Somewhere specific and they can no
> Longer tell us where that was this
> Fingertip's route from Snake Mound to
> Golden Gate Bridge

One of the reasons that Indigenous people get so upset about non-community members claiming a Native identity is that there are metric tons of misleading and incorrect material about us out there, and people who don't have an elder to ask are thought to be more likely to spread the manure around. We all have our pet irritations. I used to tell students that they would earn an F on any paper or test where they referenced Native American culture singular instead of Native American cultures plural. I have now stopped writing to make sure that I haven't accidentally done that in this piece and made myself look very foolish. Nope, I'm okay. Another thing that gets me is the word *shaman*. Yeah, some people use it. It gives me an instant rash. We all have our things that annoy us, things that we feel are wrong.

Within mixed-culture Indigenous communities, those in urban areas in particular, there is generally one tribe/band/Nation with greater representation than others. People from that culture will sometimes try to hold people from other cultures responsible for knowledge that is not relevant to them. People are often stunned that I learned to make fry bread when I got to university. My gran didn't do fry bread; she did biscuits, fried fish, and cornbread, but not fry bread. Not our thing. I think the thing that shocks non-Native people most about me is that I don't go to sweat lodge. None of these things are problems; none of them require a confrontation, but sometimes one happens anyway. Sometimes we pick up bits of one another's culture by being around each other, but that can get awkward too. At a craft fair I once walked up to a Cherokee artisan making an Anishinabe thing and selling it as "authentic Cherokee." Well, authentic Cherokee artisan, authentic thing. I don't know. I'm still working through this one. Okay, I confess I thought some very judgmental things. By the same token I could market "Authentic Cherokee" barsht from an old family recipe, Cherokee because I am, and old family recipe from the other side of the family, but for now we have such a problem with the things that people believe about us that aren't true I don't believe I ever would.

WPA bridge over the Neosho I
Stood on it in full flood with my
Dad the water just
Kissing the underside of the boards

Another reason that people are concerned about the authenticity of people's claims is money. In about 2008 I was speaking at a young women's event put on by a state assemblyman, one that I spoke at without being paid, by the way. The woman who had asked me to speak, who was not Native, set off the building's fire alarm system with some enthusiastic and, to me, confusing use of sage smoke. She also hit my identity rather hard in her intro, but I do that sometimes too, so okay. One of the teachers in the audience stood up and stated that she was an enrolled Cherokee and that she got her per diem checks every month. She said that she thought we Cherokees whine about identity too much and that the previous summer she'd spent time on the reservation in New Mexico and felt that we'd been given the best land in the country and should be grateful.

Where to start? All of this is clearly not true. Cherokees don't get monthly money. No one was "given" land—tribal lands are what was left after everything else was taken—and there is no Cherokee tribal land in New Mexico. I have heard, from more than one person, some variation of a desire to get citizenship in one tribe or another to get money. I'm here to tell you that, at least for the Cherokee, the money angle has been grossly overstated. I'm pretty sure that someone else is going to talk about people, or one person, claiming identity and getting educational benefits. I will just say that there is confusion in the general population about money, land, and status. This confusion causes some of the problems. Ignorance, particularly ignorance caused or helped along by oversimplification, is a big part of the problem.

That year the wind took the
Topsoil and the children the
Maps all changed and not
Everyone found a pair of
Magical shoes or good
Company

I do understand that as a papered Cherokee I'm painting a huge target on myself by participating in this book. I do. It's not as if I personally need more publications, but the issue is important to me. So while we're making a spectacle, I might as well mention the thing that I believe to be the other main reason for the identity bullying. Some people want to be the only acknowledged authority about things Native. It is my opinion that no one from any tribe should claim to know enough about any other tribe to set themself up as the only authority. The various people who like to trash others as being not Native enough will always attract a following. Anyone who has attended a high school has seen how this works. Someone hustles themself as the cool kid, and suddenly they have hangers on. The bullying commences. They must get some charge out of doing this. I have no idea what it is. In an age where Twitter bullies have climbed to high office, it's never been easier to watch the process. It's disappointing to see it in communities where you'd think we are dealing with enough stress already. I'm sure that there are books out there on the psychology behind all this. I'm just a poet. Here's what I've noticed. The more attention my work gets the more my identity is questioned. If you find that you are being regularly challenged, it probably means that you are making enough noise to be noticed. Congratulations. I try to take it as a compliment, as long as they spell my name right.

Deborah Miranda

Things You Can Do with Your Chart for Calculating Quantum of Indian Blood

In August 2007 I embarked on a journey into the past. For my first academic sabbatical, I headed to UCLA, where a fellowship would allow me to research my California Indian family history for a year, and—I hoped—write a draft of a book about how a few members of that family had survived a triple invasion: the violent Mission system imposed on them by Spain and Mexico and near-extermination by the Americans. Ahead of my arrival, I shipped out a wealth of materials gathered by my late mother, Madgel Miranda. While a deep dive into UCLA's archives, among others, was part of my plan, so was immersion in my mother's research from years before.

Madgel Miranda had become a dogged, determined self-taught genealogist because she loved me—and hoped to make me eligible for Native American college scholarships—and maybe because she felt a little bit guilty. I was thirteen years old when I finally asked her to tell me about my father, whom I hadn't seen since he was incarcerated in San Quentin when I was three years old. I think my mother sensed my hunger for the other half of my heritage—not just my father, but aunties, uncles, half sisters who looked like me, and a homeland whose mountains, rivers, and beaches I could name but had only gone back to visit once or twice. My mother's remarriage to a man from Washington State had removed me from all that. In that pre-internet era, she sat down and typed up a form letter explaining her quest to prove my Native blood quantum so that I would be eligible to apply for scholarships targeting Native students. I remember her sitting at the little kitchen table of our old trailer in Kent, Washington, late at night, with her stack of dittoed form letters (later Xeroxed), envelopes, stamps, and her battered checkbook. She had lists of people to write to, and in her own methodical way, between cups of coffee, she'd make her way down those lists. I still have a copy of her form letter. It was very articulate, to the point, and clear: *I need you to help me accomplish this for my daughter's education.*

She wrote to government offices for birth and death certificates and kept all the replies with useful information, first on handmade family trees, then on "pedigree" forms purchased from genealogical organizations. (Much later, she'd transfer all this onto a series of computers, using a series of genealogy software, always upgrading, always improving her methodology.) But it wasn't until my 2007–8 sabbatical—six years after my mother's unexpected death—that I had time and resources to sit down and go through what she'd left me: banker's boxes full of painstaking genealogical research and an amazing family tree that she had traced back to some of the first Native converts at Mission Carmel in 1770. It was as if my mother had stored her half of a conversation in these white banker's boxes, and I was only now coming around to hear the legacy she'd left me.

Sitting on the sofa in my small Westwood studio apartment one night, I opened one of those banker's boxes, pulling out a three-ring binder I had never seen.

A thin stack of paper was tucked print-down into the front pocket. It had been preserved there for so many years that the ink of the bottom copy had transferred to the binder cover. When I pulled the papers out, tugging as the paper and ink separated, I found a clear copy of the writing tattooed onto the plastic binder cover. Turning the pages over, I saw—for the first time in my life—a Bureau of Indian Affairs (BIA) blood quantum chart. In fact, I held a stack of blood quantum charts. Maybe ten of them. It took me a few minutes to figure it out—mother's blood quantum along this axis, father's along this one, child's blood quantum revealed where the two intersect on the page. Along with these charts, I found the form letter sent by some anonymous BIA paper-pusher, dated 1974: "In response to your query, we estimate your daughter's blood quantum to be . . . the BIA does not research individual cases . . . contact us if you have more information that might effect [*sic*] these results . . . enclosed is a chart to assist you in determining . . ."

Sitting there, I felt the weight of the task that must have fallen on my mother as she read this letter. She was starting from scratch. She had no idea how to locate the vast amount of complicated documentation needed to fill out that Chart for Determining Indian Blood Quantum. She worked full-time at a stressful job that was an hour's commute each way. I would graduate from high school in only five more years. Where to start? Was this challenge even possible?

Storytelling takes many forms. All art is, in the end, an attempt to tell a story. Looking at those blood quantum charts that night in Westwood, California, the visual impact was almost overwhelming: so much violence on a single page of tiny black-and-white rectangles, a grid of heartless numbers split up into relentless fractions. Although words have been my favorite tools for as long as I can remember, language does sometimes fail me. This was one of those moments. The legal implications and destructive potential of that chart. The heartbreak. The genocide. The weaponization of love. The nurturing of injustice. A whirlwind of emotions I could barely keep at bay: anger, grief, yearning.

My box of colored pencils was on the little table in front of me. I picked it up, shook out the royal blue. I began filling in the rectangles in the upper left-hand corner of the grid. I was not even thinking in words, a rarity for someone for whom words are the solution to everything. Another part of my mind took over, stepped in.

As I sketched, the first coherent thought slowly came to me. *This looks like the kind of grid you would use to plan out a beading pattern. A basketry pattern.*

And I began to fill in the spaces with color.

And a design began to emerge out of the BIA blood quantum chart, almost as if the chart were welling up with its own truth, its own measurements. As if something old were rising to the surface after long erasure.

My mother had probably made these copies at one of those Xerox machines at the front of the Safeway store, or in the library. Ten cents apiece. They had cost her a dollar back when that was enough money for a whole pound of ground beef. And yet, she had never filled in a single chart. Left them in this notebook for me to find, almost forty years later. I was glad that, in the moment she read that brutal letter from the BIA, my mother had no idea what she was up against, that she didn't know that the game was rigged, that in their haste to document our transformation into civilized citizens, Spain, Mexico, and the United States governments had burned our back trail.

When I finished the first drawing, I immediately began another. I thought about the ways missionization and colonization demanded that I squeeze my body into the tight grid on the page, yet had erased all the documentation that such a demand required.

I was born at UCLA hospital, on a Sunday evening late in October 1961, to a woman of immigrant stock (French and English) and a California Indian man (Esselen and Chumash).

My mother's parents, Kenneth and Doris Yeoman, lived in Beverly Hills in a small bungalow, her father employed first as a service station employee, then a mail carrier, while her mother worked as a punch-key operator for an aircraft company. My father's parents, Tom and Keta Miranda, had divorced when he was still a child; both lived in a series of rental homes, in and around their respective homelands, for their entire lives. Keta, before her early death, did domestic work and, in her last job, was a restaurant manager; Tom was a jack-of-all-trades who worked as a cowboy, factory worker at Spreckels Sugar, logger, pipelayer. All four grandparents had been born in the early 1900s, years before the U.S. government decided, in 1924, to bestow citizenship upon the Indigenous peoples living within its boundaries.[1] This, of course, made no difference to the Yeomans. I'm not even sure if the Mirandas and their parents knew they'd become citizens until employers required

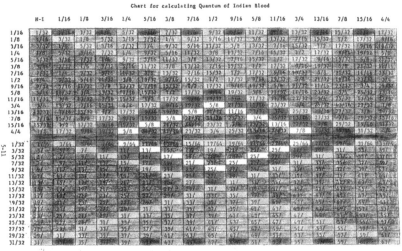

FIG. 1. "Wannabe Creations." Make up a beautiful, totally fake "Indian" design that means absolutely nothing to any North or South American tribe. Sell it for a lot of money. Tell everyone you're Cherokee. Certificate of Degree of Indian Blood, colored in by Deborah Miranda. Source: Bureau of Indian Affairs, Tribal Enrollment, App. H.

them to apply for Social Security. Tom continued to call whites "the Americans" all his life, as if he'd never quite absorbed the fact that he, too, was an American.

More important than citizenship, however, was the farce that resulted when the U.S. government sent agents to determine where surviving "Mission Indians" lived, how many of them lived, and what their needs were. While the Indian Service Bureau acknowledged the Esselen tribal community as the "Monterey Band" in 1905–1906, 1909, and 1923, it neglected to follow through with the federal trust and fiduciary relationship with it required by Congress. As scholar Philip Laverty writes, "Simply put, the [federal acknowledgment process] criteria of sociocultural and political persistence and external recognition do not account for 230 years of state-sponsored violence, crass federal neglect, expropriation, and assimilationist policies." (41).[2] As Laverty goes on to explain, although government agents "negotiated" (the term appears to have been used loosely) a total of eighteen (never ratified) treaties with various California tribes in the interior of the central coastal area of California, these same agents believed that the Monterey Band of Indians was already "civilized," thanks to the efforts of missionaries, and needed no land or treaty agreements. In 1927, the year my father was born, still another government agent, Lafayette Dorrington, misread previous populations of Esselen Indians, disregarded earlier reports of a substantial number of Esselen people, did not do any sort of onsite visitation to determine the current population and, when pressed by his supervisor for his late report, declared that the homeless Indians for whom he was responsible did not need land set aside for their benefit. "The net effect of Dorrington's dereliction of duty," Laverty writes, was an "illegal administrative termination or, as his replacement would later note, sheer 'Crass indifference' and 'gross negligence.'" Illegal or not, negligent or not, Dorrington's report was never amended, and the Esselen tribe was summarily terminated from the rolls of Federally Recognized Tribes.

Erased by a whim, by one man's laziness, by a flawed system.

On my mother's side, the family tree goes back to some of the earliest colonizers on the North American continent: English farmers looking for land in 1650 (surname Yeoman) and wealthy Huguenots fleeing religious persecution in 1661 (surname Gano). Both lines arrived in the New York area, then spread west to Ohio, Indiana, Illinois, Iowa, and Nebraska and southwest to Virginia, Kentucky, and finally Nebraska, where those two lines eventually converged, with the marriage of Kenneth Yeoman and Doris Gano. Along the way, my ancestors produced a preacher said to have baptized George Washington while serving in the American Revolution (and later a key figure in the founding of Brown University), a Confederate general who retreated to Texas (having freed his enslaved workers) after the end of the Civil War, a Mormon woman who made the trek to Utah from Illinois after Joseph Smith's murder (only to have her husband leave her when he married two other women to form a plural marriage), a family of millers who perfected the art of water wheels, a woman who found herself married at thirteen to an abusive husband (bearing him two children, and then running away with the town doctor, who had treated her injuries), a young man who became one of the earliest aviators in World War I, a postmaster, and multitudes of other European immigrants and their descendants who fought, farmed, stole, and blundered their way steadily westward across the North American continent until the moment when the two family lines met in tiny Elwood, Nebraska, in the late 1880s. Doris was born there in 1898; Kenneth, in 1900. They grew up together and married in June 1924, leaving immediately after the ceremony to drive to new jobs in Colorado and, a few years later, on into Southern California. "We thought we'd landed in Paradise," my grandmother told me once. Compared to the harsh climate of Nebraska, I'm sure it felt that way.

My European ancestors and their exploits are vividly represented in the paper archives spread across the country, as well as digital archives like Ancestry.com—and even Wikipedia entries for the more notorious, often with images of their faces. All I need to do to document my connection is trace that genealogy through an extensive network of carefully preserved and maintained records. I am qualified, therefore, for membership in Daughters of the American Revolution, Daughters of the Confederacy *and* Daughters of Union Veterans, The Huguenot Society of America, First Families of Ohio, Illinois Prairie Pioneers, Society of Indiana Pioneers, Society of Kentucky Pioneers, and Utah Genealogical Association Founding Pioneers, not to mention the somewhat questionable Continental Society Daughters of Indian Wars. ("If you are a direct descendant of a Native American, you will be recognized with a certificate and the opportunity to purchase our new insignia teepee pin that can be worn on your official ribbon.") Of course, there are applications to fill out, fees to be paid, and genealogical credentials to be submitted to join these groups, but the fact of the matter remains that my European lineage is fully documented, should I ever need to apply for a Certificate of Degree of European Blood, to gain access to the rights and benefits that the CDEB provides its members—

Oh. Wait.

There is no such thing as a CDEB. Nor is there a Certificate of Degree of Latinx Blood, or a Certificate of Degree of African Blood, nor any of the other lineages carried to me through my father's genetic gifts. Wouldn't it be hilarious if white people of European descent actually had to prove their lineage to be treated according to the promises of this nation and government? And isn't it lucky that all those archives and records actually exist and are, for the most part, accessible? The truth is, the only part of my identity for which certification of my blood lineage is required for that lineage to be "recognized" is my Indigenous line. Why do you suppose that is? Trick question. It's about the land. It's always about the land.

The CDIB (Certificate of Degree of Indian Blood) is an official U.S. document, typically a little card meant to be carried in one's purse or wallet, issued by the Bureau of Indian Affairs. This CDIB certifies that an individual has a specific degree of Native American blood of a federally recognized Indian tribe, band, nation, pueblo, village, or community. No, seriously; I'm not kidding anymore. And note the two qualifiers here: *a specific degree* of Native American blood, that is from *a federally recognized* Indian tribe.

Therein hangs the unpapered tale.

In Westwood, in 2007, I reached for another blank chart.

Let's back up all the way to the late 1760s, when Spain, already long-established colonizers in Baja California and Mexico proper, felt pressured by the presence of Russian fur traders and other Europeans closing in on what was then called Alta (Upper) California. A strategic colonizing plan was put together to quickly create a Spanish presence in the form of self-sustaining towns filled with Spanish citizens. However, the Crown had neither the ability to transport large numbers of colonists to California nor the military might to anchor such a vast and unexplored territory so far from Spain itself. The solution? Missionization, a tactic that enabled Spain to utilize the Indigenous population for its own empowerment. Spain had long practiced this method with Indigenous Mexicans. Let us be

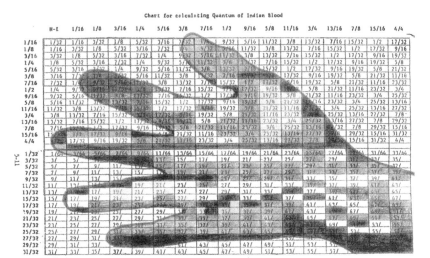

Chart for calculating Quantum of Indian Blood

Note: All denominators for lower part of scale are 64. "N-I" stands for non-Indian. To determine degree of blood of children, find degree of one parent in left hand column and of the other parent in top row. Read horizontally to right and vertically below to find the proper degree. Example: Child of parents, one 11/16 and the other 5/8 would be 21/32 degree.

Blood degree shown in enclosed area is less than 1/4.

FIG. 2. "Hand of God." What if God was one of us? What would His blood quantum be? Should He be enrolled in a federally recognized tribe? Does it have a casino? Go ahead, put your hand down and trace it; you're God's proxy in His absence. Certificate of Degree of Indian Blood, colored in by Deborah Miranda. Source: Bureau of Indian Affairs, Tribal Enrollment, App. H.

clear: the Spanish colonization project in Alta California was not a band of pioneers made up of Spanish families toiling away on small individual farms to establish self-sustaining homesteads. This was a military operation to violently force autonomous Indigenous populations into slavery under the guise of religious proselytizing. At the heart of this military operation was the appropriation of Indigenous land, labor, and resources to establish Spain's political and military power in the world. The partnership between the Spanish military and the Catholic church designed a system of missions as proto-assembly-line factories into which "wild Indians" were taken at one end and, by force or coercion, converted to Catholicism, taught Spanish language and social-cultural customs, and trained in practical trades to support Spanish colonials and soldiers. They were supposed to emerge at the other end of the missions as lower-class Spanish citizens equipped with the skills to support Spain's settlements, thus solidifying a claim to Alta California. Abracadabra! No Indians to see here! Just good law-abiding, hard-working, working-class Catholic citizens who know their place: to serve the Spanish elite.

The first such mission, San Diego de Alcalá, was founded in 1769; in 1770 Misión de San Carlos Borromeo was established. It was originally located in Monterey but relocated to Carmel the following year due to constant violent attacks and rapes of Indigenous women and children by the soldiers in the Monterey Presidio. Nineteen other missions followed, located along the western edge of California from Sonoma to San Diego. My father's ancestors were among those taken into the Carmel, Soledad, and Santa Ynez missions. And that beautifully crafted assembly-line construction of Spanish laboring citizens? It fell apart.

From the very beginning, Spanish colonization and missionization of California Indians were meant to disappear the Indigenous peoples of California. At the same time, ironically, priests at each of the twenty-one missions in California carefully recorded that erasure via detailed ledgers for baptism, marriage, and death. In these ledgers, the life of each Indigenous person passed through the hands of a mission priest. Incoming adults had their Indigenous names written down phonetically in leather-bound ledger books, along with the new Spanish names forced on Natives during baptism. It was, in fact, the last time Indigenous names would be acknowledged at all. Children born into mission life may have been given Indigenous names within their own families, but such names were never recorded in the ledgers, only Spanish names. Likewise, their parents were now noted in these baptismal records *only* by their Spanish names. Incoming adults' ages were estimated, home villages identified or guessed. Children born to missionized parents, however, did not have a home village; they were "from this mission." The Spaniards liked pinning down time: dates for births, baptisms, marriages, and deaths were recorded with care. Each Indigenous person was assigned a number indicating their chronological entrance into the community, making them traceable through those big black leather-bound ledgers. My 5x great-grandfather, Fructuoso de Jesus Cholom, was given special notice as #1000 at Mission Carmel, the one thousandth Indian baptized. Simultaneously, Indigenous ways of telling time—ceremony, ritual, music, seasonal foods—were not just discouraged, but punishable offenses. Indigenous religious customs were never seen as actual religious customs, but pagan worship of heathen gods, lowercase *g*. Indigenous practices, like Indigenous languages, were tolerated in the early stages of missionization but eventually treated as major infractions—and punished accordingly. Spanish was required for daily communication, with a mix of Spanish and Latin for church services. Again, some priests tolerated Indigenous languages for a time, even creating Spanish-Indigenous language versions of prayers or confessional templates. But that didn't last long, as priests realized these languages were far too complex and numerous for them to learn and empowered Indians, allowing them to speak to each other without surveillance. Indigenous languages were banned and went underground, where the combination of massive deaths and threat of punishment made it difficult or, often, impossible for languages to be passed on reliably to subsequent generations. Gerónimo Boscana, a Franciscan scholar and priest at San Juan Capistrano, spent over a decade researching and writing about the religious beliefs of the Indians in his care, producing a document still considered one of the most comprehensive studies of California Indian spirituality. Boscana concluded, "Indians of California may be compared to a species of monkey," adding that native beliefs and customs were "horrible," "ludicrous," and "ridiculous."

Sometimes documentation is another form of erasure.

My fingers cramped. My wrist ached from pressing the soft pencil lead so hard into the paper. But I wasn't finished filling in the charts my mother had received from the BIA.

My grandfather, Thomas Anthony Miranda, was born in 1903—just as the population of California Indians had fallen to its lowest. Current estimates of precontact population put one million inhabitants in the area currently called California; by 1903 that number had fallen to

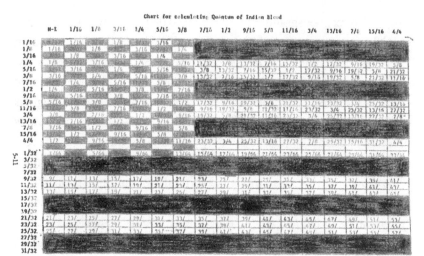

FIG. 3. "Patriotism Percentages." Why is blood quantum so important to the U.S. government? It must be a measure of Indian patriotism. Create a flag that expresses your patriotism. Whatever you do, be respectful of another nation's symbols. Certificate of Degree of Indian Blood, colored in by Deborah Miranda. Source: Bureau of Indian Affairs, Tribal Enrollment, App. H.

about 15,000. The missions, the Gold Rush displacement and murder of Indian communities, environmental devastation, resulting starvation, and outright genocide, approved of and funded by the U.S. Congress in the form of bounties for dead Indians, were to blame. Like most of the surviving Indigenous people, Tom learned not to identify as Indian except in the safest of circumstances. Rumors of him sneaking off to Indian dances in the hills, or speaking his wife's Chumash language, filtered down through the family, along with Tom's refusal to speak Spanish. In recordings of conversations in his old age, Tom's English is a soft, mysteriously accented mix of languages. As a young woman, his wife, Marquesa (Keta), still spoke Chumash with elderly women in her family, but neither Tom nor Keta ever taught this language to their sons. My father, Al, grew up speaking English and the street Spanish of his neighborhoods in Santa Monica in the 1930s. As an adult, he was ashamed of both; he felt he didn't speak either one well enough to really hold a conversation. In that, he was mistaken.

This family history did not come down to me as a child; my parents divorced when I was three years old, and my mother remarried and moved with her new husband and me up the coast to rural western Washington. I did not see my father again for ten years. During that time, my identity was a fragile creature: I knew I was "half Indian," because my mother told me so, but we didn't know what tribe, or tribes. My mother, working with what little information she'd heard, told me it didn't matter anyway: "they're all extinct now."

But I was the only dark-skinned, dark-haired girl in every classroom, in my stepfather's family, and in my birth family. (I had two older siblings, born of my mother's first marriage.) I was always chosen as the Halloween witch in school plays, cast as the Indian maiden at Thanksgiving, or mistaken for a Mexican who should speak Spanish. I stuck out like a sore thumb in the predominantly white, rural trailer courts we lived in, and when we settled at last on a small piece of land with woods and fields, I went to predominantly white schools all the way through high school.

But I knew I was Indian.

And that night in Westwood in 2007, less than a mile away from where I had been born, I sat surrounded by a genealogy that hung on the walls of my rented studio, the Indigenous names of my ancestors printed out above their baptismal names. The documentation of an erasure that had never ceased. But I thought to myself: None of this makes me any less Esselen, any less Chumash. None of this negates what my ancestors went through, the thin thread by which my grandfather's and grandmother's survival hung. None of this changes the fact that we are still here, part of the twenty-first century. None of this erasure succeeds unless we let it succeed. Oh, it's exhausting, this battle to be seen. The documentation of blood when claiming that blood could get you killed. The required birth certificates on which parents wrote "Mexican" or "white" because

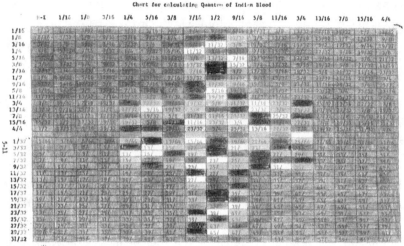

FIG. 4. "Blood Quantum: The Four Sacred Directions." The four directions come from, and lead to, everywhere; utterly inclusive, they are clearly not full-bloods. How would you put them in their place? Certificate of Degree of Indian Blood, colored in by Deborah Miranda. Source: Bureau of Indian Affairs, Tribal Enrollment, App. H.

to claim "Indian" was shameful or dangerous. The demand that we maintain a continuous presence in our homelands when our homelands are in the hands of the rich and powerful, when just renting a tiny apartment is more than we can afford, let alone purchasing land. The charts that claim to hold more veracity than memory and bodies.

My father told me this story: During World War II, his ship docked at the Port of Seattle for leave; he and his friends went out to hit the bars. But bartenders asked for his ID; seeing "American Indian," they told him it was illegal to serve alcohol to Indians in Seattle. Ever resourceful, my father went back to the ship and bribed the purser to change his ID so it read "Mexican." Went to a different bar. Flashed his new card. And passed.

Documented, and erased.

Night had fallen while I worked on these charts. I'd left the door to my studio open, and now soft evening air came through the screen, carrying the scent of the bougainvillea climbing along the fence, the sweet, almost soapy perfume of an orange tree in a corner of the yard. Crickets sang; a few birds called as they settled into the bushes. A breeze with a lick of ocean salt stroked my cheek.

My thoughts echo inside my head.
"Sometimes documentation is another form of erasure."
"Spain, Mexico, and the United States governments burnt our back trail."
"It's about the land. It's always about the land."
"Erased by a whim, by one man's laziness, by a flawed system."

Here's what you can do with your chart, I thought as I finished the last one. I taped it to the wall next to the first three, lined up under the genealogy of names I had come to revere, from villages like Achasta, Tucutnut, Echilat. From other places like Sonora, Guanajuato, Jacona, which had already been through Spain's Catholic mission machinery. From Spain itself, through priest and soldier. From tribes brought over in chains across an ocean, West Africans who married Indigenous people here, and whose descendants traveled as soldiers and laborers through Mexico and into California, married again into Indigenous families. From small villages where people had forgotten their tribes in England, Wales, Scotland, France, caught up in the grip of history.

I stepped back to take in the now-colorful designs. Smiled. I'll tell you what you can do with your chart.

NOTES

1. On June 2, 1924, Congress enacted the Indian Citizenship Act, which granted citizenship to all Native Americans born in the United States. The right to vote, however, was governed by state law; until 1957, some states barred Native Americans from voting. Library of Congress, "Indian Citizenship Act."
2. For a clear and detailed study of the Esselen Ohlone–Costanoan nightmare, see Laverty's article.

BIBLIOGRAPHY

Laverty, Philip. "The Ohlone/Costanoan-Esselen Nation of Monterey, California: Dispossession, Federal Neglect, and the Bitter Irony of the Federal Acknowledgment Process." *Wicazo Sa Review* 18, No. 2 (Fall 2003): 41–77.

Library of Congress. "Indian Citizenship Act." Today in History. https://www .loc.gov/item/today-in-history/june-02/?loclr=bloglaw.

Kimberly L. Becker

The White Box

At the DMV, I am the only customer. Having just moved to this small Southern town, I need to get a new license. I am a cisgender female of mixed descent—Cherokee (not enrolled), Celtic, Germanic. The cop on duty is white with a florid face, his gun a dull threat under his girth, but for the moment he is jocular, if not flirtatious, while exuding arrogance.

The steps seem easy enough: vision test, sign test, photo. I pass the vision test and move on to signs, but I am uncertain of the meaning of one symbol (a tractor? farm equipment?). He laughs and says I must not be from around here. I do not tell him my family has been here for generations, even though I lived away, in a major metropolitan area, for decades, pre-divorce. I don't allow him this intimacy. I say, "No sir." I smile winningly. I need to check this errand off my list. He laughs (he seems always to be laughing) and says he'll give me a pass. He says we'll be done "in a jiffy," that I just need to sign a form and have my picture taken. He says *we* as though we are allies.

He types on a computer, prints a form, and passes it over the counter for me to sign, proffering a pen. As he moves, I watch the belt with his gun strain at his waist. He taps his fingers on the counter while I read over what he has filled in. "Everything in order?" he asks, a little impatiently now that I have waited a beat too long, now that I have disrespected him by not trusting what he typed on the form for me to sign.

I notice he has checked the *white* box for my race. I want to get out of here and could just sign the form, but I am annoyed he made assumptions in assigning his own perceptions and projecting them onto me, aligning me with him. I can hear my Cherokee teacher telling our immersion class that it doesn't matter how much Cherokee you are, but if you say you're Cherokee he's going to expect something of you, and you can't be "part" Cherokee. You either are or you aren't.

An enrolled friend, now dead, advising: "Choose a path to walk. You can't be white and Indian. You have to choose."

"Actually," I say slowly, smiling, lifting the end of the word *actually* to soften it to more of a question than a demand, the way women know to do, so as not to appear to be challenging a man in a position of authority, especially a man with a gun. "Actually," I say again, "I need to make a correction." He frowns, takes the paper from me roughly, without asking. He reads off my name, address, phone. Yes, yes, I nod, but then he reads "race: white." "Well, you're white ain't you?" He laughs.

I feel my face flush. Who wouldn't want to be white? Is this his unspoken assumption? I could say yes and keep the *white* box checked that he already answered for me, but I can't. To do so would deny an important part of my identity. So I say again, "actually," as if repeating the word will make it irrefutable, "I am mixed race, white and Native American."

His face goes still. It is the kind of menacing stillness before a dog bites. People think you have to be afraid of dogs that are growling, but growls are warnings—it is the still stance and hard eyes that often precede a bite. It is then I begin to feel fear. Because he is white. Because he is a large male. Because he wears a gun. Because he is displeased. "Sir," I say (he must be used to being called "sir"), "I can't sign this one. I am mixed race, and you checked the white box. I need you to correct it."

He looks stupefied. Incredulous. His face darkens, reddens. Writing about it now, I feel again how my heart began to race and how all at once I became afraid of this white man with his red face and black gun, who did not approve of my insolence.

"Well, you look white to me!" he mutters. I do not imbue him with a further honorific. "Could you redo it, please?" I ask.

He snatches the paper from me, I am surprised I don't get a paper cut, and makes a show of ripping up the paper in front of my face, slowly, pointedly. My mind flashes to broken treaties. Never trust any paper from a white man, I think but do not say. He throws the pieces away and punches again at the computer, prints out a new form, and shoves it across the counter at me. I read the new form, feeling his eyes on me, the flesh around his eyes crinkled.

I am suddenly aware I am a woman alone in this room with him. He jabs a pen at me and orders, "Sign this one." I can tell he wants to add, *bitch*. I thank him (why do I have to thank him, except for not wanting to enrage him), sign, and force myself to smile, even though I do not like having to thank an armed man who had the audacity to speak for my identity.

I could have made it easier on myself and signed the first form, since I can easily pass for white, but I knew it wasn't about passing; it was about not passing up a chance, however small, to assert my own identity in the face of the dominant culture. This small act of defiance, of resistance, is nothing like the warriors guarding Standing Rock, but if he is guilty of this microaggression, I am going to challenge him. Until now my seemingly white skin gave me the privilege he has—the privilege to move through the world unafraid, unlike those of more evident color beaten or killed by police. I feel for my phone in my purse, but whom would I call? The police? He *is* the police. I wait. I force myself to say, "Thank you for retyping the form." I see the handle of his gun with every move. I see there is an office behind him he could take me into if he wanted to. I think of walking out, but I need my license and I do not want to have to come back.

He tells me to go over to a seat at the back wall in front of a blue backdrop. I do as I am told. I find myself fearful of this white man with the red face and black gun, and I imagine how women who are browner skinned than I must feel every day. The photo should only take a second, but he tells me to turn this way and that, to smile, not to smile, to push my hair back, and when I don't do it to his liking, I feel his hand in my hair, pushing my hair off my shoulders. His gun is close. I feel humiliated and sick, but I will not show it. He is putting me in my place as he moves my hair with his fingers. Not in a dramatic way, not in a way that will cost my life—I think of so many disappeared Native women—but in a way that nonetheless makes me pray for someone, anyone, to open the door so I won't be alone with him. I leave my body and watch, like every survivor knows how to do. I become an observer. It is safer that way.

It is then I realize I am no longer alone. Behind me, unbeknownst to him, stand other women, my ancestors, some of whose names I know and others I don't. I feel their strength, their spirit of protection.

Finally, when he sees he cannot get a rise out of me, he loses interest. He says, "You're done." Not *we*; I have alienated him, refusing to be part of his tribe. Perhaps he fears he cannot pose me anymore without risking a complaint to his superiors. He has no use for me now, nor I for him, except for needing my license.

I stand, willing my legs to support me, and go to the counter, where he completes my transaction. He thrusts my license across the counter with a smirk. I pay for my identity. I am too shaken to say anything else. "Have a real nice day, now," he nearly spits. I imagine him telling this story to his buddies. I know he knows where I live. I know I will never feel safe in this town. I also know it's only a fraction of what my browner-skinned cousins feel every day in the presence of police, and all because I refused to go along and check the *white* box. The rage in his face is the rage in the face of every white man who believes his race reigns supreme. His gun is the gun of every white man who has ever inflicted violence on a person due to skin color.

I walk to my car, where I immediately lock the doors then sit, shaken, before starting the engine. I am furious at being shamed and vow to report him as I have other abusers. But he has a gun. It is a small town. I was not (physically) harmed. It was a small offense, a petty indignity compared to what people of more noticeable color experience routinely. I start my car and drive away. I give him power every time I think about him. I force myself not to think about him. Until I move again and need another license.

Home: a place of belonging, at least that is the ideal. but what about not feeling at home in one's own skin? My encounter with this police officer is, I know, only a minor humiliation, hardly worth mentioning. It is nothing like the systemic abuse of people of color by white people, especially police officers. It is nothing like the tragedy of the Trail of Tears. Nothing like the loss of language, culture, or long hair at government schools. It is hardly a matter of justice at all, except that it matters to me. I have avoided checking the white box, but also, if I'm honest, I have avoided looking inside to examine its contents. My white box is heavy, but no hope chest. Its hinges creak resistance when I lift the lid. It is full of privilege granted me by society for the lightness of my skin. It has afforded me resources, such as education and healthcare, lacking or deficient for so many brown people. My white box is filled with ancestors, who may not have had slaves, but who nonetheless benefited from the subjugation of African Americans. They were farmers and chair caners. European men married Cherokee women, who adapted, assimilated, acculturated, hiding in plain sight or, as one of my family documents says of a Cherokee ancestor, *did not go west with the Indians.*

Instead of a Trail of Tears, there was a trail of silence. So I write to break the silence and reclaim what was suppressed, knowing full well that without "proof" I will be dismissed, yet when I praise Creator in the morning I do not have to submit proof. Still, my history is intertwined with the shameful history of the South; the slur "black Irish" was used to describe many of Indian heritage. My white box is filled with the lilt of Celtic music, indigenous people also, whom so-called Christians converted by force. My white box is filled with disease ancestors brought to this "New World." It is filled with German fairy tales and guilt by ancestral association over that country's Holocaust and the shameful knowledge that a Holocaust happened here as well. George Washington was known as "the town destroyer" for burning all those Indians.

I force myself to look squarely at its contents. If a black box contains clues to an airline disaster, maybe a collective white box contains evidence of this nation's racial record.

When I get to the bottom of what I think is the white box, I realize there is a false bottom in the box, a hidden compartment, so I feel along the seam and lift another lid and begin to unpack the secret contents. It is here I find what underlies my refusal to check the *white* box. Here I find the foundation for my insistence on not simply being white and here, again, there is discomfort, self-doubt mixed with self-recognition:

You don't look Cherokee. (At an outdoor photo shoot, for a book on Native writers, at which my light brown hair had gone to frizz and my light skin was pink with heat.)

Must be nice to get casino money. (I explained I am not an enrolled citizen of a tribe and the per cap is not for me.)

The time I was with Indian friends and the waiter did not wait on our table until after all the white people around us, who arrived after us, had been served. The time a white professor disrespected a Native professor and me as that professor's student.

Recurring comments and questions designed to discredit: *how much Cherokee are you, what's your blood quantum, what's your dna test say* (never mind that only a tribe determines criteria of its members and I do not meet those criteria; it is not just blood, but also culture), *did you grow up on a reservation?*

Thoughtless comments by coworkers who would never dare make a disparaging remark about African Americans: *low man on the totem pole, everyone wants to be chief; no one wants to be Indian.* Rooting for sports teams with Indian mascots.

Then there are the insults or threats hurled at one time or another: *Indian giver*; I'll give you an *Indian burn*. Or even the seemingly innocuous: sit *Indian style*.

In some ways, I am a dichotomy: I say my prayers in Cherokee every morning. I sing the morning song while facing East. I pray to the Creator of all for the good of all, including those I would sooner curse than bless. I go to church even though I know the inherent racism of Church as institution was part of the cultural genocide of Native Americans and indigenous populations everywhere, including the Celtic Indigenous "snakes" that Christian missionaries silenced.

Some Indian men have called my green eyes "exotic," and if I am honest, I have fetishized others for their differences as well. But there is no denying the privilege I have inherited as a person of Caucasian descent, my "white" (freckled beige) skin allowing me to pass through the world largely unchecked.

Still, if I dig deeper, to the bottom of this compartment, I can begin to smell cedar and tobacco, signifying the place where the most sacred memories are stored.

I have made many mistakes. I have, at times, failed to act honorably, and always the inner voice insists, you are not enough; you do not deserve the good. This voice was internalized from childhood, yes, but is also the message internalized by so many Indians after so much damage. Make them hate themselves for being dirty Indians, the whites said and, indeed, an Indian friend says he tried to scrub the brown off.

I give a poetry reading at a college, and I state that I am not a member of, nor do I presume to speak as a member of, a sovereign nation. After the reading a student approaches me. She says that she *is* an enrolled member of a tribe and that all her life she was made fun of for her light skin and light eyes. We hug and for a moment we are bound by blood—and pain.

I am always careful to attribute, and be respectful in referencing, what does not belong to me, at least not to the white part of me. But I am never going to be Indian enough or white enough to meet some people's criteria. So I uncheck all the boxes; the shape of the box itself is confining, linear, whereas the Indian way is the circle of dances and ceremony. Even the Western conception of time is linear, rather than inclusive of all time and space, and nonlinear narratives exasperate readers steeped in Western literature. So instead I enter the circle where I begin to dance. I do not do it well. I do not really belong, but it is a dream I have often, and always in the dream I am welcomed into the circle.

I have studied the language, history, and culture to the best of my ability, but I will never be fluent in any. To many, I will remain an outsider. Still, I try to honor my elders and betters from whom I have been blessed to learn. Their generosity astounds and humbles me.

I have looked into the white box as directly and unflinchingly as I can. I have also explored that interior compartment, not evident at first, that holds what is most precious and grounds my entire identity. Now I shut the chest and slide it, leaning my shoulders into it, back to the base of my bed. When I dream, I transcend all the boxes. I contact the spirit world. My prayer is to be useful. I think of Marilou Awiakta's mother's question to her: and what will you do for the People?[1] I think of this every time I write and consecrate my words to the service of what is true and holy.

I think of the poem "Dear World" by Paula Gunn Allen and her description of the way mixed-race people inherently fight against ourselves, often manifesting as illness—in this case, lupus.[2]

I think of the war dance or the welcome dance—the dance that can have two meanings depending on the context. I think sometimes I am at war with myself, not only physically but mentally and spiritually. I attempt diplomacy with myself. I think of Audre Lorde's poem "A Litany for Survival": So it is better to speak / remembering / we were never meant to survive.[3]

A white doctor shames and traumatizes me. My Indian doctor says there is nothing wrong with me, that my experience is spiritual, not pathological, that my trauma is also intergenerational trauma. Unlike the white doctor, my Native doctor first does no harm. He teaches me ceremony for the spirit of depression that visits me after so many losses, of loved ones, of relationships, of health. I see how vital ceremony is to me in connecting to my Indian heritage, in helping me heal so that I can be a better agent for healing in the world.

I know both worlds to a degree. If I disavow the white box, I have no influence in that world. If, out of reticence, I disown the Native box, I lose my ability to contribute what little I can, and I believe that withholding one's gifts, however modest, dishonors the Giver of all gifts.

But residual doubt lingers. Even this essay seems to take up too much space on this white page as I type, asserting my will across the screen. Will I ever be at peace? Someone asks me where all my sadness comes from, and my throat tightens on sounds of a language I know I'll never master. Master. Always the white part seeking dominance.

Fast forward several years. I move for another job, this time to a large city in the Midwest, where I rent a room in someone else's home. Once again, I am at the DMV to get a new license. I enter behind a dark-skinned woman in a hijab, my own head covered by a wig after radiation also zapped my hair. I remember a friend saying hair is strength and how she cut her hair in grief for the death of her mother. In that case, I have lost my strength, but I grieve too, for other losses. I also know my strength ultimately comes from the strength of ancestors and that strength also resides in me—when I remember to claim it.

This time the young white man behind the counter does not check the *white* box for me. In fact, as a recent college graduate and student of history, he is eager to hear about my Cherokee heritage.

Yes, times change. People, we hope, will eventually become more informed, more tolerant. And yet racism remains an ugly wound in this country, incited by the rhetoric of the current inhabitant of the White House, a house built by slave labor.

My Cherokee teacher said snakes should be respected since they can shed their skin and become a new snake, and I think of how humans shed their skin cells every seven years and become new. Seven is a sacred number. I know how hard it is to change and how some things have to die for new life to begin, but I cannot change what I have inherited.

If a black box holds the secret recordings that provide the key to interpreting an airline disaster, might not the white box hold the secret longings of a nation that refuses to acknowledge fear of non-white people and thus still punishes differences, still foments violence against those perceived as intruders, even though it is the Europeans who invaded and committed genocide? A nation that cages brown-skinned children at the border.

Living in diaspora, without tribal community, is isolating, so I have a loose community of chosen family of different tribes. We trade stories and tears. We laugh and offer encouragement and call each other "sister."

Some of my sisters are enrolled, some are not. We do not box each other in. We allow space for questions, for visions.

I am seeking integration. I am seeking to identify as human. I am in need of healing as we all are.

White is the absence of color; white objects reflect and scatter all visible wavelengths of light. I think of white people I have known who reflect deeply on race and white privilege and seek to work for justice. I remind myself that not all white people are like the white cop at the DMV who checked the *white* box for me and menaced me for changing it. I remind myself that I fall prey to the same prejudice every time I paint all white people with the same brush, for how then can I be an agent for reconciliation?

This time, at this DMV, my photo-taking is uneventful. I may look white, but I am proud to have even a drop of blood from the Real People, AniYvwiya.

After I get my license, I still have to go get my registration. I am walking downtown in this new city, where I am completely unknown. I do not know where I am going, so I am looking at my phone for directions when I trip and fall hard, skinning my knee to blood. (In Cherokee the word for *red* contains the word for *blood*.) I have also hurt my wrist, but no one stops; they walk around me on the sidewalk. I could not be more anonymous. And this makes me laugh aloud.

I hobble to the courthouse, where a young African American woman issues my registration. With my new license and registration, I am now official in a state the name of which is supposedly Iroquois meaning "the land of tomorrow." I am, however, suspicious of my inclination to romanticize.

I walk the long city blocks back to the parking garage; by now my hand is starting to blacken and swell, and blood causes my knee to stick to my black dress pants. I manage to feed the parking ticket into the machine by using two hands. The skin on my wrist is now mottled dark with bruising, not white at all. I exit and the disembodied voice of my GPS guides me onto the unfamiliar highway, where I merge and up my speed to keep up with all the other drivers.

What drives anyone? What moves us to speak up? And if we do not speak up in small things, how can we expect to find the courage to speak up in more important matters?

I am just a person who had no say in my family heritage. But I do have a say in how I honor or dishonor the Cherokee in me. (*If you say you're Cherokee I'm going to expect something of you.*) I find what I think is the right lane. I head toward my rental room in someone else's home.

NOTES

1. Awiakta, *Selu*, 132.
2. Allen, "Dear World."
3. Audre Lorde, "A Litany for Survival."

BIBLIOGRAPHY

Allen, Paula Gunn. "Dear World." In *Skins and Bones: Poems 1979–87*, by Paula Gunn Allen, 71. Albuquerque: West End Press, 1988.

Awiakta, Marilou. *Selu: Seeking the Corn-Mother's Wisdom*. Wheat Ridge CO: Fulcrum Publishing, 1993.

Lorde, Audre. "A Litany for Survival." In *The Collected Poems of Audre Lorde*, 255. New York: W. W. Norton & Company, Inc., 1997.

Steve Russell

Seeking the Indian Gravy Train

I am an old man now, twice retired, and when cancer came calling a couple of years ago, it provided a powerful motivation to take stock, to sum up, to consider the historical matrix into which I was born and evaluate how I played the hand I was dealt. Did this dropout do all he could do about the injustice everywhere he looked?

At the time of my birth, in 1947, the Cherokee Sacred Fire had been burning from time immemorial, or so those of us born Cherokee are told by our elders.

We know the Fire burned in the early nineteenth century when a Cherokee man of no schooling but great learning invented a method to put the Cherokee language on talking leaves, a method adopted by the Cherokee government in 1825. The Cherokee villages scattered in and around the Smoky Mountains had united to form a constitutional republic, and the citizens of that republic had a higher literacy rate than the surrounding settlers when the young settler nation deigned to begin calling the Cherokees "civilized."

We know that in 1838 the Fire lit the last council before the Removal in Red Clay, Tennessee. It was brought on the Trail Where They Cried to Indian Territory, a journey that is part of the blood memory of modern

Cherokees. The Fire was not extinguished by the tears, and the embers survived to light ceremonial fires in Indian Territory as it became Oklahoma in 1907.

The Sacred Fire was returned to the homelands in 1951, and embers from it were used to light the Council Fire when the elected leadership of the Cherokee Nation of Oklahoma and the Eastern Band of Cherokees held a joint council on April 3, 1984, back in Red Clay, Tennessee.

The Cherokee Sacred Fire that had turned seven woods to ashes from time immemorial in the Smoky Mountains did the same in Oklahoma as a Cherokee man named Haney Walter Teehee crossed from the Cherokee Nation to the Muscogee Creek Nation to seek work in the oil fields.

The Fire burned on impassively as Haney Teehee searched on a cold and wet day and returned without a job but with a bad cold that did not go away. Haney, like his father, Henry, had married a white woman, and his death left her with their two-year-old son, Clifford Wayne Teehee.

Cliff Teehee grew up in the Muscogee Creek Nation without the Cherokee language and became the third generation of male exogamy when he married a beautiful and headstrong child of a driller and a housekeeper. I was born, part of the baby boom, on the day the Paris treaties formally ended World War II in Europe. I share my birth year with the AK-47 assault rifle, the U.S. Air Force, NASCAR, the Voice of America, *Meet the Press*, the International Monetary Fund, India as an independent nation, Pakistan, and the Stigler Act.

The Stigler Act joined the Dawes Act and the Curtis Act on a roster of infamy for Indians, laws passed to separate us from the reservations we had gotten through an involuntary exchange for our homelands. The designation "Indian Territory" had already become a cruel irony, but Stigler was aimed at the tiny slivers of property still held in trust for citizens of the Five Tribes: Muscogee-Creek, Seminole, Choctaw, Chickasaw, and Cherokee.

The Sacred Fire burned as this additional barrier to Indians retaining their property went up.

The Fire burned as, in Cleveland, the American League baseball team adopted what the *Chicago Tribune* called "the most offensive image in sports": Chief Wahoo, a caricature that resembles the way Nazi propagandists had represented Jews, which is only now being phased out by the Cleveland Indians.

The Fire was still burning when, in Richmond, Virginia, Dr. Walter Ashby Plecker walked in front of a speeding car and departed the world he had altered for thousands of people with his authorship and enforcement of the Racial Integrity Act of 1924. That law recognized only two "races" in the Commonwealth of Virginia, "white" and "colored," effectively legislating American Indians out of existence. From his post as registrar for the Virginia Bureau of Vital Statistics, he enforced the "one drop rule" against African Americans and Indians alike, and no "colored" person, like my father, could lawfully marry a white person, like my mother, until the U.S. Supreme Court struck down the law in 1967.

In Oklahoma City, the state legislature authorized building the Turner Turnpike, a construction that would immediately bisect the Creek Nation and become part of a system that would bisect the Cherokee Nation, where the Sacred Fire was burning, and seal the economic fate of the town where I was born.

In Bristow, Oklahoma, formerly the Muscogee Creek Nation, I was born with a Cherokee blood quantum of one-eighth to keep the Fire burning.

Or not.

My first stomp dance was at a Creek ground rather than a Cherokee one but, truth be known, I would have been almost as much a guest at a Cherokee stomp ground. I had no obligation to the maintenance of any Cherokee grounds or any fixed role in the ceremonies. I was, in Cherokee parlance, an "outlander," a Cherokee citizen living outside the homelands, connected only by telephone, U.S. mail, and a chain of government paper leading to a "Certificate of Degree of Indian Blood."

To white Oklahoma, had I not been born in a small town and named Teehee, I could have passed for "part Indian." That was a status more Oklahomans claimed than not, a trace amount of Cherokee blood passed down by a many-greats grandmother who had high cheekbones but no tribal enrollment because she ran off from the Trail Where They Cried.

The Cherokee grandmother trope was a sure-thing laugh line among Indians of all tribes. I developed the habit of firing back with a quote from Paint Clan Cherokee Will Rogers, who claimed, "I have just enough white blood for you to question my honesty."

In the economic circumstances of my childhood, I might have envied many things and I suppose I did, but I never heard even distant rumors of an Indian gravy train where my blood might get me a ride.

My elderly grandparents did the best they could with their limited resources and the years they had left, but I lived in the shadow of the cold fact that they would be gone before I was educated and I would be alone, my only inheritance their constant reassurance that I was smart and I could make something of myself.

After my grandfather died, I had a conversation with my grandmother in which she warned me that she was unlikely to live to see me graduate high school. I could not break the news that I did not expect to graduate high school, but I took her point.

My grandparents' reassurance that my mind was strong enough to carry me to better days conflicted with virtually all the feedback I got in the public schools. Still, it turned out to be an inheritance of such value that I wanted to acknowledge it and perhaps pass it on. Still do. That's why I choose to spend the last months of my life writing about how I managed my material and emotional needs. Both of those accomplishments seem improbable without the legacy from the elders named Russell. In their honor, the name I wished to pass on when I started a family became Russell.

I was aware that the Teehee family has a distinguished history within the Cherokee Nation. Family legend had it that I was a direct descendant of Houston Benge Teehee, who served in Tahlequah city government, Cherokee County government, Oklahoma state government, and most famously as register of the U.S. Treasury. In that role, he signed the currency and the bonds sold to finance World War I.

My namesake was supposedly Ginatiyun Tihi, Stephen Teehee, who was Houston B's father. Ginatiyun served Cherokee tribal government in a number of capacities. I did not find out the principal role for which he was remembered until I was a middle-aged judge poring over old issues of the *Cherokee Phoenix*. Ginatiyun Tihi—whom I had known for serving in legislative and executive positions—-was primarily remembered as a fair and impartial judge. In a time when much tribal business was done in English, Tihi stayed with Cherokee.

While it's an honor to be thought associated with such a man, he was not my namesake. According to my mother, Stephen Teehee was a living friend of the family when I was born, although *he* certainly might have been named after Ginatiyun Tihi. Houston B. Teehee is a collateral rather than a direct ancestor.

The family story about Houston B. did not hold up, but a look at the Cherokee section of the Dawes Rolls—the master rolls that determine eligibility for Cherokee Nation citizenship—-showed more Russells than Teehees. While I am not related to the Cherokee Russells and I am related to the Teehees, being publicly called Russell would not imply I am unlikely to be Cherokee.

At the very end of my air force hitch, I hired a lawyer to change my name. I never told him why and he never asked, because the only reason a judge could deny a name change is if the purpose is fraud.

When the order was signed, I was required to take it and a copy of the pleadings to my squadron commander so my military discharge would have the correct name on it. While waiting in the squadron business office, I peeked at the petition and found that the lawyer had attributed a reason to me: that the name Teehee had subjected me to ridicule. While that was true, it had nothing to do with why I would give up a fine old Cherokee name.

I first learned of that embellishment while I was waiting to meet the officer who had taken over my squadron while I was in a military hospital for seven months. My turn came quickly, and I was ushered to the inner office. I saluted and then shook hands with my new commander . . . Maj. Eugene Tehee. The spelling difference was not significant. He was Cherokee; I was mortified.

Major Tehee was very kind and began a discussion of possible relatives in common. I had no graceful opportunity to explain that I wanted my discharge papers to say Russell and the degree I hoped to earn to say Russell and the children I hoped to have to carry the name that had come to mean so much to me.

It was impossible to not notice the color of Major Tehee's skin. My own complexion varied greatly, so greatly that I grew up thinking my Cherokee blood protected me from sunburn. I proved otherwise in an act of stupidity that left me past well done and toward crispy. Time spent at the white end of my spectrum conferred no social advantage, because if you live in a small town in Oklahoma and your name is Teehee, everybody knows you are Cherokee.

When I left Oklahoma, "Teehee" became "Indian" and when I changed my name to Russell, I gained the ability to pass among the settlers as one of them. For almost twenty years, the only people who knew I was Cherokee were the people I chose to tell.

Well, not the only ones. I have been accosted by older Indian people several times who either asked me a question that they could not expect a white person to answer or who just started speaking in Cherokee. That would lead me to beat a quick retreat to English but also to wonder what was going on. More than once I asked and got only a chuckle and some remark about a lucky guess.

Came the day when I gave some legislative testimony for the Texas Indian Bar Association and the Austin newspaper covered it. I thought nothing of being outed since my friends already knew and I wasn't hiding my dual citizenship.

Being a citizen of the Cherokee Nation suddenly became significant.

An elderly man came and looked me up at the courthouse to tell me it was not right for me to hold public office because "Indians don't pay taxes." More disturbing, my IQ seemed to have dropped twenty points overnight. I found myself dividing lawyers into those who treated me differently and those who did not.

I learned through the courthouse rumor mill that I had only been admitted to the University of Texas and then Texas Law because of affirmative action. Ironically, the only time I had consciously played white was to avoid that very thing, the affirmative action stigma.

I've never looked, but I would bet my records at UT do not list me as Indian. My transcript contains no racial information, and the only time I remember mentioning my tribal affiliation was when I asked that a graduation notice be sent to the *Phoenix*. I did not want any affirmative action, and I did not want UT to be able to claim they recruited me for diversity's sake.

While I favor affirmative action as public policy, I must admit that the very existence of it causes white students to assume they arrived with better credentials—true in my case because I arrived with *no* credentials, but I did not use my tribal affiliation to finesse that problem.

Another result of the newspaper mentioning I am Cherokee was I started being regaled with Cherokee grandmother stories. I could not understand who they thought had appointed me arbiter of Indian authenticity or how in the world the limited number of Cherokee women gave birth to so many white people and then somehow lost touch with their offspring in just a couple of generations.

A common story was that Grandmother ran off from one of the removal parties on the Trail Where They Cried. Since Grandmother was not around, she never taught them that literacy in the Cherokee Nation was nearly universal and there were lists of who went with which removal party and whether they arrived in Indian Territory.

None of the real history mattered once my identity became public. I relearned what I had learned as a child and forgotten. For modern Indians, our experience is all stereotype all the time. After a short flash of novelty that attended the news, and opinion adjustments applied to address the puzzle of how an ignorant savage got to be an elected judge, I was back to my courthouse routine.

Since he is now retired, I will not cause trouble when I divulge that another enrolled Cherokee was also an elected judge in Travis County, Texas, but he had the good fortune not to get noticed by the newspaper. It was odd, after fifteen years on the bench, to have lawyers slowly explaining matters that a first-year law student would know. I would not wish it on anyone else.

My new social status was not why I quit, but it certainly made quitting easier.

I had always wanted to teach. After the kids were grown, my wife was not just willing to take the pay cut—she was happy to never have to go through another election. When I put together my résumé for a teaching position, I was still reeling from the sudden drop in my IQ when my tribal identity became public. Once was enough.

I figured that if the Indian gravy train existed, there had to be a depot in academia. The happenings that had shaken my judicial career had taught me that I could not escape the affirmative action stigma by not letting on I was Indian.

I was also concerned that my teaching résumé would look a bit thin for a man of forty-eight. I had taught as an adjunct at St. Edward's University and I had about half a dozen academic publications, but only two were outside of law journals. I had a master's on top of my law degree, but I was not sure PhDs would understand that a Juris Doctor was required for admission to my master's program because the degree hierarchy differs in law.

Weighing all that, I made the conscious decision to let it all hang out on my résumé. I mentioned that I had the blood and I mentioned that I had the paper. I lost my qualms about riding the Indian gravy train, because I understood that the people around me would think I had been riding it anyway. Having experienced the downside, I was ready for the upside.

I was short-listed at three universities, two in Texas and one in California. I was hired by the one I would have chosen, and as I went through the pro forma interviews with the chain of command, mention was made of my publications and the fact that I had a graduate degree in addition to the J.D. Not a word about my ethnicity.

The next year, as luck would have it, I was appointed "affirmative action officer" for a search committee. I thought it would be prudent to read the affirmative action plan. When I did, I found that the plan mentioned Indians but contained no hiring goals for Indians because, it said, there were not enough qualified Indians. That is, Indians with terminal degrees.

This reminded me of when the Indian Bar in Texas wanted to form a section of the State Bar. There were not enough of us. We had to recruit friendly non-Indians and accept the fact that we could only have the section as long as unfriendly non-Indians did not decide to join to vote us all out of leadership roles.

Given my experience with the Indian Bar, I realized that the remark about too few Indians with terminal degrees could be correct. The next time we had a search, I was appointed to chair the committee. I used my personal contacts to generate applications and came up with over half of the applicants being Indians. Of course, none of them were hired, proving I was not the only one unable to find the Indian gravy train.

There is, without a doubt, a problem in academia called "box-checkers" on the student level and "Pretendians" on the faculty level. Some of them have managed to board an Indian gravy train that appears to elude real Indians. They are an employment problem only if you take them to be in a zero-sum game, where they are taking spots that would have gone to real Indians. That is seldom the case, except when an Indian studies program seeks to hire an Indian to facilitate research in Indian communities.

The first thing two Indians discuss upon meeting is relatives. Then friends and acquaintances. Is it too much to ask that an Indian hired for Indian community connections have some?

My suggestion for those rare cases when you must have an Indian is you can seldom go wrong by using the papers to allocate the burden of proof, but the real issue is connection to an Indian community.

Should a university hiring an Indian be asking for papers? That would not work because not all Indians have papers, but they do have some connection to some Indian community somewhere. There is a truism that keeps coming up in discussions of Pretendians: "It's not about who you claim; it's about who claims you."

If an individual who claims to be Indian is not tribally enrolled, it's reasonable to ask them for proof. Nobody thinks twice about asking a non-Indian for references, so why would it be wrong to ask an Indian?

If an individual who claims to be Indian is tribally enrolled, the person who claims they are not Indian should provide proof—that is, why they think the applicant is a faker.

Colleges and universities have bureaucracies that can smoke out fakers if that's an issue. The other place where faux Indians find fame and fortune is the literary world, where only individual publishers have bureaucracies and their purpose is generally to sell books to the exclusion of checking the bona fides of authors.

The literary world has had some Pretendians who really got some daylight under their wheels before they were outed. Carlos Castaneda and Nadijj come to mind. Others, like Margaret Seltzer, got caught early. I suspect all will get caught eventually, either by the tribal relatives falsely claimed or by real relatives who are offended by the whole enterprise.

This brings me to my last experience of the elusive Indian gravy train. All three of the Pretendians named above were producing fake memoirs. Earlier this year, I won what I perceived to be a race with my own mortality to write my dropout-to-professor memoir, which I hoped would do good for dropouts and people who work with dropouts. It's almost funny that I got tenured twice in the realm of publish or perish and I never considered publishing that big a deal . . . until now, when I've got a manuscript so close to my heart.

So what, though? I do not think for a minute that my reality is being crowded out by somebody's fakery. It's simply not true that the Indian gravy train is pulling out of the station with some faker in my seat.

Am I angry? You bet.

Am I disappointed? Of course.

Some of the things I said about myself are that I am enrolled Cherokee, a disabled air force veteran, and emeritus faculty from Indiana University. When I started out to peddle my memoir, I made a document containing my tribal identification, my VA identification, and my IU identification. All those cards have my picture. I should not have bothered. I've not been asked to prove anything.

My life experience offers two explanations for this last futile search for the Indian gravy train.

It could be that my story is just not as interesting as I thought it was, either because that's the fact of my life or because embellishments are expected and I did not embellish.

It could be that there really is a gravy train, but the name stenciled on the side of the engine is not "Indian"—it's "Luck."

Diane Glancy

Unpapered

I want to begin by quoting from "Motion of Fire and Form," *Mixed Blood Messages*, by Louis Owens, University of Oklahoma Press, 1998:

> Not a real, essential Indian because I am not enrolled and did not grow up on a reservation . . . I have learned to inhabit a hybrid, unpapered, Choctaw-Cherokee-Welsh-Irish-Cajun mixed space in between. I conceive of myself today not as an "Indian," but a mixed-blood, a person of complex roots and histories. Along with my parents and grandparents, brothers and sisters, I am the product of a liminal space, the result of union between desperate individuals on the edge of dispossessed cultures and the marginalized spawn of invaders. A liminal existence and tension in the blood and heart must be the inevitable result of such a crossing.

I can relate to Owens's "liminal existence and a tension in the blood and heart" because I have a similar "unpapered" background.

From the perspective of the Cherokee Nation, I am not Cherokee because my paternal great-grandfather, Woods Lewis, is not on the Dawes Rolls. And that determines Cherokee citizenship. My great-grandfather is not on the rolls because he was not in Indian Territory when the

1898–1907 rolls were taken. According to stories of my father, his sister, and their cousin, Woods Lewis fled Indian Territory just before the Civil War. There were disagreements and infightings in the upheaval of resettlement that followed the Removal Trail. The new territory, Indian Territory, was a fierce place. I could say that Indian politics still are.

But I want to continue with the many disputes in Indian Territory and the many disputes in my family chronicles. The details have varied, but the story has continued along two versions. My great-grandfather was born near Sallisaw in what is now Oklahoma. Or my great-grandfather was born in Tennessee. There was trouble in Indian Territory, and he fled to Meigs County in eastern Tennessee (some 600 miles to the east). He enlisted in the 4th Cavalry, Company L, Union Army, Tennessee. That information is in the Civil War Records in the National Archives in Washington DC. He was five-foot-eight and had black hair, black eyes, and an olive complexion. He marked himself "White." The only other choice was "Black."

After the Civil War, he married Margaret Blevins in Meigs County, December 6, 1865. That also is written record. When they migrated west, word got out that he was back, and he could not resettle in Indian Territory. They went to northern Arkansas. Their daughter, my grandmother, was born in Viola in 1887. My father was born in Viola in 1908.

Each generation married Anglo-Christians. It is what I am more than Cherokee. But there is a Cherokee part also. I do not have Native language or tribal contact. I live in an over-branch of heritages. I live in a shadowland. A marginal land. A lateral Native background. An interfacing. A confluence. A left out of both worlds. A not Indian but somewhat banished Cherokee. My great-grandfather was a fugitive who could not return to Indian Territory after the Civil War. He was part of a family that came from Tennessee and tried to settle in Indian Territory and faced expulsion. His mother, my great-great-grandmother Arvezena Crawford Lewis, is buried in Paw Paw Cemetery in Sequoyah County, Oklahoma. I have visited her grave. She went to Candy's Creek Mission school, established by Dr. Samuel Worcester, a missionary to the Cherokee. That is on record also.

I have been to sweat lodge ceremonies and the Sun Dance held in South Dakota. I was at Standing Rock during the pipeline protest. I remember the thought "I am not one of these—the traditional, tribal Natives." I did not belong, though I believed in the protest.

Further, as Joseph Brad Drowning Bear said, an Indian is only Indian in relation to a tribal community. I am not in a tribal community. I have been an outsider, as my family has been, living in the Anglo-Christian community. My father left Arkansas and went to the Kansas City stockyards for work. In those days, companies transferred their workers. It seemed we always were leaving. Sometimes mid–school year. Uprooted. A new classroom in another state. A new teacher. Different curriculum. We were disconnected. We grew self-contained. But there was the continuity of going to school. To church. I have continued in both all my life. They also have been uncomfortable places from the beginning.

Further still, all I have are my father's story, a wedding photo of his mother, Orvezene Lewis, my mother's photographs, and a letter from Aunt Effie, my father's sister, whom I saw only a few times in my life. I wrote to her in the early 1980s, when I started writing. Was the story true?

Her letter is dated June 10, 1981—

Dear Diane, I received your letter & will try to answer some questions for you. Grandpa and Grandma were married in Tenn, & he was also Cherokee Indian, but he was borned at Sallisaw, Oklahoma. Uncle Charlie Lewis lived at Pauls Valley he & Aunt Rosie are both dead but they have three sons that live there Don Earl and Jim of course the girl Dixie I don't know her last name. Grandpa had one brother and one sister she married a Key's they live at Okmulgee. I called Charlie Lewis here & talked to him he said you come to see him when you are in K.C. he can give you more information. I talked to Edith on the phone and gave her some information for you. Come to see me when you are in K.C. Love, Aunt Effie

I don't remember my mother, Edith, giving me any of Effie's information. My mother was not fond of Cherokee heritage. I lived in Tulsa at the time and did not visit Aunt Effie or Charlie Lewis.

Recently, I had a poem accepted by *Mud City*, a journal at the Institute of American Indian Arts. The password they gave me to look at the poem was *pretendian*. I understood what they meant. I have taken flak over the years. It began as soon as I started writing. I was only one-eighth Native. Then recently, in the upsurge of authentication, I have been accused of not being Native at all, which is true if you look at Drowning Bear's statement: a Native only in a Native community.

There are shadows on the wall from which I write. Similitudes. Adjacencies. What will I liken them to? Petroglyphs on a wall—the original meaning of which has been lost, other than hunting rituals—or the boxy outline of someone walking toward you with the sun behind their back. The drawings are representations of what I had not seen the originals of. This backed-up, undocumented heritage is the source of my work.

I think the recent movement against "Pretendians" is necessary and valid. I know many "unpapereds" who are being challenged over their cultural identity. Native heritage is not simple, nor always clear and documented. Indian rolls did not get everyone. But if self-claiming Native heritage includes being involved in the Native community, then I do not have authenticity because I've always lived in an Anglo-Christian community. My first feeling of being excluded came from them.

Many people think they have Native heritage. I don't think I've ever given a reading at which someone didn't tell me afterward they had Native heritage—usually Cherokee. I think in some cases it could be true. Some of the Cherokee fled the 1838–39 Removal and stayed behind. Some Cherokee disappeared along the 900-mile Trail of Tears that crossed Tennessee, Kentucky, a corner of Illinois, the nearly 300 miles across Missouri, and a corner of Arkansas into Indian Territory. There were also orphans given to farmers along the way.

After a DNA test, I had an email from *My Heritage* that a first cousin once removed had shown up on my chart. This cousin, who was from Arkansas, contacted me and sent an article that another family member had written after his research. Parts of it did not fit with the parts of the story I had known. Apparently, Woods Lewis was born in Tennessee and not Indian Territory. He may not have come to Indian Territory until after the Civil War. His mother, Arvezena Crawford Lewis, who was from Tennessee, came to Indian Territory to register as Cherokee in 1887. Actually, it was one of her sons-in-law, a white man, John Kesterson, who came first, by himself, to "receive land" because he was married to a Cherokee, and it must have irritated them. I talk about her experience in an essay, "Jump Suit," in *Island of the Innocent: A Consideration of the Book of Job*. Arvezena's mother's name was Mary Waters Crawford. Mary's father was Michell or Michael Watters; his name is on the Cherokee Henderson Rolls of 1835.

Michell Watters, my paternal great-great-great-great-grandfather
Mary Waters Crawford, my great-great-great-grandmother
Arvezena Crawford Lewis, my great-great-grandmother
Woods Lewis, my great-grandfather
Orvezene Lewis Hall, my grandmother
Lewis Hall, my father
Helen Diane Hall Glancy, myself

Now there are two stories of indeterminate nature instead of one, with no way to know which one is true.

I am quoting Louis Owens again, this time from his essay in *Contemporary Autobiographical Authors Series*, Volume 24, Gale Publishers, 1996: "Everything I'm interested in, every problem I want to explore or question or try to resolve, revolves around being of mixed ancestry, crossblood, in-between. When I begin to write, it seems that my words always move in that direction . . . Perhaps it's the uncertainty, self-doubt, fear of inauthenticity that drives me to words, sentences, pages, stories."

Again, I can relate to Owens's need to write. To establish place. To explore the middle ground between cultures. To work with the unsettledness of uncertainty. It is what many of the essays in "Unpapered" are about. A free-range collection of different experiences with documentation and authentication.

I write in the liminal space between spaces in which I find other liminal spaces. An overlap of versions that lend their grace to the bifurcated past of which I may never be sure. And why my paternal aunt, Effie, was sure her grandfather, Woods Lewis, was born in Sallisaw. And how he got from Indian Territory to Meigs County and how his mother was in a mission school in another county, though still in Tennessee, and how they strung themselves along to Indian Territory and how many times he had been there and back. And my own wanderings from place to place. Could I go back and remember each trip I have taken—all the travels? A pending heritage. A clouded thought. These grasses here. Those hills over there. It is in summer or winter their longing for each other. I know I belong somewhere else when the full moon wakes me with its light. Phrases insert themselves. A lost heritage. The pieces of belonging—often contrasting.

After hearing Dr. Kim TallBear's talk at Michigan State University's 2022 English department conference, "Unsettling Genealogies: Unmasking Pseudo Indians," I felt an elemental response of permanent dislocation and indecisive placement click together like the seatbelt when I buckle my travel box into the passenger's seat. It is a singular story with multi-folded parts. A mystery of "mixed space in between." An uncertainty I know to be my story. An absence.

Many of my ancestors made their way across the ocean from various places, leaving their shadows moving on my wall in the morning sun. Some of my ancestors were here when they arrived. They are the same shadows I see unmoving on the moon in the dark of night.

FINDING THE WAY

In this section, you will find essays dealing with the experiences of unpa-pered Natives, distanced from their communities, trying to settle into some sense of belonging with both the tribal nation that is their heritage and other tribal nations around them. These authors interrogate not only their family histories but their own motivations and behaviors, as they try to find a home for their deepest selves.

On Chumash Land

For the record I am not Chumash. I am an unpapered, undocumented mixed-blood, with roots in Oklahoma. Why am I not tribally enrolled? Grandpa was Cherokee, Lenape, and Seneca. All her life Grandma had been a Cherokee, but in 1953, the year I was born, the government decided Grandma was Lumbee. Uncle signed up right away. But Grandma refused to let me get enrolled. She said it was just folks talking and a piece of paper from the government couldn't change anything.

Squinting at me, Grandma said, "Child, you're a Cherokee and the Cherokee people have been divided and scattered into odds and bits, yet we're determined to keep our life ways alive."

And for forty-three years I lived in California, near the ocean, in an area that makes up the traditional Chumash homeland. I'm walking gently, a guest on this good land, and I hold the culture, traditions, and history of the Chumash people in my heart. For my Chumash friends, divided only by enrollment defining the federally recognized Santa Ynez Mission Band Chumash and Coastal Band Chumash, who applied for recognition in 1981, this is their landscape of time.

When I return from Limuw, Santa Cruz Island, with my Chumash friends, at first I only want natural light. It is past ten when I rinse the salt water from my hair. Moonlight falls from the open window, a flood of light from above. I am still under the influence of sea tides springing strong.

I spent four days and nights on the island, to let come what may. I wanted to be helpful to my friend, in her eighties now. A much loved, respected elder. Sometimes she needs a tiny bit of help fetching things and getting from here to there. I'm learning as she teaches me how to be helpful and grow old in a beautiful way.

Used to be, when you walked on the island of Santa Cruz and looked around, all the land you could see was Chumash Indian land. The island was once home to the largest population of island Chumash, with a highly developed, complex society and life ways. This included marine harvest and trade with the mainland. Island Chumash produced shell beads used as currency. Grasses and roots for making baskets and other necessities for living were there for the taking. And so, apparently, was the land. Historical records show that by 1853 a large herd of sheep had been brought to the island. The Civil War significantly increased the demand for wool, and by 1864 some 24,000 sheep had overgrazed the hills and valleys of Santa Cruz Island. Some of the early buildings from sheep ranching still stand.

During my four days on the island, instead of sheep, Indians again filled the area. We came to honor the Chumash peoples' annual channel crossing from the mainland to the Channel Islands.

A camp village is put up, where basket making, cordage making, song, prayer, and storytelling take place. On day one about fifty Indians have gathered. By Saturday, the day the Tomol arrives, there will be nearly two hundred of us, and the quote "a single bracelet does not jangle alone" describes us. The connectedness we have to each other is so much a part of our lives, it can't be distinguished from our lives.

Too often in our community there is a division between those who are federally recognized and tribally enrolled and those who aren't. Yet while we are on the island, this is not important. We are all Indians and we listen to the elders; they lead and we do as they instruct.

There's real power here on the island. When we leave the campsite village and walk to the rim of the island, first there is silence. Ravens and seagulls at the water's edge dip and wheel and dive. Under a sky turned pink we go for a sunset swim. With so much island and ocean and so few people, there is a lazy wag of space. I float in the sea with my head surrounded by gulls and fledglings.

At dawn we wake to sunrise singers. A high, sweet trill of voices, abalone beads swaying, carrying songs from the ancestors. The singers are letting us know it is time to gather for sunrise ceremony. Next, we wait for the paddlers to arrive. I stand with others on the shore and feel the sun rise from my heart. I've known two of the paddlers, a male and a female crewmember, since they were babies, and I've watched them grow to strong, beautiful, kind, and responsible young adults. Now I'm a grandmother, in my late sixties, moving toward elderhood, and I know the world that I will one day leave behind is in good hands.

If only in my mind, I am again in 1997, back when these two young paddlers were small kids and our community put together the American Indian Education Project series "Tomol Trek." After much hard work, we put together an academy with federal (Title V) funding, producing a modern-day recreation of a tomol. Our modern-day tomol was built by the children under the guidance of Peter Howorth, in his backyard tomol-building workshop. There was a perfect balance between master and apprentice as the children sanded pieces of the vessel throughout construction. A dozen hands move slowly across the handle, moving toward the paddle end of an oar. Small hands, young hands, skin so smooth, and maroon, peach-colored hands, muted brown, every child with an Indian community–belonging circling her or his heart.

Remembrance weighs heavily on my mind, as it does for most Native people seeking to affirm cultural identity in a high-tech world. There is a comfort in being with those who understand. Our kids did not have to trade in their Indian values for education; the project carried ancient memory and cultural knowledge into their lives today. And now two of those children, now grown, are making the crossing.

The paddlers leave the mainland at 3:00 a.m. There will be a careful change of crew three times. The moment the paddlers in the tomol come into view, my heart breaks open and I'm ageless and timeless and feel the welcome arms of the ancestors. The tomol is brought forth from the sea, and there is song and prayer.

Back at camp we prepare dinner, while island fox keep a steady eye trained on us. A near–Harvest moon rises. We eat, talk, joke, and tell stories of past crossings to the island, and "the old ways" move through our evening together like dancers, stirring to the same rhythm. All the people, the paddlers and those that help make the crossing and camp village possible, are honored. The day fades into liquid dusk and moonlight.

Time is a continuous loop until our stay on the island comes to a full-circle closure. Thankful for what I have been given, yet reluctant to let go, I prepare to leave and make the rounds to say goodbye to everybody who welcomed me.

On the boat ride to the mainland, we are soaking wet, laughing. A humpback whale is sighted in the navy blue ocean. In the Chumash language, my friends sing in the whale, and she surfaces.

At home in earthen shadows, rinsing off the salt water and sand, I feel the light from the moon, full and wan. I braid a pungent memory and fill my lungs and my heart with it, knowing it will permeate my body and cling to my soul as a reminder of what I can feel when we are all together on the island. The land, the culture, and the people I will always carry within.

Abigail Chabitnoy

A Salmon-Fishing Story

"Common among Alaska Natives, people who were either raised away from our home villages, or who had to leave at some point during our lives, and had to remain away for some length of time, displaced *Unangan/ Unangas* have a deepened sense of the sacred value of our origins. We feel a loss for what we have been missing."

—Barbara Švarný Carlson, "There Is No Such Thing as an Aleut"

The truth about stories is that's all we are.[1] At least that's what Thomas King says. So this is my story. Only the beginning is true. That is, only *beginning* is true.[2] I am from the place where the world began. In our language, the word for the sea is *imaq*. It is the same word for "a liquid contained inside" and "contents." The root word appears also in the words for "it is full" and "it is empty," to feel sad or downhearted, or to have a sinking or foreboding feeling. The word for "I am sad" translates in English as "I am searching for my contents." So I've read. I'm still learning my language. It was lost, or it was taken, when my great-grandfather was removed from his home, where the world began. I was born in absence, removed. Blood, the saying goes, is thicker than water, but water and, by extension, the sea—by extension, *imaq*—draws me home where liquid I am one among the ghosts of my family, my people, my culture, haunted and haunting, sinking, lost, and ultimately carried back to shore, ultimately still living, more than ghost, water *and*. My grandfather was called "half-breed," and for a time no one talked about "the Indian." My family did not tell stories. Still, the current carries on. I am still learning how to be "of the water," Alutiiq, of the liquid contained inside. I am still learning how to say that I am.

"So, what are all of you?"

It was my second year participating in Colorado State University's Native American Cultural Center's Women's Circle, though I knew only a handful of the women's names. I enjoyed their company, and the beading projects were a welcome tactile relief from the constant barrage of existential quandaries posed in my graduate courses, but when fingers paused too long, messier questions with oscillating answers threatened to wrinkle the patient work. A Navajo woman, new to the community, had asked the question I'd been too timid to voice. Most of the women already seemed to know each other, where they came from, what their positions were as Native women. I didn't know if such a question would be appropriate, and I didn't know if I would have an appropriate answer when the question was bounced back.

I was contacted by the center the summer I arrived in Colorado for graduate school, because I had filled in a box on some standard application form's list of intrusive, irrelevant demographic questions. I didn't remember doing so, not because this didn't sound like something I would do, but because this was something I did inconsistently. I didn't know the motives behind the list of ethnicities, and I didn't trust the motives behind my answer. The list of given prompts, too, seemed to treat the subject unevenly. *Caucasian,* for example, as it has come to be used and is understood in the context of such questionnaires, alludes simply to race, to a color. Not a place of origin. It does not distinguish between nationalities.

Why did it not matter that a long time ago my family was German? Or at least some of them were.

What if you were white but were born and raised in Alaska? Could you say you were Alaska Native? (I'd gotten into more than one heated debate in college with a few smug Northerners who thought you could.)

Why, if it did not matter that a long time ago some of my family was German, should it matter that somewhat more recently, but still a long time ago, a smaller portion of my family was Alaska Native?

And these are only the motives I question behind the choices that are offered. Why do I sometimes absently check the obvious box (obvious to my mind, *Caucasian*) and move on to check the next obvious box, when other times I linger over that *Native American/Alaska Native* box before checking *More Than One*?

Who isn't more than one?

What if I were just to click that one? Who would I be helping—or hurting—with my answer?

Even now, I can't tell you which one I mean by that one.

Wish-wash. Arnat qutmi et'ut. Aturaatnga.[3]

"What are you?"

My family doesn't tell stories. Or rather, my family tells one. Pieces of one. It begins with a boy and an island. There are deaths in the family, and trains. There is a baseball jersey with a large red *C*. *C* as in Carlisle, as in the Carlisle Indian Industrial School, where that boy played baseball with Jim Thorpe, a name I'm always surprised isn't familiar to every household. My great-grandfather's name was not Jim Thorpe. It was Michael Chabitnoy (though on a recent visit home with the rest of my dislocated cousins, the Pennsylvania Chabitnoys, I heard Jim was at his funeral). He was Aleut, from Woody Island, Alaska, and the family name meant "salmon-fisher" in Russian. I had known these precious few facts as long as I had known how to say our name. Besides a vague understanding of a period of Russian occupation of the Aleutian Islands (thus, the name), I didn't know what it meant to be Aleut. Michael never left Pennsylvania. He got a job in a chocolate factory, married a girl in Lebanon, Pennsylvania, and died shortly after my grandfather was born.

My family knows this story, tells this story, holes and all. It might have ended there, but in 1971 the Alaska Native Claims Settlement Act was passed so that oil extraction could progress in the state. My father enrolled in the Koniag Corporation, corresponding to Michael's last known whereabouts before Carlisle, and when it was time to apply for colleges, my siblings and I were enrolled as descendants. It was only later, as adults, that my sister and I enrolled in the Tangirnaq Native Village, and though we met the Tribal Council's criteria for citizenship, I had been reluctant to do so. I was writing my first poetry collection, very much concerned with questions of belonging, historical erasure, generational trauma, and who gets to tell the story, and I was nearly paralyzed by a self-imposed burden to question my motives at every turn, to hold the limits of my understanding of my culture and history accountable, to question whether or not I belonged.

"You have such a lovely complexion—and those cheekbones . . . Do you have Native blood?"

It's a question I'm asked frequently, but only in the summer, after my skin has had time to fully bronze. But the Aleutian Islands, off the Alaskan coast, aren't known for their summer sun, so even then I'm not sure which of my physical features can properly be attributed to my ancestors. Do all Natives tan easily? The confidence of my response when asked about my ancestry depends on the ancestry of the questioner. I am learning motives matter, and bilateral microaggressions do occur, though they are stealthier.

If it is a matter of blood, I am fractionally Aleut. Other than my cheekbones and questionable complexion, I don't look terribly different from a non-Native person, especially in winter. Do I look "Native enough" to answer, "I am Aleut?" Do I look "Native enough" to say this to a full-blooded Navajo from Fort Defiance? Do I look "Native enough" to say I am Aleut to a half-blooded Ojibwe from Milwaukee? What must I do to be "Native enough," and why is this a lack I am concerned with?

My great-grandfather, Michael Chabitnoy (also listed as Chabotnoy, or Shepednoy, according to various records, all incomplete) was born in 1885 on an island without trees, along the Pacific Ring of Fire, with wind no man could walk against, without "modern conveniency," where it rains two hundred and fifty days out of the year. At least he was likely born on such an island, though some of the nearer islands do have trees, and both Russian colonizers and American soldiers, at various times, have planted trees to mask the foreign fact of their presence, to make the seemingly inhospitable chain extending from the Great Land toward Russia smaller, more like home. He was last registered at the Baptist Mission Orphanage on Woody Island, which suggests the presence of trees. But he wasn't born there. His mother had a bad heart. His father was traumatized. No one seems to know what this means as a cause of death, but shortly after his parents died, Michael, my great-grandfather, full-blooded Aleut and orphan, left—or was removed—from those islands for good.

I say he was full-blooded. That is, we say he was full-blooded—my family and I. That is, his papers say he was full-blooded. But I'm learning that genealogies can be tricky in Alaska, first colonized by the Russians, then by the "Americans," who transplanted unwanted Indigenous peoples from otherwise homogenous nations in Northern Europe to herd reindeer, which had also been transplanted in an early effort to replace the Alaska Natives' economy of subsistence with that of commerce. The result of successive waves of colonization and Indigenous imports was an influx of Scandinavian and Norwegian names to further clutter genealogies already impregnated with Russian.

If I can say with confidence that I am this much Aleut, it might be enough, though I'm having trouble articulating what it might be enough for. In the summer of 1942, shortly after the Japanese invasion of Pearl Harbor, 831 Aleuts were forcibly relocated from their villages on various islands of the Aleutian chain to Southeast Alaska with little to no warning, and no information about how long they would be gone. Eighty-five would die in the hastily planned internment camps. White settlers serving military personnel and their families were allowed to remain on those islands; anyone with as much as one-eighth Native blood was moved to the camps, no matter whom they were related to. In their absence, the Aleuts' homes were looted (by American soldiers and civilians—not the Japanese, who never landed inland past Attu, the second most western island), and the villages were burned to the ground so Japanese troops wouldn't be able to use them.

I'm not sure whom my flippant use of quotation marks earlier, around "American," is meant to offend, or will possibly offend. It's possible my intention to offend, in itself, is not clear, is easily overlooked or dismissed. It's possible this ambiguity is intentional. It allows me to refrain from taking a firm position, making a declarative statement, an act of ethnic warfare. "Genocide" is not a word I grew up hearing in association with the grand founding of these United States. I'm not sure to what extent I have the right to offend or be offended, but that number, that fraction—in light of the events during World War II—begins to matter in ways I never gave thought to before.

I have a card, cheap laminate, flimsy, no photo, that says, "The owner of this card is an Alaska Native as defined by Section 3(b) of the Alaska Native Claims Settlement Act of 1971, as amended by Public Law 100–241, passed February 3, 1988." This act established thirteen regional corporations to manage resources and profits to be distributed—if the corporations were managed well, and there were, in fact, profits—among shareholders. I didn't have this card when I was a kid. I had a nice summer tan, an athletic build, hazel eyes I wished were Indian brown like my sisters', and a faulty translation. When I was a kid, I would talk the ear off of anyone not in a position to get away. I can still remember explaining our last name to restaurant hostesses and anyone else caught in the vicinity. (I was also loud.) *Table of six for Chabitnoy. It means salmon-fisher. My great-grandfather was Alutiiq. They're from Alaska.*

Even today, people of the Islands go back and forth on *Alutiiq* versus *Aleut*, versus *Unangan*, versus *Sugpiaq*. As though they were the same. Maybe, after all this time, they are more similar than different. Maybe we remember what is convenient. Maybe we stick with what is easy.

Aleut was the name the Russians gave the Unangan people of the Aleutian Islands. Meaning *people of the water*. (Though, conversely, I've also heard it translated as *people of the islands*. So which are we? The land, fixed and separate, or the water that moves between? The contents or that which contains?) Alutiiq is the Sugpiaq term for Aleut. The meaning is the same, but the word *Alutiiq* is spoken in their own tongue. This was an attempt by the culturally distinct people of the Alaska Peninsula and Kodiak archipelago to take ownership of the name the Russians foisted on them and to assert their own identity. Before the Russians, they called themselves Sugpiaq, "the real people." But this, too, depends on geographic boundaries of distinct cultures that were indiscriminately lumped together as one when they were "discovered" by the Russians. Were my ancestors included among the Real People? Alutiiq was the name we were given when my father registered. Aleut is the name on my great-grandfather's records from Carlisle. Aleut is a name that reflects the history of colonization that has shaped the people, that allows for my own shape to fit into that story. Unangan and Sugpiaq are the names that honor those still living in those places, to whom I am bound. *Aturaatnga.*[4]

When giving our name and (hi)story to restaurant hostesses, in memory, I am wearing my father's green Koniag jacket—a gift upon registering with the corporation—with the state and its iconic constellation outlined in blue on the back, sleeves hanging well past my hands. But memories can be convenient that way. Like water, they adjust to the shape we ask them to fill. What a lovely detail if it's true. An Alutiiq boy came up with the design for the Alaska state flag, but I didn't know that then. When I was a girl, those stars were just the big dipper. Ursa Major. Benevolent and beckoning. Just a bear cut out of stars, not a shovel seizing resources to extract and export to the United States proper, the Lower Forty-Eight. Then I hadn't heard of words like "resource colony" or "settler colonialism." Then I thought the Aleutian chain was small enough that we were related to every person on that island. Distantly, but related. Variably, it was only one island when I told this story. At that age my understanding of geography was based on a literal interpretation of the maps in my history book, and I understood the whole state of Alaska to be slightly smaller than Texas and only slightly bigger than the sprawl of Hawaii, similarly boxed and relocated on the map of the United States.

This was before I realized those eager greeters at the hostess stand were only looking for a first name. Something easy to pronounce, preferably one without a backstory. *Bob, party of six. Your table is ready.*

This was also before we learned my great-grandfather's name did not mean salmon-fisher. I don't know where this origin story came from, or who started it. I don't remember learning it. It was something I always knew. My father, similarly, doesn't remember where it came from. In the genealogy a cousin has traced it to the initial point of Russian encounter. Mikhail Chebotnoi (d. 1856) is listed as a local *baidarshchik* (a village chief approved by the Russian powers that were), occupation: walrus hunter. While this strikes me as more impressive, more primal somehow, it lacks the elegance of "salmon-fisher," the symbolic significance attached to the fish. (Though as sea levels rise and ice in the Bering Sea falls, jeopardizing the future survival of these great sea mammals, perhaps salmon skins fit better after all.) Its origin could not have come from my great-grandfather. He died in Lebanon, Pennsylvania, of tuberculosis shortly after my grandfather was born, 3,000 miles from anyone who might have known. My grandfather and his brother were called "half-breeds" in school, but both identified as white, teaching their children to do the same. Maybe one of them made up the name's history to console themselves.

Of course, my grandfather and great uncle had little choice in the matter of identity at the time. It's hard to identify with a culture and land you've never been introduced to. It's hard to identify as an Alutiiq, or an Aleut, even if you know the land. So much of the population was lost so quickly and, with it, so much of the culture. There wasn't time to write it down. That bit about the name, about being salmon-fishers, was all my family had to relate to. That, and the Carlisle Indian School.

In 1901 my great-grandfather was sent from the Baptist Mission Orphanage on Woody Island to the Carlisle Indian Industrial School in Pennsylvania, 50 miles from where my family settled. I don't know how I learned about the Carlisle Indian Industrial School. Perhaps in elementary school. It may have been a blip on some otherwise brightly illustrated page in our history books. I'm sure the teacher tread with caution. Or perhaps my father took us to visit, that summer we toured all the battlefields, and told us that was where his grandfather came through. A boy, fifteen years old, crossing the whole of America by train. That was where our family began. And it was, in one sense. But I can't remember when or where I learned what happened to the children when they spoke their Native tongues. I don't think it was from my father. There's never been much animosity in the little he's told. The thought of losing one's entire family and almost immediately afterward being shipped, alone, a world away, practically to another country (Alaska was not yet a state at this time) fills me with terror. But there is almost awe in my father's voice when he tells us this story. To this day, he loves train rides. My great-grandfather was an orphan. Who knows what would have happened to him had he not come to Carlisle. Alcoholism and abuse threaten any impoverished, broken space, and the fishing economy's never fully recovered from Exxon-Valdez. There are too many factors to give much thought to the what-ifs. *What if* could be a whole lot worse. It could be. Or it could not. *Gui taugna ikani. Aturaatnga.*[5]

From 1879 to 1918 the mission of the Carlisle Indian School was to assimilate Native children to white culture, to teach them trades to be successful in the white man's world. Captain Richard Henry Pratt wanted to show government officials in Washington DC that, given a "proper" education, Indians could be the equals of whites. They could be civilized. (At least enough to do the laundry, contribute to the humming machinations of society—literally—in its factories.) Sounds nice, if you don't mind being told your way of life—your way of living in this land that has served you fine for generations—is at best quaint, at worst savage, and it's a good thing these foreigners are finally here, with their true god, to show you how to make this land, this life, worth something, after having brutally beaten your people into submission and effectively cutting off all means of sovereign subsistence. Put another way, the mission of Carlisle was "Kill the Indian: Save the Man." Children as young as five were taken from their homes on the reservations—some more willingly than others—so they would be free of the influence of their people. Their hair was cut, and they were punished for speaking their Native tongues. They were made to choose white names, Christian names.

When Native American children came to Carlisle, it was customary to take before-and-after photos: one when they arrived, in full traditional regalia—feathers and braids and buckskins (sometimes authentic)—and one in their new suits and dresses, in the style of the "civilized" world. This was before the word *propaganda* left such a bitter taste on one's tongue, and these photos were used to show the skeptics in Washington that the Indian could be civilized. In my great-grandfather's file, at least in what has survived of his file, there is only one photo. One photo of a boy, perhaps small in the dress suit he was given but standing tall and straight, pleased with himself. Perhaps there was no need to "civilize" him. After all, he had been sent from a Baptist mission, and the Russian encounter had left such an impact on the people of the Aleutian Islands that unraveling what practices make up "traditional" Aleut culture or, indeed, even which people should be called Aleut, which Alutiiq, Sug-piaq, Chugach, or Kodiak, remains difficult enough. Perhaps he already looked "white." He may have already spoken English. (He may have even spoken Russian.) He already had a "proper" (Christian) name. If he had any other name, which I suspect he did, it has been lost. I wonder if he ever told a soul, after Carlisle. I wonder if he would have told his sons, if he would have given them secret names, if he hadn't died from tuberculosis, a common casualty of the Carlisle experience.

This mix of history and legend, fragmented as it was, was handed down imprecisely, shrouded in all the mystery befitting a relic. But it was intact enough that when Congress passed the Alaska Native Claims Settlement Act in 1971, when my father was a graduate student in Washington DC, conveniently located to access the National Archives where Michael's student records were held, he was able to register as an original share-holder. Born before 1971. Therefore fully recognized.

Legal settlements with the Natives were later in coming to Alaska. Perhaps because not too many people had a desire to occupy that wild land. They only wanted its yields. In 1968 oil was discovered in Prudhoe Bay, encouraging Congress and those similarly business-minded to settle the score once and for all, eliminating the possibility of inconvenient land claims in the future, as the rest of the world became more familiar with the riches of the Great Land. All Alaska Natives born before 1971 were assigned a corporation based on their village location. In return, the Alaska Natives gave up any future claim to ancestral lands—and their resources. Shareholders could then bequeath their stakes to anyone they chose. You can be 100 percent full-blooded Alaska Native, but if you were born after 1971, you don't get shares. You get a flimsy plastic card and an enrollment number.

I was born after 1971, hence my plastic card. Assuming my great-grandfather was, in fact, full-blooded, I am Native enough to qualify for certain corporate and tribal scholarships, but not Native enough to own shares. At least not yet. My father might bequeath them to me. Or some of them. How this new understanding of ownership will affect my personal sense of Native identity, I don't yet know. Will owning shares make me finally feel at ease in my own skin? There's a chance I won't get any shares. I have three siblings. Three nephews, one niece. Theirs is the last generation that will qualify for enrollment. (At least with the corporation. The Native village to which my sister and I belong traces membership through lineal descent. Cracks continue to grow; more water moves to fill them.) After them, unless through marriage, there will be no more hesitation when checking boxes. My own children, should I have any, will not even carry the name *Chabitnoy*. Upon my wedding day, I surrendered it for all legal purposes, though truth be told my husband's name has never fit quite like my own skin. I still identify by my family name, my great-grandfather's name.

My father didn't even have to provide a birth certificate to prove he was Michael's grandson. I've never asked, but I suspect he, too, identifies as white (though he, too, is proud of his heritage, has asked me where he can learn some Alutiiq words). Perhaps this suspicion is why I've never asked. If my grandfather identified as white, and my father identifies as white, what right have I to claim otherwise? The way bloodlines were generally treated in the early days, when Uncle Sam thought the Indian problem could be solved through breeding, was if your father was Native, you were Native. If your father was white, well, you could maybe pass for white too, depending on skin tone. You were at least one generation closer, though I doubt it was as simple as "you are white," just like that. The last time I was home in Pennsylvania, a palpable unease filled the dinette, the only room in our house my mother had hired an interior designer for, and thirty-plus years later refuses to update, to change— blues, geese, and pineapples dominate the setting. I was old enough, finally aware enough, to ask the hard questions. It was one of a handful of times I ever heard my dad speak about his father.

As the blood thins, this need to understand what it means to identify as Unangan/Sugpiaq, as an Aleut, or as a person of "more than one" ethnicity grows more persistent. I need to know what it means to have descended from a disenfranchised people, what it means to recognize that words like *genocide* do exist in my country's past, that my country does have a past, and had a present before that past, and in that present my forefathers drew life from the water. I've never had to catch my dinner, or clean it. I didn't have to watch my family and neighbors massacred and enslaved. I didn't have to ride a train across an entire country, fifteen years old and alone, for my inheritance. I simply present my plastic card, and a world of affirmative action opens to hold my hand through my first-world hardships, depending on who you talk to. But I carry these ghosts nonetheless. *Tuci ikani.*[6]

I've always harbored a certain amount of guilt for accepting funds in reparation for a tradition of exploitation I've only inherited, and worry I am unworthy of receiving. The summer before my senior year in college I was given a highly competitive internship position for the Arctic Studies branch of the Smithsonian Institute in Anchorage. It was a research assistant position, and the project involved combing through archived interviews and conversations with Elders from the near Aleutian Islands. The islands my great-grandfather was from. I suspect my lineage and the narrative I wove through my application essay played more than a small role in this achievement. My job was to look for anecdotes, descriptions, or explanations to accompany pictures of artifacts the Arctic Studies Center was going to post online as a virtual museum exhibit. Not a lot of people make it out to Kodiak Island, where most of the physical artifacts are housed in the Alutiiq Museum.

"Are you Sugpiaq or Ugpiaq?" my roommate's mother asked. They were Sugpiaq. I had never heard these names before. As I've since learned, it's complicated. Mostly because the Islands were so heavily impacted by colonization. Even the United States government contrived domestic arrangements, supervising marriages and relocating able-bodied Natives to cash in on the fur business in what could hardly be called anything other than conscripted labor.

I didn't spend much time with this roommate that summer. She was an older, non-traditional student, wife, and mother who had grown up in Alaska. I was a young bright-eyed tourist eager to learn about my elusive heritage but not yet aware of the right questions to ask. I came across variations of my family name in the archives on rare occasions, but it turned out we were not as well-connected as I'd thought. There was, indeed, more than one island. There was more than one corporation for the Islands. If my father had registered according to some of the information later uncovered by his cousin, based on the island my ancestors lived on before the Russian economy rearranged the demographic landscape of the chain, we might be in a different corporation.

When I wasn't combing archives, I was hiking with a local Meet-Up group of mostly middle-aged transplants and real estate agents in high-end outdoor gear. We never really left Anchorage, but I felt a thrill discovering that land. Land that was almost home. Back in Pennsylvania, my parents weren't the outdoor type. These Alaskan field trips were my first real forays into nature. It didn't matter to me that the landscape was entirely different from what my great-grandfather and his fathers would have known. (I don't even think I really knew this at the time.) The other members of the group were kind, parentally protective, and equally unsure of their status as Alaskans.

If you're white and were born and raised in Alaska, are you an Alaska Native?

If I don't ever go back to Alaska, if I don't make it to the Islands, can I say I'm from Alaska?

Does it count if I just visit?

What are the motives?

I don't know. *Gui taugna ikani.*[7]

I've come to learn everyone has motives, on both sides of the question. I don't know at what point I became aware of language as a reflexive act, as a vulnerable presentation, but sometime around high school, maybe college, I stopped talking. Not altogether. Not to everyone. But to strangers. To hostesses and cashiers. To new acquaintances. To people who might not know my motives for speaking, or whose motives in listening I might not know. A classmate once told me I was not an Alaska Native because I had never been to Alaska. This was before the internship. He was the haughty, self-assured New England type who insisted the New England accent was *the* American accent. Well, I've since been to Alaska, so I suppose that makes it alright. Though I'm still not sure. I haven't seen that green and blue coat in years. All we had was knowledge of a name, incorrectly—or, I like to think, imprecisely—translated. (Chabitnoy, it turns out, is Russian slang, Shebutnoy, for "mischievous" or "energetic.") For most other Natives I've met, it's a non-question. My family was relocated. An entire oral tradition was lost and is only recently being recovered. We didn't know what we had lost, and if I don't ask these questions, it may be lost for good.

I don't know which box I *should* check. I suppose it still depends on who's asking, and why. Over the last month alone, I've been asked what I am several times, and the answer has not usually felt any more comfortable passing through my lips. At least as summer approaches, I'm beginning to look more the sun-kissed part. But I still feel uncomfortably voyeuristic at powwows, and I'm still not entirely sure what I'm doing beading once a week with the Native women from the Lower Forty-Eight, who learned their beading from their fathers on their traditional lands.

Did the Aleuts bead in this way? I know they wove—weave—beautiful baskets, baskets I did not appreciate when I was at the Anchorage weekend market looking for exotic, authentic, readily identifiable souvenirs.

Can I say that I was one raised away from our home villages? Can I say "our"? "We"? I, too, feel a loss for what I have been missing, but I'm still not sure I know what exactly that entails. What have *I* lost, and is it something that can be returned through archives, digging up memories that may or may not have been painful, that either way I was not present for and would not be present for now but for those moments invoked in memory? And what can be recovered, for how long? For my generation? For my children's? What are any of us looking for in our enthusiastic internet searches for ancestors? I suppose I'm looking for a way of being in this world. A way of being worthy of the opportunities and stories I've been given. A way of being deserving—and belonging.

"So, what are you?" the woman asked.

Since the question was posed, I've finally made it back to Kodiak, where I still felt foreign, and to Woody Island, where stepping on the black sand beach, waves lapping my bare feet, I could feel my ancestors in me, the stories, with all their holes (wholes?) I carried, still carry. Born and raised landlocked, I've learned to feel them each time my body meets the water. Each time I enter the water is a prayer. I don't need paper or plastic to feel the cracks in my *sua*, my being, fill. I've spoken to tribal members, young and old, experts and academics in Alutiiq studies, western trained with indigenous sensibilities, Native and non-Native but with an appreciation of the culture and the people, their spirit of survival, of living with the water. I've met cousins I never knew I had, could not trace on a family tree how we're related, but felt akin to the moment they opened their doors to me and all my insecurities. I am learning to speak my language—or at least one of them. I am learning that my story is not my own, is not a litmus test for suffering or belonging, but one among many, as valid and complex as any, not in need of or eligible for validation by anyone but those to whom I belong. *Aturaatnga. Aturqutartua.*[8]

I don't hear "Aang, Unanga!" or "Cama'i, Sugpiaq!" often (or ever). I'm still learning what it means to be Aleut, through the relatives and experts I've met, through the research I've pursued in writing poems, through books, and through the writing itself. Through stories. Had I not chosen to become a writer, to write the particular collection that would become my first book, *How to Dress a Fish*, I wonder if I would have an easier relationship with my Indigenous identity. I still worry I get it wrong in those poems, but I am learning daily how to be Sugpiaq, Aleut, a real person of the water, of the islands, container and contained. I don't think I'll ever let go of that fear, but I've come to terms with it. That fear keeps me honest, holds me accountable. Through my writing, I am building community. I am writing what it's taken for me to arrive at a place where I can say I am Aleut. Where I can say I am Aleut *and*.

I am a salmon-fisher, *x*-times removed. I am mischievous and energetic. I am an Alaska Native as defined by Section 3(b).

I am my great-grandfathers' great-granddaughter on both sides. We don't spend our lives in the places we are from, but we never stop belonging to those places.

Cama'i. Gui Abigail Chabitnoy. Pennsylvaniami sullianga. Maamaqa Valerie. Pennsylvaniami sullia. Taataqa Robert. Pennsylvaniami sullia. Ilanka Tangirnaqmiut. Cali Ungamek, cali Germanymek. Ilanka imaqmiut. Aturaatnga.[9]

I am of the water. They sing to me.

NOTES

1. Švarný Carlson, Barbara. "There Is No Such Thing as an Aleut," in *Alaska Native Writers, Storytellers & Orators: The Expanded Edition*, ed. Ronald Spatz, Jean Breinig, and Patricia H. Partnow (Anchorage: University of Alaska, 1999).

2. Thomas King, *The Truth about Stories* (Minneapolis: University of Minnesota Press, 2008), 2.

3. *The women are at the beach. They sing to me.*

4. *They sing to me.*

5. *I am that one there out of reach. They sing to me.*

6. *They are those ones there out of reach.*
7. *I am that one there out of reach.*
8. *They sing to me. I will sing.*
9. *Hello. I am Abigail Chabitnoy. I was born in Pennsylvania. My mother is Valeria. She was born in Pennsylvania. My father is Robert. He was born in Pennsylvania. My family are Woody Island people. Also from Unga. Also from Germany. My family is of the water. They sing to me.*

Jeanetta Calhoun Mish

Confessions of a Detribalized Mixed-Blood

In 2012, when media stories of Elizabeth Warren's claim of Cherokee ancestry became widely disseminated, I experienced immediate and conflicting intellectual and emotional reactions:

Dang, another Cherokee Wannabe.

Oh, crap, have I ever stated my ancestry as a way to gain some slim advantage?

Oh, crap, am I like her?

Pocahontas my ass. *(Some called Warren "Pocahontas," and not in a good way.)*

To the first reaction: Yeah, it's always Cherokee. Even my Cherokee friends say so.

To the second reaction: As several caught-in-bad-acts politicians and televangelists have reportedly done, I promised to search my heart and my memory to find the answer.

To the third reaction: What would my communities say?

To the fourth reaction: Wow, insulting Matoaka, a kidnapped historical person with more courage than you'll ever have while, at the same time, insulting all Native people, and women, too, you ass.

Once the emotional storm over the Pocahontas comment had subsided, and on the way to writing this essay, I thought my way through the morass of ancestry and identity. It wasn't an easy task since it required absolute honesty and a thorough examination of the facts, something like AA's fourth step, which requires that recovering alcoholics make "a searching and fearless moral inventory of ourselves." I embarked upon a searching and fearless inventory of my Native ancestry, whether I'd used it to my own benefit, whether I was just another pretending like Warren (and *so many* others), and whether there was a Native community that recognized me. As recently as May 2019, Warren still insisted that 1. her claim of Native ancestry did not benefit her in any way, including on her law school application and 2. "that's what my family always said." I wanted to make sure I wasn't guilty of her transgressions. And, if I am guilty, to move on to the fifth step: admitting "to God (whose?), to ourselves, and to another human being (to Native people) the exact nature of my wrongs." I don't know how else to go about this inventory except to tell stories.

So far as I understand, being Native American has several essential components: Blood, Culture, Language, Ceremony. So I've examined these components, one by one.

BLOOD

Part of the problem with Wannabes is that they can't say who their people are. Among inhabitants of Oklahoma (and the Deep South), no matter what ethnicity, race, and creed you are, it's near a sin to not know your family—to four generations. When two people from my part of the country meet up, after names are exchanged, the first question is: "Who's your people?" Folks who don't know who their people are get looked at with a serious stink-eye. Warren could not name any of her Native relatives—nor can other Pretendians. Did anyone ever ask her if she could name a couple of generations of her white relatives? I bet she could but found nothing odd in the fact she couldn't name her Native relatives. Throw her a stink-eye.

When I was in elementary school in Wewoka, during the second week of class, there was a "blood quantum countdown." The countdown was used to establish Wewoka Public Schools' eligibility for Johnson-O'Malley funds:

> The Johnson-O'Malley Program is authorized by the Johnson-O'Malley Act of 1934 and the implementing regulations are provided in Part 273 of Title 25 of the Code of Federal Regulations. As amended, this Act authorizes contracts for the education of eligible Indian students enrolled in public schools and previously private schools.[1]

In practice, in our school, at least, the census of "eligible Indian students" was carried out like this:

> The homeroom teacher would tell students to stand beside their desks.
>
> They would begin the countdown at $\frac{1}{32}$—everyone who was *not* at least $\frac{1}{32}$ Indian (terminology at the time) or more would be instructed to sit down.
>
> Then $\frac{1}{16}$ then $\frac{1}{8}$.
>
> Then $\frac{1}{4}$ and so on.

By the time the teachers reached one half, the only kids left standing were high-quanta mixed-bloods, many of whom were Black, and full-bloods, including many who were more than one Nation, Seminole and Creek, mostly. I don't remember the countdown occurring after elementary school—the administration probably added a "blood quantum" line on the enrollment forms.

My mother told me I should sit down at one-fourth, affirming that I was one-eighth Indian. Or thereabouts. But my grandpa's enrollment says he's one-fourth Delaware, which makes me one-sixteenth Delaware plus likely unproveable fractions from other tribes.

Recently, I shared the story of the quantum countdown on Facebook. The general reaction was one of horror: How terrible! Weren't the students embarrassed? How dare they call out students like that? To me, it was just a common part of the first few days of every school year. I can't speak to how the half- and full-bloods felt.

My family history, like that of many mixed-bloods, is complicated, in part because of the fracturing of the Delaware into several different tribes as they exist today. The tribe up to Bartlesville, known as Delaware Tribe of Indians, consists primarily of descendants of the Delaware who settled on lands purchased from the Cherokee. And the Kansas Delawares, those who stayed behind when most of the people moved to Indian Territory. There are also the Delaware Indians of Idaho and the Munsee-Delaware Nation and the Moravian Delaware of Canada and Delaware members of the Stockbridge-Munsee Band of Mahican Indians. The multiple tribal entities are a result of the many forced and so-called voluntary removals the tribe and tribal members endured.

My grandpa, Luther Sanderson, is enrolled in yet another group of Delaware: the Western Delaware, also known as the absentee Delaware, known today as the Delaware Nation, with headquarters in Anadarko. Anyway, I think he's still enrolled—there was a "rectification" of rolls a while back. His grandmother was Louisa Ellen Exendine, daughter of Archibald Exendine Jr. and Rachel Nations. Louisa is cousin to Jasper Exendine (who raised Pistol Pete after his parents were killed). She is second cousin to Jasper's son, A. A. Exendine, who was elected to the College Football Hall of Fame (as a player). He played and coached for Carlisle and several other colleges and later became a BIA lawyer. The Exendines and the Sandersons were neighbors in central Missouri—several families of each. Family stories about Louisa's father and his brother, Johnson (Jasper's father), dying in the Civil War have been confirmed.

Louisa was four years old when her father died in 1861. No one knows for sure when her mother, Rachel, died, but by 1870 several of Rachel's younger children were living with other families. Because Louisa was orphaned when she was very young, she had little memory of her childhood. To complete her Eastern Cherokee application, Louisa contacted her oldest sister, Marguerita Exendine Bledsaw of Black Gum, Sequoya County, Oklahoma, to find out what her parents' names were. Marguerita's reply is included in the application. In it, Marguerita said that their mother, Rachel, was Cherokee, and we know that their father was Delaware. Louisa's sister said their father was also Cherokee. At the time, Delawares who enrolled with the Cherokee were often called

Cherokee. On the 1860 census, Louisa, her siblings, and her parents are listed as Black—the only choices were white, Black, or mulatto. This is not uncommon.

In 1913, after her husband died, Louisa Ellen lived with my grandpa and his parents, Henry Owen (H. O.) Sanderson and Iness Little. My great-granny, Iness Little Sanderson, held Louisa's traumas against her—she was a dirty Indian, she was an orphan whose family didn't take care of her, she lived "with this one and that one." They did not get along when Louisa came to stay with the Sandersons.

My grandpa, Luther, remembered her well since he was fourteen when she passed in 1929. Grandpa told me that Grandma Louisa gave stories to his father, her son, Great-Grandpa Henry. She also shared these stories with Grandpa because, as a child, he had plenty of time to listen. My grandpa gave them to me. He also insisted that I would be named after his grandmother—my middle name is Louise. On Ancestry, I discovered that one of Louisa's sisters was named Jenetta. I always assumed I was named after my mother's mother, Jeanette. Maybe it's both. Like many people, I didn't ask enough questions of my elders, although Grandpa and I were so close that I was known as "Luther's shadow."

I know my other people, too, and have six generations of stories about them. We went to Great-Granny's Little-Lowery family reunions. My Granny Jeanette gave me stories of the Wallings and Chisms and Rodgerses and Robertses (a few mixed bloods in that line, too). But we didn't go to Sanderson or Exendine reunions.

When I was in junior high, I asked Grandpa why there weren't Sanderson reunions. In his quiet, nonconfrontational way, he sauntered off to the other end of the house, as if he hadn't heard me. Once Grandpa was out of earshot, my grandmother whispered to me that her mother-in-law, Iness, wouldn't allow *those Indians* in her house, so Great-Grandpa went to theirs. Yet Great-Granny knew full well that she was part Cherokee, from the Lowerys. As a result, I didn't know any of my grandpa's daddy's people other than Grandpa's many siblings and his father (who died when I was three).

My paternal grandmother's paper-name is Ola Mae Miller. My mother told me more than once that her mother-in-law, Ola, was "half Indian."

I now know that Ola was the daughter of a Creek girl who, as family whispers say, was raped by the white man she cleaned house for. Whispered stories are often reliable because they are about shameful things—telling them puts the family's reputation at risk. My father and other members of his family that I met as an adult confirmed the story. The lack of enrollment in my family extends to my son. My son is not enrolled, because his father is 7/16 Southern Cheyenne and 1/16 Lakota, making him 7/16 Cheyenne, 1/32 short of qualifying for the Southern Cheyenne rolls. My measly documented 1/16 Delaware (my son's 1/32) doesn't count toward his blood quantum any more than the 1/32 Lakota he got from his father. But last year, for the first time since he was five years old, my son's father came back into his life, and my son went to ceremony with his father and half-brother.

How much, you ask, of this information did I have before the existence of Ancestry.com? I started with my grandpa's stories, all of which were confirmed and expanded by later research on Ancestry and elsewhere. How is my claim to Delaware ancestry different from Warren's Cherokee claim? Our stories weren't vague—names and places and tribal affiliations were not forgotten by later generations. And I've worked to confirm them through family, genealogy, various archives, and others' stories.

Instead of doing the work to establish her claim to Cherokee ancestry, Warren took a DNA test while running for president. Supposedly, the results showed Native ancestry six to ten generations back. But she didn't bother to discover who her purported Native relatives were. Her ancestry claims were investigated and disproven by the Cherokee Nation; the Nation also explained, in a press release, why DNA tests didn't prove Cherokee ancestry and heritage.

For us mixed-bloods who weren't raised in traditional families, documenting Native descendancy is complicated and sometimes impossible. If it's impossible to document, it shouldn't be claimed.

CULTURE

I am a fourth-generation Oklahoman and, like many Okies whose families lived in Indian Territory and Oklahoma Territory before statehood (1907),

I have always understood myself and my families to be mixed-bloods. When speaking to outsiders, I have a shorthand statement about my identity: "Scots-Irish, three tribes (Delaware, Mvskoke, Cherokee), no card." I don't name the tribes, though, because I know that the second I say "Cherokee," there's gonna be a princess story. There's never a princess story for the Delaware and Mvskoke. This quip leaves out my paternal grandfather's English and French ancestors. It's hard to imagine oneself belonging to those groups when growing up in Wewoka, Oklahoma, a place where many (most?) people were—are—either full-blood Natives or mixed-bloods of one sort or the other: Native and Black; Native, Black, and white (often Scots-Irish or Scots); Native and white; Black and white; and other combinations I haven't the inside knowledge to identify.

Wewoka was founded by John Horse, a Black Seminole, and it was entirely an Indian town until a few years before statehood. It's also the capital of the Seminole Nation of Oklahoma where, in 1899, two Seminole teens, Lincoln McGeisey (18) and Palmer Sampson (17), were kidnapped on suspicion of a white woman's murder. To escape Seminole Nation jurisdiction, the lynch mob took the young men a few miles west, just over the Indian Territory–Oklahoma Territory line. The teens were tortured and burned alive. According to Daniel L. Littlefield's extensively researched history of the event, it's unlikely that either was guilty.[2]

(How can I transition to the next paragraph with lynching on my readers' minds? I suggest you cleanse your spirit, in whichever way your tradition instructs, before we return to the quotidian.)

I was a Head Start kid in Wewoka, from the age of four until the end of first grade. Perhaps some don't know what Head Start is—an educational program for poor kids that was established in 1965. The economic standard applied meant that most of my fellow Head Start denizens were African American and Native American—there was also a handful of us poor "whites."

A moment here: the word "denizen" in American English is defined as "an inhabitant or occupant of a particular place." The British English definition is "a foreigner allowed certain rights in the adopted country." The word carries both my genesis and the colonization of Indian Country.

I got in trouble at Head Start during the first month I was there, for cutting off a Mvskoke boy's hair. He asked me to, honestly. It was 100 degrees in July, and he asked me to cut his hair off—perhaps he was inspired by my pixie cut. As I remember, I used a pair of blunt-end children's scissors to do the deed. Needless to say, his family was justifiably angry. I stood in a corner for a week's worth of recesses, with my nose in a circle drawn on the wall at the right height to keep me on my tiptoes. I later learned this punishment was also inflicted by government boarding schools. I was a nontraditional mixed-blood child and had no idea I'd done something terrible. I still mourn my actions today, that I was so damn ignorant of the pain the haircutting would cause to his family. Wewoka Head Start is now administered by the Seminole Nation.

In my memory, by the 1970s there wasn't much friction between the Natives and the non-Natives in Wewoka, maybe because that would mean feuding with your cousins. However, in 1977 (or thereabouts) a teacher told a Mvskoke student that he couldn't return to school until he cut his hair—the teacher threatened to cut it off if he didn't. I remembered my Head Start lesson, that to do so would be a grave injustice. To my fellow students' credit, almost everyone participated in the walk-out protest and, afterward, the young man was allowed to return to school with his waist-length blue-black hair intact.

One of the best bar fights I've ever seen (I've seen many) was when I was in Traverse City, Michigan, visiting my mother, Myrna, and my stepfather, DeWayne (one-fourth Choctaw), who was up there pipelining. My brother, Phillip (some Choctaw on his daddy's side), was also visiting. There were a couple of rednecks at the bar, and they asked my stepfather where we were from. DeWayne answered, "Oklahoma" whereupon one of them said, "What are you guys, a bunch of blanket-asses?" My brother and DeWayne whupped those guys and made them apologize for their slur, in front of everyone at the bar, to my momma, me, my brother, my stepfather, and to Native people everywhere.

Then there were the years with my son's father, a *Tsitsistas* (Cheyenne) native speaker. His family's allotment home out at 12 Mile Point (near Calumet) was the site of the incorporation of the Native American Church on October 10, 1918. We were kinda wild—I met him in a bar on the Paseo in Oklahoma City during an open mic where he was reading poetry. I was instantly enamored because he was a poet. A for-real poet, published and everything. I picked him up with this line: *I have a new car and two twelve-packs on ice in the back—wanna hang out?* We spent the next seven days going to every NDN bar in Oklahoma that he knew. And he knew a lot. Perhaps I should make a load of cash by turning our story into one of those romance novels with the hot (fake) Indian guy on the cover.

My ex and I traveled to Europe and New York and Ohio and, back home in Oklahoma, we spent a lot of time at Bogies Bar in El Reno and the Crazy Horse in OKC and the 49s at Wheeler Park, where the National Indian Softball League Finals were held. And where, one 49-night, a cop car cruised through—the People turned the cop car over and ran the officer off.

My ex's Cheyenne and Arapaho running buddies accepted me, in part because I was useful. I did all the driving and was never subjected to random stops or searches. I went into convenience stores after midnight to buy beer and cigarettes and cheap cigars. I was never followed around the store by cashiers, and they didn't call the cops on me. In 1998, against my ex's better judgment but because I was hangry, we stopped at a diner outside Clinton, Oklahoma. Clinton is in the middle of Cheyenne country, and some old non-Native folks still tell stories about "depredations" inflicted on their families. When we walked into the diner, it was like a Western movie when the bad guy steps through the door of a saloon. Everyone stared at us—it was quiet as a grave. Once we found a place in the back of the diner, one of the farmers said, in a stage whisper, "I wonder if that white girl's daddy knows she's with a prairie-n——."

What I'm trying to say here is that even though I'm not a traditional or enrolled tribal person, I grew up in a Native-inflected world and remained among Native people when I got older. I mean, my mother said to us, "mvto" for "thank you," and she wasn't even Seminole. She also said, "put the *ki-bosh* on it," a variant translation of a Celtic word that Seamus Heaney used in a poem. It was just part of our town's mixed Mvskoke–African American–British Empire shared language. By the 1970s, class was more a divisor than race, at least on the surface, and only among the young people. Black, po-white, Indian kids all on one side, the Socs on the other—a division physically manifested at class reunions as late as 2000. Some elders were still traumatized by racial animosity and violence and, therefore, banned having white kids in their Black or Native houses and their kids in white houses. Some, but not all, older members of white families maintained racist boundaries. But growing up working class (sometimes poor) in a Native-inflected community does not make me Native any more than it does Elizabeth Warren, who also grew up in a sometimes middle-class, later working-class family in Oklahoma.

LANGUAGE

In the fifth grade in Wewoka, we—the entire grade—studied Mvskoke language for a semester with Mr. (Tuskahoma Brown "Mutt") Miller. When I knew Mr. Miller, he had retired from teaching and serving as a school principal. He spent his time teaching Wewoka students Mvskoke while also serving as cofounder and first curator of the Seminole Nation Museum. Our Campfire Girls troupe, recruited by Mr. Miller during those Mvskoke lessons, served as docents at the Seminole Nation Museum shortly after it opened. The museum still exists, and when I'm there, I can still serve as a docent, reciting the history of the Seminole Nation as I learned it from Mr. Miller.

I want to apologize here for my Campfire Girl costume, to which we affixed the badges we'd earned. The costume was a pseudo-Indian rough-cotton imitation of a buckskin dress with fringes. There's probably a yearbook photo of me wearing it. There was one full-blood girl in our troupe, Merilee—I wonder, what did she think of that? I would ask her except she left this world in 2001.

Wewoka is a Mvskoke-language word meaning "barking water" or "roaring water," named for the rapids in the deep creek. Towns down the road are named Weleetka, which means "running water," and Wetumka, "tumbling water." Wetumka is pronounced in Wewoka like it is spelled in Alabama, "We*tump*ka," which is the ancestral home of the Mvskoke Nation. Major north-south street names in Wewoka are Mvskoke words or references. Muscogee Street refers to the Mvskoke Confederacy. Okfuskee, Okmulgee, Mekusukey (Miccosukee), Hitchiti, and Eufaula Streets are named for tribes that were part of the Confederacy. Seminole Street is named for the tribe; Wewoka was—and is—the post-removal capital of the Seminole Nation. Brown Street was named for John Frippo Brown, the last chief of the Seminole Nation before the Dawes Act. His sister, Alice Brown Davis, was appointed in 1922 as the Seminoles' first woman chief.

I grew up on Ocheese (O-*chee*-see) Street. Verner W. Crane's much-cited 1918 article, "The Origin of the Name of the Creek Indians," gives the history of the term "Ocheese" and the genesis of the tribal appellation, "Creek":

> Ocheese ("people") was in origin the Hitchiti term for their Muskhogean [*sic*] neighbors. Prior to the Yamasee war the chief towns of the Ocheese, Kawita, and Kasihta were located on the upper Ocmulgee river. As was frequently the case, the stream took the name of the folk, so that the Ocmulgee river above the approximate site of Macon, Georgia, was known to the English as "Ochese [*sic*] Creek."[3]

Our high school's talent show was called "Katchu-Tal," combining a phonetic spelling of the Mvskoke word for "tiger" (panther or cougar) with "talent." In 1990—after blessing my pregnant belly, which he said (correctly) was a boy—Yuchi-Creek poet Louis "Little Coon" Oliver reminded me that *kaccv* was his clan name.

Here's a trivia question for you: Which U.S. golf tournament has a Native-language name (place-names don't count)? The answer can be found on the Wewoka Golf Course website: "*Pokkecetu* was the name given to the tournament in 1951 by Isaac Walker, a local Seminole Indian and avid golfer. Translated it means 'play ball'."[4] The tournament is held at the Gil Morgan Golf Course, named for Wewoka's famous PGA golfer, who often comes home to play in the tournament.

In my hometown, even golf, a middle-class sport, has a Native accent.

I can still count in Mvskoke (and have some other random words), which I learned from Mr. Miller and from Seminole and Creek friends. In 2009 my husband and I went to Dead Center Film Festival in OKC to hang out with my friend Richard Ray Whitman for the Oklahoma premiere of Sterlin Harjo's film *Barking Water* (the protagonist is going home to Wewoka). I found myself counting along in Mvskoke during the scene with the girl and her uncle (Whitman) on the porch swing. I didn't know until that moment that I remembered how.

My grandpa used the Mvskoke word for the "ghost or shapeshifter owl," which I won't repeat here. It wasn't to be spoken aloud except under dire circumstances. The Delaware had (have) a dread of owls, similar to the Mvskoke and Cherokee. I was with my grandpa when he saw a pair nesting in the western eave of his parents' house—his face blanched and he took a sharp breath. "Not good," he said. His father died in his sleep that night.

I have some *Tsitsistas* language from my son's father and from keeping camp for him and, once, for his brother during tribal ceremonies. I don't have any of my ancestors' Lenape language, except for a few phrases learned in book study or from the online Lenape Talking Dictionary.

CEREMONY

I've never had the opportunity to participate in any ceremony that belongs to the Delaware (Lenape). The last complete Big House ceremony was held west of Copan, Oklahoma, in 1924; according to some sources, there were "partial" ceremonies held in 1944–45 after traditional leaders tried to revive the practice for many years. There is no story about my grandpa, born in 1914, attending Big House ceremonies. Some Delaware, due to their long-time proximity to Cherokee and Creek people, attend Green Corn ceremonies. A Yuchi friend took me to a Green Corn once, because he said I should attend ceremony, having just discovered I was pregnant with my first child. It's not my prerogative, as a guest, to name the grounds.

I have, more than once, attended Cheyenne ceremony and participated as a family member (camp keeper). Because it's a community ceremony, families of those who are sacrificing have particular duties and rituals. I won't explain what they are—the rituals belong to the tribe.

However, living among tribal people, attending ceremonies and honor dances and powwows—Pretendians often claim they've attended ceremonies because they've attended powwows—and learning a smattering of various tribal languages does not make me a Native person.

DETRIBALIZED

It should be clear by now what I mean by "detribalized." I do not have the language, ceremony, or culture of my family's tribes. And, one could say, the blood is mighty thin although, I suppose that so far as Okie mixed-bloods go, I'm not at the tail end of the pack.

To the question of whether I have cashed in on my Native ancestors. I determined that I *have* benefitted from the opportunity to spend time with Native people, to learn about indigenous ways of being, to expand my literary horizons, and to cultivate long-lasting friendships. I have never put "Native American" on college admissions forms or financial aid forms. I have not dipped into funds set aside for Native businesses to support my small press. It never occurred to me to claim Native ancestry for advantage, having been aware for a long time of the struggles, historical and contemporary, of Native people. The tribal people I know have had to fight to be treated as full members of American society and to maintain their culture, land, and sovereignty.

Thinking back to the question of what would my communities, my Native friends, say about my status as a mixed-blood—would they say I'm Pretendian? I won't speak for them here—you can ask next time you meet up with them. However, unlike many Wannabes, I have had and continue to have close personal friendships with Native people of many tribes. A couple of years ago, I was taken as a Comanche captive—I have the T-shirt to prove it. I take that very seriously—most of my Comanche friends are women, and you don't mess around with Numunuu women. Or with that Pawnee woman whose children call me Aunty. Or, for that matter, *any* Native woman. I suppose I could do the paperwork to petition for enrollment with the Delaware Nation since they do not require a minimum blood quantum, but I'm not sure I want to. It feels somehow Pretendian, even though my ancestry would suffice.

It's obvious that some people think that "Native" is merely a mantle to wear when it's useful and to remove when it's not. I am not one of those people. I know who I am: an Okie of mixed white and Native ancestry; my sense of self is not troubled by desires to be something else. Moreover, I recognize my privilege as a whiteish woman—my years with the Cheyenne made that clear to me in my twenties. Instead of petitioning for enrollment, I think I'll continue to use my color and educational privilege to give back to the People. I have had opportunities to promote the work of Native writers through projects like editing Native issues of *World Literature Today* and the *Journal of Working-Class Studies*; by reviewing books by Native poets for *Transmotion*, *American Book Review*, and *World Literature Today*; and by publishing a number of Native writers through my small press, Mongrel Empire (named, of course, for all us mixed-bloods out there). Perhaps the most important way I give back is hidden from the public: Because I am known as a writer with Native ancestry, I have been asked, often, to speak *for and about* Native people and, once, *for and about* Oklahoma African Americans (!). I steadfastly refuse to do so and, instead, give requestors a list of the Native and African American writers and activists they *should* be contacting. Let's call it a giveaway.

NOTES

1. Bureau of Indian Education, "Johnson-O'Malley."
2. Littlefield, *Seminole Burning.*
3. Crane, "Creek Indians," 342.
4. Wewoka Golf Course, "History."

BIBLIOGRAPHY

Bureau of Indian Education. "Johnson-O'Malley." U.S. Department of the Interior. Accessed April 12, 2022. https://www.bie.edu/topic-page/johnson-omalley.

Crane, Verner W. "The Origin of the Name of the Creek Indians." *The Mississippi Valley Historical Review* 5, no. 3 (1918): 339–42. https://doi.org/10.2307/1888814.

Littlefield, Daniel F. *Seminole Burning: A Story of Racial Vengeance.* (Oxford: The University Press of Mississippi, 1996).

Wewoka Golf Course. "History." Morgan Municipal Golf Course. 2012. http://www.wewokagolfcourse.com/history.html.

Carter Meland

Thinking with Bigfoot about a Jackpine Savage

Cryptogenealogical Reflections

Along the Embankment

The trees of the northwoods, white pine and red pine, bend at the edge of her vision as the car speeds down the road. From that peripheral perspective, they seem to dip toward the ground as she passes by, but then they rise again from the earth if she glances into the rearview mirror. She aims to make Bena before too long. Capital of the Leech Lake Anishinaabe Nation in what is currently known as northern Minnesota. Bena is her home. Perhaps.

The trees press against the road, keep her car focused forward, moving toward something in Bena, but the story doesn't make it clear why she's heading there. Maybe she's heading to an ailing grandparent or toward ceremony; perhaps she's been away from her community for a year or a decade or a lifetime and is seeking to renew connections she'd neglected for too long, even if she's maybe only really been gone three months. She's moving toward something in Bena is all we know for sure.

Deep in the woods around her, back where the soil thins, jack pines grow from some of the most unforgiving ground. Pawprints, hoofprints, and footprints cross and recross one another on the paths back there amid the pine, evidence of the lives in the forest encoded in the twisting helixes of trackways in the dirt. These traces conjure familiar deer and chipmunks, but also the rarer moose and wolf and, perhaps rarest of all, Bagwajinini. The wild man, elder brother to the Anishinaabe. His footprints are as long as a tall man's forearm, longer even. His stride covers five or six feet at a step. The earth holds all these tracks, including Bagwajinini's, memories of moments from passing lives that swirl away in a stiff breeze or are pounded deep into the ground when the thunders come.

Ahead is a break in the trees, that sort of break that barely even registers consciously when we've been on the road for a while, but that still draws the eye. A railroad line crosses the two lanes of the state highway. No bells are ringing, no lights flashing, so she approaches at speed and, again in that unthinking way we get when on the road, she glances down the tracks and sees him there, standing at the top of the railroad embankment, rising from the stones along the tracks. Really, he towers there, taller than any person she's ever seen, dark hair covering his body. He looks straight into her eyes, his head turning to follow her as she speeds past, and she begins to cry. She feels the weight of his gaze as the railroad tracks recede and the trees rise again in the rearview mirror.

We don't know whether her tears come in great heaving sobs or as a gentle release of pent-up emotion. The story doesn't go that far, but she will later tell people that she cried because Bagwajinini had looked into her soul.

Her soul.

He took it in as she sped by, saw something valuable nested there, I think, and so the tears came. He saw how real she was.

Cheap Paperbacks and Harrowing Death Marches

There was a spinning wire rack at the local public library, ripe with cheap paperbacks, some held together with rubber bands to keep their pulpy, light-yellowed pages from fluttering down to the carpet as just so many dead leaves. As a kid in the seventies, this rack was always my first stop at the library. It was the rack of teen idols, sports heroes, and monsters. Yeti. The creature in Loch Ness. Bigfoot. I read as many of those monster books as I could. Even if they most often just rehashed the same few dozen stories time and again, they captured me. To me, Bigfoot seemed especially—how can I put it?—distinctive. The mysterious way they moved in the woods, evading discovery, known only by their enormous footprints and a handful of pictures that were suggestive, but not conclusive, images of something in the shadows. I'd stare at those pictures, rehashing the rehashed stories in my mind, until it seemed the creatures might step out of the page, transported from that uncertain dimension of theirs into mine. I wanted to know them, not just about them.

It was around that same time, in the mid-seventies, that I learned my grandpa Ralph was my dad's adoptive father.

Maybe we were driving home from the library when Dad mentioned it. Maybe a stack of Bigfoot books was under my elbow on the back seat. At least one was sure to have been open on my lap.

"What happened to your real dad?" I asked, too young to realize that Grandpa Ralph was his real father; he did the work of parenting and provided the love that this other man couldn't.

"He died in World War II."

Grandpa Ralph had fought in the war, too, from the pilot seat of a B-17 bomber, flying missions from England to German-held territory on the continent. I knew Grandpa Ralph, the treats he bought us, how he was always adding rooms onto his and Grandma's cabin in the northwoods, but this other man was not known to me at all and was dim even amid the trees of Dad's memory, barely even a shadow. I learned later that he had abandoned the family when Dad was around two, when Grandma was pregnant with my uncle Ted.

"How'd he die?" I asked at some point, but not on the car ride home I'm imagining here. I remember I was sitting next to Dad when he told me that this man none of us knew had died on the Bataan Death March.

Though I was a regular champion in classroom spelling bees, I had no idea how Bataan was spelled. I heard "baton," but that didn't matter because "death march" said everything I needed to know. From Saturday matinee movies on TV, I could see rows of troops marching down rain-slick roads, slipping and falling in the slop and being beaten by the enemy if they failed to get up quickly enough. I'd seen many such Hollywood deaths, so I could see that of this never-known man.

"A lot of soldiers from Brainerd died on that march." Dad grew up in Brainerd, Minnesota, so it made sense his father was from there, too, and that he had died along with some of the young men he had grown up with. While not known to me and hazy at best to Dad, this story added a layer of interest to this shadow man, giving him at least one remarkable dimension, his death.

From the White Earth

This father-shadow, though a hazy memory in Dad's lived experience, is, of course, a deeper presence in our DNA.

Some forty-plus years after the Bataan Death March, another dimension to this never-really-known man emerges with the passage of the White Earth Land Settlement Act of 1985 (WELSA). WELSA was designed to clear the clouded titles to land on the White Earth Anishinaabe reservation, titles that had become muddy through various shady land deals, with the result that by the 1970s and 1980s most reservation land was in non-Native hands and those messy titles were interfering with the ability of people to buy and sell the land. To resolve the problem of the titles, the U.S. Congress decided to pay off all the surviving allottees and heirs to the clouded land. Sometime in the late 1980s, my dad and uncle received phone calls informing them of their heirship. Even though, by then, they had the last name of their adoptive dad, Meland, whichever branch of the government was in charge of tracking down the heirs found them under the last name of their biological father in the school registration records in Brainerd.

Suddenly something not-known was known. This shadow in our DNA was a descendant of White Earth Anishinaabeg, his mother was Anishinaabe, and her mother was too—and then all the way back.

As a writer, this shadow's genetic footprint raised an interesting question in my mind, one that I would later come to realize is the wrong one. Given this genetic link, I thought the question to ask was, What does it mean for people like us, raised outside the community, without any knowledge of our Native heritage, to be Anishinaabe? Elders told me that even if you only had one drop of Native blood, being Anishinaabe was written into your physical DNA, as well as what they called your spiritual DNA, which is a concept not yet known to Western science. While such DNA may be there, I hadn't been raised with any sense of Native community, responsibility, or culture—and I was going on thirty years old when I learned of this connection. What did this mean to me? Did it mean I was Native? I mulled over questions like this as I undertook my graduate studies of contemporary Native written literature and then moved into my position as a faculty member of the Department of American Indian Studies at the University of Minnesota, Duluth. Today I participate, albeit fitfully, in Anishinaabe language learning tables and continue to explore the philosophical depths of Anishinaabe thought with cultural people, but I realize these things, while rewarding, are not really addressing the question I felt at the center of my explorations.

The question, I realize now, is not about what it means to be Anishinaabe. Rather, the question is what does it mean to *not know* you are Anishinaabe? Not-knowing raises questions: Why don't you know? What should you know? Not-knowing in this situation is a form of uncertainty, both of where you came from and where you might be headed. Not-knowing is one way of being lost.

DNA provides an uncertain sense of connection but proves nothing. Not-knowing anything about Dad's biological father made him an absence in my life, but when I learned a little bit about him, and about our Anishinaabe descendance, suddenly that thing that had been a not-known became an unknown. Really, it is sort of impossible to think about a not-known, but the unknown is a mystery, a problem, perhaps, inviting a certain kind of reflection, even if there is no solution. It's like the pictures of Bigfoot tracks I've seen. Those traces suggest something, something you might know, maybe should know, but don't; the tracks point to possibilities, to the unknown.

Lost

Bagwajinini looked into that woman's soul as she sped past, and she began to cry. That's all we know about her. Donald Sherman, an enrolled member of the Leech Lake Anishinaabe Nation and a Bigfoot researcher, told the story to a newspaper reporter in Duluth, Minnesota, about fifteen years ago.

Why does she cry when she sees him? What does it mean that he looked into her soul?

Sherman explained to the reporter that Creator sent the Bigfoot people to the Anishinaabeg for many reasons, including to warn people of impending illness. Illness may be not just a physical ailment, I'm supposing, but could also speak to a loss of spiritual balance, that harmony you seek to maintain within as well as with your greater community (which includes all the other-than-human lives around you) and with the ancestors that is the key to living mino-bimaadiziwin. Mino-bimaadiziwin is how you say "the good life" in Anishinaabemowin, that life of harmony and balance that reflects both spiritual and physical well-being.

Sherman also told the reporter that Creator sent the Bigfoot beings to guide and care for the Anishinaabeg. "Bigfoot teaches us medicine through our medicine man," Sherman said.[1]

I am trying to understand this Bigfoot trait of guiding and caring, of teaching medicine, as pointing to the sort of abiding compassion that some might call a blessing. It is the sort of compassion that comes without conditions and is weighted with the sort of keen concern someone has for those who may need help. Later I learned that Bagwajinini also comes to people who have lost their way in the woods, particularly those who are seeking medicine. If such a person has good thoughts, Bagwajinini will help them find the medicine they seek and, if they are lost, will set them on the path home.

Knowing this, we can begin to see why that woman may have cried. Maybe she was heading to Bena to be good medicine for an ailing relative; maybe she was heading back after spending years living an other than attentive or harmonious life; maybe she felt lost; maybe she was lost. When he looked into her soul, though, she felt his compassion enter her.

Cryptid

A cryptid, like Bigfoot or Yeti or the creature in Loch Ness, is an animal undocumented by science; they are unpapered. They live in stories that, no matter how compelling, frightening, or mysterious, are only suggestive of their actual existence in the physical world. Their habitat in wild and seemingly inaccessible places coupled with their ability to elude capture allows them to remain uncertain and unknown.

Cryptozoology is the study of cryptids, and the *crypto* part of the word literally means "hidden." They are creatures hidden from science, from documentation. Loren Coleman, one of the leading cryptozoologists of the last half century, points out that people like himself don't actually study cryptids. Cryptozoology is, as he puts it, "the study of the *evidence* for hidden animals." Since they can't study the animal itself, cryptozoologists are really only studying the evidence they find, which suggests the existence of some not-known life. Tracks, traces, tufts of promising hair, scat, photographs, and film footage are all part of the evidentiary record, but what dominates are the reports. Stories like those of the woman driving to Bena.

Dad's biological father is also a cryptid. We have tracks and traces, evidence of his existence, but no living memory of his presence in our lives. He was hidden from us for decades; rather, I should say, he hid himself away from us, given his abandonment of my grandma, dad, and uncle. We don't have him in our lives to study, so we have to turn to the traces and try to discern the shape of some sort of narrative in the evidentiary record if we want to find what was lost to us.

A Jackpine Lothario

Like the hidden connection to the White Earth Nation in our blood, what else did we *not* know about this cryptid, this biological father who never even really knew his own children?

There's no reason to believe he was an entirely bad man, but almost everything that we've learned about him is bad. Grandma's petition for divorce busts him out for not providing for his family and for "riotous living," which is the mid–twentieth century semiformal and legalistic way of saying he spent more time carousing and chasing skirt than he did fulfilling his responsibilities at home. Their fitful union seems to have begun at the end of a shotgun—not really, but you get my point—when Grandma was a few months pregnant with my dad, and it pretty much ended less than two years later when he punched Grandma with a clenched fist. According to the divorce petition, the blow caused "her to fall against the wall and floor, thereby inflicting painful bruises upon her and swollen areas and black and blue marks." Grandma was not anyone's doormat; I don't see her cowering following his assault. Those who knew the couple in those years reported that they were, in the words of the family history my uncle later wrote, "constantly arguing and disagreeing with one another." Stories I've heard include that he often demanded she give him money so he could go out partying (not a very 1940 word, I know, but I feel like it is the one that conveys how I understand his, um, character). It was household money and I'm guessing it was just enough to keep the family fed, and I know Grandma probably kept a tight grip on it. He also seems to have spent many nights someplace other than at home. Members of his own family described him as a charming womanizer, which may explain how he landed with Grandma in the first place, as well as why he didn't last. No one described him as a devoted family man.

Reared at the southern edge of the northwoods up there in Brainerd, Grandma grew up hearing the phrase "jackpine savage" and, though I never heard her refer to him as such (I really never heard her refer to him at all), I think this absent man fits the category. I am trying to find a way to speak of him without bringing his name into all this. I know his name, but names are for people who live up to them. What he did to my grandma, dad, and uncle renders him nameless. Let's let him be a jackpine savage.

The *savage* part of "jackpine savage" points to the sort of animalistic and backward ways of living non-Native people invented to pin on Native people, to derogate them and justify thieving their homelands. The *savage* part of the phrase points to a notion that some people devolve socially, whether by environment or by choice, when they move among the jack pine, which is to say that the *savage* part plays into notions that Native people are less evolved socially and that, under the right conditions, anyone who steps out of "civilized" life to live back in the woods becomes more animalistic and backward, morally and behaviorally, whether Native or not.

We have to keep in mind that this word is weighted with these implications when we see the phrase "jackpine savage." It stinks of the sort of racism we dream we've moved beyond. But the phrase, as I grew up understanding it from Grandma, while still burdened with such racist overtones, generally had a lighter touch and was directed only at people who were, as far as I recall, not Native—or, in my case, didn't know of their Native descendance. Grandma teased me with the phrase when I'd come back filthy after playing in the woods, or she'd call one of the neighbors such a thing if they somehow managed to prank her. While mostly used as a joke by Grandma, there were times when the words were used to lay low some lunkhead, even if they were completely unknown to her. When Grandma heard of something particularly egregious, like some backwoods criminal and their half-assed backwoods criminal enterprises, like breaking into lake homes to steal liquor or paddling up to a dock under the cover of night to siphon gas from someone's boat, she'd drop a snide "jackpine savage" on them that was empty of all tease. To be teasingly called a jackpine savage by her and to really be called one were two entirely different things.

Like "redneck," I know some people use "jackpine savage" as a way to honor those folks whose schooling in the woods, on the water, and along rutted gravel roads of northern Minnesota have given them a hard-knock insight into life. I'm talking about the sort of people who are so tough that they could, in the words of blogger R. Scott McCoy's father, "beat your ass til it barks like a fox."[2] Grandma never saw it this way, as I remember. Forgetting the tease, Grandma would likely join with those other people who take a dimmer view of jackpine savages. She'd have seen the sense in the words of the anonymous commenter on McCoy's blog, who says that jackpine savages spend their days and nights "at the bar getting wasted, fighting, and trying to get laid."[3] Grandma would also likely stand with that person at the *Urban Dictionary* who describes a jackpine savage as someone who "does all things to satisfy their instantaneous desire." Both of these latter definitions capture some of what we know about Grandma's first husband. Asking her to give him money for his riotous living is a hella jackpine savage move. It's the sort of move that makes you want to cock your fist and launch it at about jaw level, or maybe a little lower. Like the throat.

At some point in 1940, I imagine he came looking for some of that cabbage of hers, and I'm sure she refused to give him any, no doubt telling him she needed it to buy things for my then-toddling dad and the child she was pregnant with at the moment, my uncle Ted. I want to think she told him to get out and never come back, adding, I hope, something to the effect of, "Chase your little hussies, swill your beer, shoot your mouth off and see where it gets you, but don't come back here sniffing around for me or any money." I like to think these were the sorts of things she said as she showed him the door. Because Grandma had a sailor's mouth on her, in a later era, like now, she'd have just told him to fuck off. Perhaps she said it that day as well. It's not like we invented the phrase out in the schoolyard in 1977.

As a cryptid, this jackpine savage was hidden from my dad and uncle. I imagine that when they got a little older, back there in the early 1940s, and wondered why they didn't have a dad, Grandma killed him off, telling them that he had died on the Bataan Death March, as so many soldiers from Brainerd had. Such a death could be seen as that of a hero, or of a martyr at least, and I can only suppose that Grandma must have decided it was probably better to have them think they had a dad who died in service to the country, rather than having them know they had a father who had abandoned them.

She hid him there in the historical record.

Mayak Datat

The most iconic image we have of Bigfoot is probably that of "Patty," as the female Sasquatch filmed in October 1967 by Roger Patterson and Bob

Gimlin is known. Breasts clearly visible, she is seen in three-quarters rear profile striding away from the camera, but at one point in the roughly minute-long film she glances over her shoulder and stares straight into our eyes. This image has been reenacted, mimicked, and parodied until even those who have no interest in Bigfoot know who Patty is, even if they don't know her name. (Of course, that's just the nickname given this being; we have no idea of the name her people know her by, or if they even use names.)

Another iconic image, one that has escaped parody (at least in my experience), is that of *Mayak Datat*, the Hairy Man. The Hairy Man is a pictograph in a rock-shelter located on the Tule River Indian Nation, in what is now central California.

The Hairy Man is not alone in this rock-shelter; it is a famous pictographic site filled with images of beaver, bear, frog, condors, eagles, and geometric designs. Also present with the Hairy Man are pictographs of a female and a child Bigfoot. The three together are known as the family.

Let's just look at the father, the Hairy Man, as that is the one most often discussed in Bigfoot studies. His figure is rendered with red, black, and yellow paints. He is about eight and a half feet tall, and his outstretched arms measure nearly six and a half feet across, as big as contemporary stories report Bigfoot as being. (Patty's arms, famously swinging in the Patterson-Gimlin film, are estimated to have been forty-two inches long, giving her a similarly daunting wingspan.) The Hairy Man stands upright on two legs, he has a long torso, and his arms, as I said above, are spread open, sort of in the manner of the early George Romero *Night of the Living Dead* zombies. There are lines coming out of his eyes, which the Yokut people at Tule River identify as tears. The Hairy Man is sad, according to their origin story, because even though he helped make the first people, when they saw him "they were scared and ran away." According to the origin story, the rock-shelter is filled with pictures of all sorts of local animals because they all "drew their pictures on the rock . . . so People would remember them." Like the animals, the Hairy Man drew himself as well. "Hairy Man was sad because People were afraid of him, so he drew himself sad."[4]

In other Native pictographs, lines emerging from the eyes or the top of the head are also understood as indicators of spiritual power, as someone channeling energy from the dimensions beyond this familiar one. Whether sad or in a state of great spiritual attention, the Hairy Man appears to be lumbering out of the rock face toward us. His eyes, like Patty's, like the Bigfoot spotted by that woman along the railroad tracks in northern Minnesota, are fixed on us.

Why are these beings looking at us?

Many Indigenous traditions say the Bigfoot people are, in fact, looking out for us. In a story collected in 1975 at Tule River, elders said that while children were warned that the Hairy Man might eat them if they wandered off, they also said, "He was good in a way, because he ate the animals that might harm people. He kept the Grizzly Bear, Mountain Lion, Wolf, and other large animals away."[5]

He took care of the people he created; even if he might be threatening, he was also compassionate. In that sense, he was not so different from the living environment itself.

Dying

The story about the jackpine savage dying on Bataan is powerful evidence, proving the existence of a man who might have been a stand-up dad had he survived. Some sort of hope for two fatherless boys maybe, a track pressed in the damp earth that points to something bigger, something dreamed of.

What was hidden, though, has since come forth: we know now that this man had served in Europe and North Africa during World War II, nowhere near Bataan in the South Pacific, and died, about three years after V-E day, of testicular cancer. (Feel free to draw your own conclusions about riotous living and cosmic justice.) Neither hero nor martyr, he was in the end, perhaps, a victim of his own unrepentant jackpine savagery.

Interestingly, at least in the public record of a local oral history project, my dad sticks to the story that his biological father died on Bataan.[6] I don't know why; maybe it's that track in the earth, that dreamed-of something that he never had. Sometimes a lie is easier to believe than the truth, but I don't think it's a lie that Dad still holds to this story. It strikes me more as a personal myth, the sort of symbolic story we all elaborate in an attempt to maintain some sort of order in the chaos of our lived experience. When we can, we all edit out those hidden weights that could threaten our internal sense of balance.

I can only guess why Dad chose to edit the story this way. The explanation I've chosen to settle on is that it might be easier to not know that dead soldier than it is to not know the absent father.

Manidoo

The Hairy Man lumbers out of the rock face, moving toward us, arms extended. Is it a threatening posture or an embracing one? We know he is sad, but is he mad about our neglect of him or is he reaching out to us?

Bigfoot researchers eye him as proof. He was known to the Yokut people at Tule River, just as the eagles, bears, and beaver also pictured in the shelter were. He is, thus, as real as those other creatures, or at least was at one time. Such researchers seek proof of a material being, as demanded by Western scientific standards. What if that is missing the point of the Bigfoot experience, though? In an Indigenous context, we might see a different way to understand this experience.

Many cave art, pictograph, and petroglyph scholars tell us that the stone faces that carry these images were likely understood by ancient artists as a membrane between our physical world and other spiritual ones.[7] Despite its solid appearance, these artists understood that stone is permeable. In clefts in the rock in the caves of Europe, you can find half-formed animals emerging from such gaps, spirit animals being born from other dimensions into our own, a record perhaps of an artist's visionary experience. Some rock art scholars speculate that the hands famously stenciled on the stone in sites across the world are not simple statements of "I was here" or "This is mine"; they are not the territory-claiming tags of ancient graffiti artists. Instead, scholars think those hands are touching the membrane, marks of love perhaps, in acknowledgement of the dimensions within—and beyond—the stone. Those hands are telling that other world, "I know you are there. Remember me here."

Anishinaabe people also understand that stone is a living thing, that it possesses a spirit. One friend told me that there are rocks, which are inanimate, and stones, which are animate. "How do you tell the difference?" I asked and he responded, "A stone speaks to you, a rock doesn't." The stones in the sweat lodge are not even called stones, but are referred to as grandfathers, as they are elders possessed of great spiritual knowledge—and they speak of it.

These understandings of stones as living things or as a membrane between ourselves and spiritual realms makes no sense in a rigid understanding of Western scientific knowledge. The physical sciences focus on the material world and rock is, generally speaking, a very hard material, one whose chemical composition can be parsed, whose age can be measured, whose origins in the seas or in the crucible of the earth can be reconstructed. Rock can be crushed and ores extracted; it can be made useful to humans in all manner of ways in this materialist way of seeing and understanding the world. What the sciences seek to offer is some sort of definitive answer to puzzling questions, answers that may open up new questions to research but that still manage to resolve some sort of mystery. Many, if not most, Bigfoot researchers follow in this tradition.

In that world where stone is a membrane between our world and the ones of the spirit, where stone is understood as a living being (rather than a dead object), we can find a differing context for understanding such mysteries as living stone and Bigfoot beings. In Anishinaabemowin, the language of the Anishinaabe people, this context is called manidoo.

Manidoo is generally translated into English as "spirit" and, while that is not incorrect, it is too limited an understanding from an Anishinaabe perspective, where the connotations of the word range further.[8] *Manidoo* might also refer to a, for lack of a better word, deity or it may be that mystical sort of feeling that comes over you in certain places or at certain times; it is an essence that makes a thing what it is; and, at least as I have been told, it is best understood as a mystery.

Unlike the Western scientific perspective, mystery, in the manidoo sense of the word, is not a problem to be solved; it is a presence, not a problem. Manidoo is the mystery behind the world and within the world. It is ineffable, in the words of Anishinaabe cultural educator James Vukelich. It is incapable of being captured in words and so is a mystery, a true unknown; we know it exists but not what it is. It is part of that reality from beyond the physical dimensions we live our day-to-day lives in. Manidoo lets us know that the physical world is only one facet of our experience.

Manidoo is beyond the reach of human understanding; our reason and logic are too limited to grasp what is going on in the unseen realities surrounding us, though at times we may see a being emerging from the stone face of a rock-shelter or a hulking figure standing along a railroad embankment. Mysteries like these may never be fully known, but they can be meditated upon, prayed over, and thanked. Our engagement with them may lead to epiphanies and self-understanding.

Never Really Known

I think about Mayak Datat, this sad Hairy Man who threatens the people he helped create but also cares about their welfare. As the story tells us, all the animals drew pictures of themselves on the walls of the rock-shelter so the people would remember them. We know from the story that the Hairy Man did, too, but there is also a female and child Bigfoot pictured there. Did they paint themselves, or did the Hairy Man paint them? The story doesn't make that clear, but either way they are together there in that shelter. Archaeologists think the pictographs at Tule River were made anywhere from five hundred to one thousand years ago. For dozens upon dozens of human generations, this family has been together, intact, and looking out for the people they created.

I wish the same could be said of the jackpine savage. While we have photographs of this man now, he left no clear image of himself in his children's minds; he didn't paint a picture of himself by which the people he helped create would remember him. This man seems to have only looked out for himself. Like cryptozoologists and their elusive creatures, I'm constructing this man, and myself to a degree, from scant evidence, including that trace of Anishinaabe ancestry.

When I was a kid, Dad told me he had a dim memory of seeing this man one time, but nothing conclusive stuck from the encounter. Unlike the woman who saw Bagwajinini along the tracks, there was no meeting of the eyes, no looking into the soul, no raw emotional exchange. Just a man-shaped image, but not a fatherly one, wispy and indefinite. Never forgotten, but never really known. Cryptid.

Mishomis Stone

Sweat lodge stones are known as grandfathers. The core teachings of Anishinaabe people are called the Seven Grandparent teachings.[9] The Seven Grandparents help Anishinaabe reach mino-bimaadiziwin, that good life of balance and harmony in all things. Each Grandparent teaching has a manidoo associated with it. The Eagle is the manidoo of love, and the Bear is the manidoo of courage. Bagwajinini, as the Bigfoot being is named in some dialects of Anishinaabemowin, is known as Sabe (pronounced sah-bay) in other dialects of the language. In the Grandparent teachings, Sabe is the name we most often encounter, and they are the manidoo of honesty.

Anishinaabe Knowledge Keeper Nii Gaani Aki Inini explains the Anishinaabe concept of honesty through a story about Sabe appearing to a young boy in a vision.

Sabe tells the boy that if he is honest in his life, he will become as tall as a Bigfoot. Height here is measured not in feet and inches, I believe, but in integrity.

The jackpine savage abandoned his family.

The Bigfoot being tells the boy, "Don't deceive yourself or your fellow [humans] with lies, gossip, or words that could hurt anyone."

I can only imagine the tales the jackpine savage must have told my grandma as he tried to get her to give him some of the household money or as he tried to justify why he hadn't come home the night before.

In Nii Gaani Aki Inini's telling, Sabe continues his lesson to the boy. "As you reach to live a good life, always be honest with yourself and your fellow [humans]. . . . Be honest with who you are, and whatever you speak, make sure your words show kindness for all of Creation."

The jackpine savage punched my grandma, knocking her to the floor and leaving her face swollen and bruised.

Before leaving, Sabe touches the boy's head, a loving sort of gesture as I see it, an elder offering comfort, and tells him, "I live in the trees, watching and listening to see if you are honest. . . . I am always there to help you."[10]

Perhaps the Hairy Man's arms are best understood as reaching out to us.

Running from a Vision

Stories like these about Bigfoot and absent fathers are full of what ifs.

What if Bigfoot is real and a body is brought in next week/month/year? What new revelations about the hominid family tree will be forthcoming as the secrets in that massive body come to light?

We also have the personal what ifs. What if the absent father had been an upstanding dad, sticking with the family and raising his boys? Would we have been raised in the knowledge of our Anishinaabe grandparents and great-grandparents? What sort of changes in our family's experience would have come from his presence, rather than those experiences we have, which were shaped by his absence?

What if the story remains much as it has so far played out, with the absent father still absent, still twice dead, but with one crucial difference? What if we learned about this Anishinaabe story of ours earlier? What if we grew up knowing it?

As he promised that young boy in the story, what if Sabe is always watching from the woods and is always ready to help us should we need it?

There's also the question of what if we aren't ready for help.

When I was about ten, I was staying with my maternal grandparents at their farm in southern Minnesota. I suppose it was in late July or early August because in the summer heat the hog farm on the other side of the swampy woods that edged Grandpa's property reeked so badly that at times it actually made my eyes water.

I have forgotten much, if not most, of this particular visit, except for that hog stench and what may have been a visit from Bigfoot. It started as a typical evening of going out and visiting Grandpa and Grandma's friends that ended, back at home, with ice cream and the ten o'clock news from the Austin, Minnesota, television station about a half-hour down the road from us. The closing story of the newscast that night, that lighthearted story that is supposed to send you off to bed with a smile, was about Bigfoot. A group of young people had seen a Bigfoot crossing the lonely country highway in front of their car the night before and had slowed down to see if they could get a better look at the creature. They got more than they bargained for when Bigfoot jumped out of the ditch and pounded on the roof of the car. The driver gunned it, but Bigfoot tore after them, glaring at the kids through the windows while trying to gain a grip on the door of the speeding car. The creature kept pace with the car until it hit about sixty, and the kids pulled away with their hearts in their mouths. Their report to the sheriff ended up as a glint in the newscaster's eyes and a sly smile. "Sleep well, everyone," he said before signing off.

The road where this encounter happened was only about twenty miles away, Grandpa said, and that was too close for me to sleep well. I knew sixty miles an hour was a mile a minute, and that meant Bigfoot might be only twenty minutes away. A slant of the hall light hit the closet door in my bedroom, and the patterns in the wood there became a membrane through which Bigfoot's face emerged, and he seemed angry. He had pounded on the roof of the car and had chased them with a speed beyond human. My mind raced with these thoughts, the images of them as real as the face in the closet door. Was he mad that they had seen him? Mad that they knew where he might live? How big was his hand as it smashed against the car? What would he have done to them if they hadn't sped off?

It took a good long time to slow the spill of my thoughts, but sleep finally overtook me.

The next day I was out at the far end of the farm, separated from Grandpa and the hired hands, a good three or four hundred yards from the house, alone along the edge of the woods that separated us from the hog farm. These woods were not particularly dense, and the trees were not particularly towering, but it was dark back in there, even in the full light of day—and swampy. The boggy muck of the forest floor made a green stink in the summer heat, the musk of the earth blending with the humid stench from the hog farm. Not that Bigfoot would notice. Those cheap paperbacks I checked out of the library said that Bigfoot smelled awful. Could I be sure, really sure, that what I smelled was swamp muck and humid hog shit and not Bigfoot? At that moment I wasn't so sure, so I turned around and began to trot, hurriedly, back to the house.

Late afternoon sun cut through the dark at the top of the trees, spilling some of that golden farmland light into what was otherwise twisted and scrubby and dim. A blue so vague it was kind of gray shone in thin strips between the trunks of the trees: the sky over the field on the other side of the woods. In the space of about ten strides, I shifted from that hurried trot to a brisk jog and then into a full-bore run. The newscaster's report swelled inside me. They hadn't got away until they hit sixty!

I ran so hard that I couldn't hear the creature I was now certain was there. I couldn't hit sixty, but I would get as close as humanly possible. I was a kid who liked to run, and the gym class blue ribbons in my sock drawer at home would testify I was a strong runner.

Risking a glance toward the woods I saw nothing, but the stink was dense and he was paralleling my steps, I knew, keeping just inside the tree line, just out of sight, a clever hunter. The story of Albert Ostman leaped to mind. He had been kidnapped by a family of Sasquatch back in the 1920s and held captive for days or weeks. I couldn't remember which, but the length of his captivity hardly mattered if I was the one who was now going to be abducted. I was running away from certain capture. I vaulted the gate at the farmyard, sprinted past the pond and a couple of outbuildings, and crashed through the door of the house to the comforting sight of Grandma at work in the kitchen. Collapsing in a kitchen chair, I struggled to regain my breath.

I didn't know the story of Sabe and the boy then, about the loving way the wild man had placed his giant hand gently on the boy's head and told him how he lived in the trees and was always there, ready to help. I didn't know that Sabe is the manidoo of honesty. I didn't know about the Anishinaabe teachings, and I ran as hard as I could, not wanting the outstretched arms of that hairy woodland being to be the last thing I saw as they reached out and carried me away. I didn't realize then that, like that boy, I might have been having a vision. I might have been meant to see this manidoo, but I ran from it, not yet ready for the stories that we had never known.

Honesty

Sabe, that wild person of the woods, that giant, is the manidoo of honesty. Honesty is integral to integrity, to being honest with oneself.

To be honest, as a writer these stories of our never-known family, with all their known and little-known facets, fascinate me. Unlike the family stories I grew up hearing from the people who lived them, people I could see, question, and laugh with, people with known forms and dimensions, these stories of our Anishinaabe ancestors are vague, suggestive. Their form and dimensions are pictographic, existing only in secondhand reports and a handful of photos, just outlines and silhouettes. Just as cryptozoologists scan photos of Bigfoot, searching for similarities to our bodies, and elaborate stories about the way these unknown beings live from secondhand reports about their behavior, I scan the photos of the jackpine savage and parse the reports about him. His long face is similar to mine and Dad's, as is his dark hair. His build is lanky, as is ours. Army records show he was five-foot-eleven, a good four and six inches shorter than Dad and I, respectively, which I hope indicates, as Sabe taught the boy, our greater integrity.

I elaborate stories about his riotous living, his abuse of his wife, his abandonment of his children from known facts, and I do my grandma one better by killing him off not once, but twice.

Still, being honest, while we have little experience in sharing the ancestral story with those who lived it, there is my engagement with my fellow Anishinaabe language learners and there is my life as a teacher and writer in Native Studies.

In the end, honestly, I don't know what I am. Human, son, father to be sure, but what of it? Honestly, too, I am an unenrolled person of

Anishinaabe heritage—unpapered, reflecting the title of this anthology. Honestly, I am the immediate descendant of Anishinaabe people who made choices to leave their community, to move into cities, to abandon their families, to die a fictitious death in a war and a real death in a hospital ward. Honestly, I am the outcome of generations of assimilation, sometimes coerced and, I suppose, sometimes chosen. In some sense this body I am in is, honestly, one way to see what the genocide of Native people in North America looks like and, honestly, that is both true and way too blindingly melodramatic and sentimental to be true. Honestly, too, those unknown people did what they needed to do to survive. Honestly, I don't think I am the subject of those stories, though my Anishinaabe ancestors are.

Grandfather Asin

I do not speak Anishinaabemowin at all well. I recognize words and I know some simple conjugations and I try to piece things together, but I am not at all confident that what I am about to write is correct, but even if it's not, here goes: DNA is asiniiwan, "it is of stone." DNA, like stone, is made of carbon; it is carbon-based; it is of stone; asiniiwan. As Gerald Vizenor said, DNA is the story in our blood, a stone that speaks, and some elders will tell you that even one drop of blood carries that Anishinaabe story inside you.[11] Some stones are grandfathers and will speak to you, offering stories and teachings. My DNA is such a stone, a gift from a cryptid, that unknown grandfather. Tracks in our blood are the genetic equivalent of those cryptozoological plaster casts. With them we can trace backward along the trackway toward something we once knew, and we can follow it forward toward something we should know now. Though I am not sure what it is that we should know now, I am convinced that it has something to do with making sense of this story in our blood. These tracks are some sort of evidence pointing to some sort of potential story, perhaps this one you are reading.

That woman speeding down the highway didn't expect to see Bagwajinini among the stones along the railroad tracks. We don't know if she was road-weary or perhaps in some state of heightened emotion as she approached Bena, but when she saw him, his gaze reached into her and touched something that startled her to tears. He offered her a striking moment of epiphany, an insight that belongs to her alone. It's a story of compassion and hope, as I see it. He reached out to her with his vision.

My speeding car has no wheels, my country highway has no railroad crossing, and I have no route to Bena, but Sabe still found me, tracking me for years upon years upon decades, pursuing me through the pages of cheap paperbacks and frightening me in those rank farm woods. I used to think I liked Bigfoot stories because of their eerie atmosphere, those uncertain shadows moving under tall trees, not realizing that the sense of mystery they evoke is actually a form of teaching, manidoo visions that lead to insight when the stories are really powerful. Sabe found me when I was spinning those public library book racks and found me again as I tried to make sense of the jackpine savage and the twisting helixes of the tracks in our blood.

NOTES

1. Sherman shares this story in "Bigfoot or Big Story?" *Duluth News Tribune,* October 13, 2007, https://www.duluthnewstribune.com/news/2368058 -bigfoot-or-big-story.
2. McCoy, "What Is a Jackpine Savage?"
3. McCoy, "What Is a Jackpine Savage?"
4. Strain, *Giants, Cannibals, and Monsters,* 67.
5. "Big Foot, the Hairy Man," *Tule River History.*
6. Norman, "Interview with Keith Meland." In this interview with the St. Louis Park Oral History Project, given in September 2012, Dad tells the interviewer, "My biological father was killed in the Bataan Death March" (2). He later says, "I didn't have any memory of that other man [his biological father] at all" (2). This interview was conducted more than twenty years after we found out that man died of testicular cancer.
7. I am basing my discussion of pictographic art on David Lewis-Williams's book *The Mind in the Cave* and the book he coauthored with David Pearce, *Inside the Neolithic Mind.* Both books are careful to distinguish Paleolithic and Neolithic peoples from contemporary Indigenous peoples, while being attentive to the fact that both peoples used rock art in sophisticated

ways to both represent spiritual experiences and to activate them. Other than a section that briefly devolves into a discussion of evolutionary psychology in *The Mind in the Cave*, both books strike me as thoughtful and insightful engagements with the questions of human consciousness and the role of art and ritual in making sense of lived experience.

8. I am basing my discussion of manidoo on the great Anishinaabe scholar Basil Johnston's work in *The Manitous*.

9. These teachings are most often referred to as the Seven Grandfather teachings in English, but more and more I see them referenced as the Seven Grandparent teachings. I have chosen to use the latter term in keeping with what seems to be an emerging trend among Anishinaabe writers and thinkers.

10. Nii Gaani Aki Inini, "A Story of the Seven Sacred Laws."

11. I can't even tell you anymore where I first or most recently heard Vizenor use the phrase "stories in the blood," so I can't give a direct citation. Was it in *The Heirs of Columbus*, in his autobiography, or a collection of his essays? I don't know. No direct citation will be forthcoming, but all thanks go to Gerald Vizenor for the memorable words. Miigwech!

BIBLIOGRAPHY

"Big Foot, the Hairy Man." *Tule River History*, August 22, 2019. http://tulerivertribe-nsn.gov/wp-content/uploads/2014/04/big-foot.pdf.

Coleman, Loren. "The Meaning of Cryptozoology." *The Cryptozoologist Loren Coleman*, August 16, 2019. http://lorencoleman.com/the-meaning-of-cryptozoology/.

"Cryptozoology." *Paranormal-Encyclopedia.com*, August 16, 2019. https://www.paranormal-encyclopedia.com/c/cryptozoology/.

Johnston, Basil. *The Manitous: The Spiritual World of the Ojibway*. New York: Harper Collins, 1995.

Lewis-Williams, David. *The Mind in the Cave: Consciousness and the Origins of Art*. London: Thames & Hudson, 2004.

Lewis-Williams, David, and David Pearce. *Inside the Neolithic Mind: Consciousness, Cosmos and the Realm of the Gods*. London: Thames & Hudson, 2009.

McCoy, R. Scott. "What Is a Jackpine Savage?" *Jackpine Savage!*, May 17, 2010. https://rscottmccoy.blogspot.com/2010/05/what-is-jackpine-savage.html.

Nii Gaani Aki Inini. "A Story of the Seven Sacred Laws." *Cultural Survival*, October 17, 2018. https://www.culturalsurvival.org/news/story-seven -sacred-laws-0.

Norman, Jeff. "Interview with Keith Meland (1938–), Urban Exodus: St. Louis Park Oral History Project, Minneapolis, Minnesota." Interviews September 10, 17, and 18, 2012. http://cdm15160.contentdm.oclc.org /cdm/ref/collection/jhs/id/1007.

Strain, Kathy Moskowitz. *Giants, Cannibals, and Monsters: Bigfoot in Native Culture*. Blaine WA, Hancock House, 2008.

IDENTITY WARS

This section is concerned with Indian Country's internal battles between those who accept their unpapered relatives and understand the difference between them and Pretendians and the hardline opposition to anyone who does not hold a card of tribal citizenship recognized by the federal government and even, in some cases, those who do. The editors have tried to present multiple perspectives on the identity issue throughout this volume, but especially within this section, where we have commentary from Michele Leonard, who has battled courageously for years against the damage Pretendians do, while still valuing her unpapered relatives; Trevino Brings Plenty, who represents, in a more reasonable and palatable form, the most rigid stance of the hardliners; Ron Querry, a card-carrying tribal citizen who lacks the genotypical and geographical characteristics that many people expect from a Native person; and Geary Hobson, who offers a satirical view of the entire battlefield.

Michele Leonard

"You Don't Look Indian"

I am an enrolled citizen of the Shinnecock Indian Nation of Southampton, New York. Having to include the word *enrolled* when I state where I come from and my relationship to my tribal nation is a reflection of the times. It is the additional burden those of us who are indeed real, bona fide, legitimate Indigenous people generally include in our introductions so as not to be mistaken for the myriad of individuals who are "playing Indian."

Many years ago, I attended the Hamptons Film Festival, a festival that is held in the town that comprises the Shinnecock reservation and territory. One of the movies the festival was screening at that time was *Edge of America*, based on a true story about an African American man who arrives at a Native American school in Utah to teach English and ends up coaching the girls' basketball team. It was the quintessential Hollywood "savior" film. After the screening, citizens of my tribe who had been given guest passes, myself included, were invited to go backstage and have a meet and greet with one of the actors, a white male who had a significant supporting role. During the discussion, this individual stated something to the effect that during his stay in the Hamptons, he had met several citizens of my tribe. He went on to say that he hoped we didn't mind if he commented that we "don't look like Indians." This phrase was not new to me. It has been stated in my presence so many times that I am often tempted to respond, "Really? Well, you do not look like an Irishman"—or whatever ethnicity would spring to mind and align itself with the commentor—in an attempt to magnify the rudeness and ignorance that surrounds such a comment. Once again, I didn't state the obvious. Instead, I remained cordial.

What is an Indian supposed to look like? For decades Hollywood has attempted to define Indians by casting numerous non-Indians in leading roles. Individuals like Rock Hudson, Burt Lancaster, Natalie Wood, and even Audrey Hepburn have played Indians on the big screen at various times in their movie careers. As Native people we have had to watch television commercials touting actors protecting the environment with an Italian man dressed up as an Indian and canoeing in a stream littered with garbage as he sheds a single tear. Any child could deduce from the myriad of westerns and/or John Wayne movies that it was always the cowboys and not the Indians who were going to be the winners, despite who was hired to act out the roles of the Indians. Hollywood's domineering role in establishing and perpetuating ethnic stereotypes of Native Americans contributes to oppression and the forming of opinions, such as the one expressed by this actor at the film festival, of what an Indian is supposed to look like. These stereotypes also make up many people's definitions of who is, in fact, an Indian.

While driving home from the film festival, I tried to think back to the first time someone blatantly questioned my appearance because it differed from their understanding of being Indigenous. I believe it was when I entered college. It was the '70s and I was sixteen when I began studying at Wellesley College in Massachusetts. A mere freshman, I was recruited along with other Native students into the New England collegiate environment. This was at a time when institutions of higher learning wanted to diversify their student bodies. Indigenous students arrived in the Boston area from tribes and communities all over the United States, but predominantly from western tribal nations. For most of these students, not only was this the first time they had ventured to the East Coast, but it was also their first time interacting with individuals from Eastern tribes. While it was to be expected to hear non-Native students say, "you don't look like an Indian" or "all Indians are out West," it was unexpectedly disheartening to hear those very same sentiments from Native students from Western tribes. Those of us confronted with these comments had to offer history lessons to the ill-informed, and it was burdensome to constantly explain one's cultural and ancestral legitimacy. But explain we did. As friendships developed and practices and traditions were shared, a greater understanding of the ordeal suffered by both Eastern and Western tribes due to colonization inevitably ensued. This was also a time when I developed a deeper understanding of what it meant to hail from a tribe that had not been "removed" from one's original territory. Additionally, I wanted to learn more about other tribes, especially other Eastern tribes, and made it somewhat a personal quest to know the histories, struggles, and current challenges facing them. This manifested in a continuation of and deeper commitment to activism in support of Native issues.

After college I continued to build on existing relationships and developed new ones with Indigenous leaders and other activists throughout Indian country. My reputation for being a supporter of and advocate for Native issues held me in good stead when, many years later, I was hired as the executive director of the financially strapped urban Indian center in Philadelphia. Urban Indian centers, or Indian community centers, as they were often titled, were established in many major cities throughout the United States after the Indian termination policies of the 1940s through the 1960s. Termination was another in a series of historical attempts to force Native peoples to assimilate and give up cultural traditions. It was also a policy that resulted in the taking of more Native lands and ultimately forcing large swaths of Indigenous people to live in and around major U.S. cities. The Indian Relocation Act of 1956 played an even more significant role in increasing the population of Indians in urban areas. Unlike the Termination Acts—which attempted to absolve Congress of their responsibility to Native peoples, financial and otherwise—the Relocation Act eventually redirected much of the obligated funding for social programs from reservations to urban Indian centers, making them responsible for providing still-needed social services. For several decades most urban Indian centers were funded by Congressional grants, which allowed them to remain functioning until the Clinton administration's and Congress's policies of the '90s. Urban Indian centers got caught up in the welfare-to-work policies and Congress's desire to cut funding for social services and quickly saw their funding streams diminish.

The United American Indians of Delaware Valley (UAIDV), the Indian center in Philadelphia, had been struggling financially for many years, initially due to a series of failed audits and accounting procedures. When I was asked, in 1993, to assume the position of executive director of UAIDV, I had already established myself as a successful administrator of federal funding and expenditures. Prior to my arrival, UAIDV had received several warnings that their funding would be halted if they didn't find someone who could keep their funds in compliance with federal audit requirements. Having lived for several years in Pennsylvania, I was aware of the importance of the Indian centers to the state because Pennsylvania no longer had any tribes or reservations within its boundaries. The last legitimate tribe was the Seneca, who were forcibly removed in the '60s to allow for the building of the Kinzua Dam. Despite the reality that there weren't any tribes or reservations, Native peoples from legitimate tribal communities were attempting to exist in Pennsylvania's urban areas. In this state, many Native children had been caught up in the scandalous practice of forced adoptions of Indian children by non-Indian families. Nationally these adoptions, and the faulty process, ultimately resulted in the need for the Indian Child Welfare Act of 1978. For many of these individuals living with their adoptive families in Pennsylvania, the urban Indian centers were a connection to a tribal and cultural community.

To identify additional sources of revenue for the struggling center and the wider Native community, I applied for several grants from area foundations and service organizations. During this process, I discovered that we, the legitimate Indian center, were in competition with a group calling themselves the Eastern Delaware Nation (EDN).

The EDN was conjured up by several individuals, one of whom had

had a contentious relationship with UAIDV. This man, who went by the name of "Chief" Carl "Wyandaga" Pierce and originally self-identified as Nanticoke, had a disagreement with the leadership of UAIDV and decided to break away from the organization. Before Mr. Pierce ventured out on his own, his involvement with UAIDV gave him general knowledge of the organization's structure, programming, funding, and ways that, should he want to start his own organization, he could attempt such a venture. I was informed of this adversarial history between Carl Pierce and UAIDV when I assumed the executive director position in 1993 and was reminded several years later when faced with funding challenges.

In many areas around the country, predominantly where forts and national historic sites are located, people participate in a hobby called reenacting, and they are referred to as reenactors. These roles require them to "dress up" in costumes to portray their chosen roles. Many of the reenactments are of Civil War battles, but every now and then there are attempts to reenact battles between colonists and Indians. These have occurred frequently in Pennsylvania, primarily due to the location and history of the colonies and the presence of Independence Hall and other historic sites in the greater Philadelphia region.

Several of the individuals who joined Carl Pierce in establishing EDN were reenactors and often took on the roles of Indians. Reenactors are paid for their performances, and these "jobs" are usually scheduled on weekends, allowing them to also hold down regular employment. The income they receive enables them to fully outfit themselves in not only the costumes, but also the accessories. People portraying Indians generally have more regalia, including more expensive pieces, like elk skin or deer skin clothing, with handmade beadwork to assist in fooling an audience that they are, in fact, who they are portraying. They have even acquired ceremonial items, including but not limited to headdresses. And because they are "playing Indian," there is little regard for how offensive their depictions and behavior might be to actual Native People.

As EDN grew in notoriety, a lot of what they represented to the public was a stereotypical portrayal of Indigenous people. They held weekend gatherings in which the public was invited to participate as long as they were willing to pay the admission fee. Again, most of the motivation to play Indian was the economic advantage for a small group of individuals and their families. One of those individuals, who banded with Chief Wyandaga, was a man by the name of Michael Taffe. Taffe's family lineage was later clearly established as hailing from Ireland. To enhance his role as a fake Indian, he would eventually go by the name of Michael "Medicine Shield" Taffe. EDN incorporated as a 501 (c) 3 nonprofit, allowing the organization to fundraise and apply for grants. They welcomed other individuals into the organization who pretended to be Indians and falsely claimed descendancy as Lenape, Shawnee, and other tribes no longer existing in the East. They were always careful to not claim heritage from the tribes that, while no longer having a land base in Pennsylvania, still maintained their tribal composition and accurate tribal rolls and could clearly identify them as frauds. Claiming to be, for instance, Seneca would quickly expose the falsehood because the Seneca Nation knows who their legitimate members are.

Fake Indians would come and go within the structure of EDN, and some of them simply dropped their fake identities and went back to their non-Indian lives. Some regrouped and figured out ways to continue to perpetuate fraud by seeking other opportunities to fulfill their need to be front and center as fake Indians. In 2009 some of these fakes elevated their presence and were embraced once again, by unsuspecting and desperate people, as being Indians. I say "desperate" because, in my opinion, there has been a growing tendency for individuals, especially those aligned with academia, to "look the other way" and not question whether these claims to indigeneity are legitimate. I speculate that this perpetuates a seedy foundation within academia and further exposes a level of laziness with scholarly research as it pertains to Indigenous studies and the accuracy of that genre.

For example, in 2009 Abigail Seldin, a senior undergrad and master's degree candidate at the University of Pennsylvania, was to give a lecture at the Kalmar Nyckel Foundation in Wilmington, Delaware. The university described her as "a celebrated young anthropologist and Rhodes Scholar." A news release offered by the foundation stated the title of the presentation as "Flying with the Fourth Crow: A Reflection on Curating Fulfilling a Prophecy: The Past and Present of the Lenape in Pennsylvania and Delaware." It continued with the foundation's director of education, Samuel Heed, stating, "We are delighted to be bringing Abigail Seldin to the greater Wilmington community, helping to sponsor her extraordinary work with the Lenape Nation, promoting the astonishing and poignant Lenape survival story which Miss Selden has brought to light after two centuries of cultural secrecy and neglect."

"This is a story for our time, for all time, and for all Americans," Heed writes, describing the significance of Abigail Selden's work. "We at the Kalmar Nyckel Foundation, are dedicated to preserving and promoting the cultural and maritime heritage of Delaware for the education and enrichment of all, feel a special obligation to raise awareness about the Lenape's ongoing history within our midst, to recognize and further a reconciliation that Abigail's work has done so much to foster." The statement goes on to name two co-curators: Chief Bob "Red Hawk" Ruth, currently serving his second term as chief of the Lenape Nation of Pennsylvania, and Shelly DePaul, language director of the Lenape Nation. The press release also acknowledges that most accounts present the Lenape people as having been driven completely from Pennsylvania and Delaware by the early nineteenth century, with any local survivors expiring shortly thereafter or becoming fully assimilated into the prevailing Euro-American culture. In working on an undergraduate project titled "Native Voice," which originally planned to focus on the Lenape peoples' trek from Pennsylvania to their current locations in the Midwest and Canada, Abigail discovered otherwise. Many Lenape, it turns out, often children of Lenape-European marriages, stayed here in secret. Hiding their tribal heritage for more than two hundred years, they consciously avoided discovery by both the government and their neighbors. The press release went on to state that Abigail had gained the trust of these descendants and was eventually invited to their tribal council to hear their version and their stories, led by Bob Ruth and Shelly DePaul. What a bunch of garbage!

Eventually Ms. Seldin, who—as a student in the anthropology

department—had access to the University of Pennsylvania's museum collections, would curate a fully funded and backed exhibition utilizing items from the university's collection that were ceremonial in nature. Her access to and use of these items should have been in compliance with the Native American Graves Protection and Repatriation Act of 1990 (NAGPRA). But by allowing these Pretendians, Bob Ruth and Shelly DePaul and their followers, access to these items, the university and Ms. Seldin had literally violated NAGPRA.

The university went on to develop marketing materials for the exhibit and issued postcards with the fake prophecy "We now know that the first Crow was the Lenape people before the coming of the Europeans. The second Crow symbolized the death and destruction of our culture. The third Crow was our people going underground and hiding. The fourth Crow was the Lenape becoming caretakers again and working with everybody to restore this land."

In my opinion anyone who had done an ounce of research, even at the high school level, would have realized that there was no validity in the false claims of Ruth, DePaul, and this fake Lenape Nation, but to see an Ivy League institution, the University of Pennsylvania, fail in such a big way was appalling. It was another indication of how rampant fraud and fakes are in the Delaware Valley region, the Commonwealth of Pennsylvania, and academia.

I decided to attend one of the presentations that Ms. Seldin was going to give about the exhibition. During the presentation she again stated that she had found this group of people and had ascertained, through their stories and ceremony, that they were indeed an American Indian nation that had been hiding in the hills of Pennsylvania. She had some of the promotional materials provided by the university and offered them to members of the audience. Ms. Seldin then proceeded to ask the audience to sign a treaty that she had prepared, which had been endorsed by the university museum. The entire presentation disgusted and appalled me to such a degree that I was compelled to speak up during the question-and-answer portion of the event. I proceeded to let her know that her research and her findings were false, that she was dealing with fraudulent individuals who were perpetuating a fraud of being from a culture not their own. I also let her and the audience know about the well-researched book *Playing Indian* by Phillip J. Deloria. I reminded everyone that this was not the first time individuals had perpetuated fraud by claiming to be something they are not. I referenced Grey Owl, aka Archie Belaney, who fooled the queen of England with his fake Indian status in Canada. I was well aware that my comments during this lecture would probably not be well received, especially because of the host venue, which included an audience full of people wanting to see and hear about Indians at any cost. It goes without saying that members of the audience attacked me for daring to speak up and speak against, and for challenging the information that Ms. Selden was offering. I was heckled and screamed at to leave the lecture. Recognizing that she had full support from not only the individuals who had invited her to speak but also from most of the audience, it was another indication of just how rampant the desire of non-Indians and non-Indian institutions to support Pretendianism was—and how much they benefit from doing so.

Ms. Seldin went on to be a Rhodes scholar and study at the University of Oxford. As I watched her academic pursuits being realized due to this false "scholarly" research, I was reminded of the many Native students who were denied those same academic opportunities. It also made me question whether speaking out against fraud and these fraudulent occurrences was worth the vitriol and violence hurled at me. When I had confronted and exposed EDN for competing for funding with UAIDV, my daughters' lives had been threatened and they had to receive several months of protection from the Philadelphia Police Department until the threat was minimized. Receiving threats is always a byproduct of speaking out against the Pretendians. I knew the university was wrong and they were in violation of NAGPRA by allowing these frauds to have access to items in their museum collection and to remove those items for these fake Indians' self-proclaimed ceremonies, but I also started to worry that I had again put myself in an unsafe environment. The museum went on to maintain this false Lenape Nation's exhibition for several months, and I'm sure many people attended and walked through the halls and were given false information. For me, and for my efforts, at least I had spoken up and refused to let this go unnoticed.

I would speak out again in the fall of 2015, when I was notified that Dartmouth College had issued a press release announcing the hiring and appointment of a new Native American Programs director, Susan Taffe Reed. I was immediately appalled because I knew the name Taffe Reed was associated with the fake Eastern Delaware Nation and that she was a member of the family that had founded this fake group. Earlier that summer the country had been faced with the exposure of Rachel Dolezal, a white woman passing as an African American woman. With all the publicity that surrounded Dolezal's "outing," I found it astonishing that Dartmouth, with its reputation for supporting and encouraging Native students to attend its institution, would have hired someone to run the Native American program who hailed from a fake tribe. This announcement was especially disheartening because when I was a junior in college and an exchange student from Wellesley, I attended Dartmouth. I had great pride in studying in the Native American Studies Department, which was fairly new in the '70s, and over the years I've watched the college become even more dedicated to the education of its Native student population as an attempt to recognize and live up to its founding principles. To see a member of a family who had fraudulently promoted their status as fake Indians being given such a high position in academia, with all the accolades and monetary support that comes with that, angered me to no end. I immediately went through my contact list and started replying to the press release and the Dartmouth campus newspaper and anyone who would listen to me and the information I had that could expose the false premise that Ms. Reed was Native. Most notably, after several of us exposed this, an article published in the *Daily Mail* referenced my concerns and those of other Dartmouth Native alumni regarding an ethnic fraud being hired by the institution. Suffice it to say that after a week or two of "bad press" Dartmouth decided to withdraw the appointment of Ms. Taffe Reed to the Native American program, but they still retained her as the dean of students, with the salary and perks that come with that position. Remember, for these people, these fakes, it's the economic gain that keeps them perpetuating fraud. In my attempt to fully understand how something as egregious as this could happen, I conducted a web search of Taffe Reed and came across her credentials and CV, which are readily available on the internet. In reading through Taffe Reed's CV, it was appalling to see just how many awards, grants, and certificates she had been given because of her fake Indian status. These were clearly things that should have been awarded to real Indigenous students and not the child of individuals who fabricated a nonprofit corporation and called it an Indian tribe. The blatant exploitation of Indigenous culture to benefit individuals falsely claiming Native ancestry is truly disgusting. This should make everyone step back and take a deep look and analyze why this is happening, why it continues, and why it's even tolerated and, unfortunately, sometimes supported by other members of our Native community.

When Dartmouth announced the hiring of Taffe Reed, the photo that was used was so stereotypical, showing her in braids, in front of a blanket, with beaded earrings, and so forth, and it brings me back to my first question: What is an Indian supposed to look like? If you choose to fit the stereotype, does that mean acceptance into a world that will advance your career becomes easier? I wonder if this was why no one ever thought to question whether Taffe Reed was truly Native—because she showed up looking like the stereotype. I don't think I'll ever know the answer to what an Indian should look like, but I do know that for all the times I've been told "you don't look like an Indian" and I definitely am, I wish the same standard would be applied to those who are Pretendians. If they had been told this as often as I have, would they still pursue a false identity? In the case of Rachel Dolezal, she did all she could to look like a Black woman, and for a very long time it worked. I guess that's one of the main criteria for claiming an identity not your own. First and foremost, make sure you look like the stereotype. That's your easy-access card to acceptance.

Pretend Indian Exegesis

The Pretend Indian Uncanny Valley Hypothesis
in Literature and Beyond

Social media avatars of the Pretend Indian variety disrupt flow, but it's only a pebble unrippling in a massive confluence. Pages of profiles enhanced by Indian imagery are bait to attract a group of people to add or like them. It's the selfie ethnic wound licked by its victims, used by its predator.

We have the academic Indian lecturer who is not tied to any Indigenous community. A system validates them and meets inclusion requirements of diversity and multiculturalism. Would this create an Indian if non-Indians who bestow Indianhood unto them validate them? They are suspect when they have never stated any story at the beginning of their careers of Indianness. They steer in tribal education systems only to later find themselves some sense of Indian descendancy.

We are told to be brave in writing and telling our stories. Is it braver for a settler-colonial operating writer to colonize a Native American narrative? To pepper their work with enough suggestion to have its readers conclude its authorship is true? To wear an underrepresented people's skin is enticing. I get it: to feast on struggle, to explore imagined roots, to lay the foundational work for academic jobs and publishing opportunities.

If I'm to consider myself a Native American writer, a Pretend Indian is taking my potential success, taking away and dismantling opportunities for my peers and future generations. I guess this makes my work a consumable flavor for a Pretend-Indian-Ethic-Munchhausen individual. I'm not offended. I acknowledge the tactic, another tendril of colonization. We know the dangers of inviting a settler-colonial agent into the group. We hope they don't steal our stories; we hope better of them; we hope they don't set to default and rip apart communities. We hope they don't prove a disappointment.

Then the Pretend Indian's work is published; then they are hired to a coveted academic position; then there is a movie or made-for-TV show about their overcoming adversity as a Native American surviving in two worlds. Then they Zach Morris the shit out of their story (see episode "Running Zach"); then they Thunderheart a vision to the stronghold; then they John Dunbar a blanket and a woman; and so forth. . . .

So I guess what are the next steps? Are they allowed back into the group after their abusive behavior?

To honor ancestors is to absolve the Vague Indian Family Lineage Narrative (VIFLN). It served, for whatever mental health reasons, a family-held origin connection to place. To honor that vague story is to exploit it, but leave it be. No documented records, evidence of adoption, or severed family oral history cloud the VIFLN. The concerted effort to genocide a people and the continued erasure from intuitions and dialogue, we get that. How does a VIFLN decolonize and strengthen resistance to the dominant settler-colonial narrative? One could construe the VIFLN as another tactic for colonization. VIFLN is a shadow untethered to communities and people. It continues to say the past then Indigenous people live now and are future-bound.

Honor how the current tribal group identifies itself. If they say descendancy (patrilineal or matrilineal) or Blood Quantum as part of its identification, this is your language. Know who you are related to in the group identified. Who are your relations? They make you who you are; they are the stories championed in your narrative. If you don't know your relations, leave them alone. Don't bother them. Don't parasite the experience.

VIFLN is not the language of abundance; it doesn't instill thrivance for a people. Generate your own VIFLN ceremony to unsettle it from your mind. Be critical of your VIFLN. Everyone else is, because it's not just a feeling—it's deeper and more widespread than that.

As shitty as it might sound, there is a part of me that appreciates the Pretend Indian. PI. They are tricksters who antagonize a hard life. I have to check my eye roll when they relay their noise. In hearing them I imagine a live choose-your-own-adventure story unfolding. Usually, they start out west with tribal affiliation, but if you press them for more details of the claimed identity, their claim starts to move east and/or becomes more fantastic and prestigious. It's an inverse Manifest Destiny, masticating people's stories for how the PI builds cultural cachet. It's a deep-seated white-privilege thing to feel underrepresented as a luxury, slumming tragedy and exploring plight. When they say it's not our way to do something, I know they feel privileged when I discuss decolonizing settler-colonial institutions with them. This validates them in thinking they are part of the group when really I might be talking about them indirectly.

I appreciate the PI as the ultimate assimilated Indian. Their vague descendancy is magical. I imagine unicorns in the story or that those rumored ancestors walked with dinosaurs.

I do fear the PI; they can pass for non-Natives. In that, they can be deadly. They can use your information to pad their story. It's literate scalping. They collect their bounty. They ingest you—entrails and all. Rim the skull's eye cavity. They wrap your skin over their face, tongue the inside of your mouth. They cultivate your image. Prop you up in bed and slide their body next to yours. Wire-frame your brown body seated in a landscape of their own invention. I can appreciate that kind of image colonization.

The Pretend Indian does not fear tribal disenrollment.

How does the Pretend Indian decolonize?

To say they have Indian blood in their family without evidence or actual tribal criteria eligibility, the Pretend Indian has this story to feel more American than plain white. The Pretend Indian, in all their heart, is trans-ethnic.

The Pretend Indian, in exploring their Native roots, emerges from their chrysalis thinking themselves butterflies when they actually are moths.

If Native Americans are 1 percent of the U.S. population, the Pretend Indian is 1 percent of said 1 percent. But a 1 percent based on a story or a feeling. So a 1 percent imagined.

The Pretend Indian is an alt-reality. Their operating system is calibrated through a magical pan-Indianism experience. A Pretend Pan-Indian; a Pan-Pretend Pan-Indian. There is nothing to stop the Pretend Indian from grabbing on to other identities.

The Pretend Indian collects other Natives on social media to validate their existence. The Pretend Indian steals Native dialogue to better hone their rhetoric. The Pretend Indian feeds on brains.

I cringe when the Pretend Indian poet drops Native words and themes in their work. Then say we are all related. No. I don't think so. You are all on your own. That's all you. That's your hot mess. I can't wait until we are post–Pretend Indian. "It's not working," I will tell them. "All of it. Jus' stop."

The Pretend Indian is a construct of non-Natives' poorly imagined people. A coffee table book people.

P.I.: I heard my great-great-great . . . grandmother was Indian.

Me: Mine was too. Now leave me alone.

The Pretend Indian has their identity as a core belief, which generally is difficult to change. I get it. The imagination of a story took root. And when inserted into an urban community, there is general acceptance or at least some tolerance. The Pretend Indian uses the identity to build themselves into the urban community narrative. This is a bit more difficult to do in a direct Indian Nation; there are people who will remember you and your family, depending on the strength of the community.

Because I can't pass for white, I'm deadly aware wherever I go to not stand out much, to be cautious in my actions.

To be a Pretend Indian to an individual who might suffer personality disorders, must offer some sense of relief. To be special among other white people while still benefiting from a racist system, it's like a life "theme" or "flavor." I get it. I could, if my ethics were absent, pass as some other Native American theme or flavor. But what would the benefit be?

Be critical of the Vague Indian Family Lineage Narrative. As in this case, a memoirist used that narrative to become an authority to write of an Indian relationship without it appearing to be a white captivity story.

The Pretend Indian gets a double whammy. They get to enjoy the wonderment, delight, and dangers of a narrative from a people who are the subtext of the American Dream: genocide. And not really be a part of the said group, only their wet dream of their participation in that group. Then discard that to be bothered with further inquiry into the Indian group. Then Pretend Indians rage hard. Pretend Indian anger at those Indians who call them out. It is lateral oppression and violence when it is Pretend Indian on Indian prejudice? Is it a "divide and conquer" tactic when Indians fight among Pretend Indians? The Pretend Indian is the kitsch and tchotchkes of the American experience.

It feels like sand in one's underwear when Indians hear the Pretend Indian talk about us. The Indians, in their mind, tell the Pretend Indian, whatever you are saying, that's not my tribe. That's all you, creeper.

The Pretend Indian wants all the Indian glory without all the Indian gory.

The Pretend Indian doesn't correct the mistake when referred to as Native American. The Pretend Indian will go into details about their features that might hint at an imagined Indian. The Pretend Indian secretly wants to kill any Indian that questions their Pretend Indianness.

Construct the perfect Indian name. Must have a Christian worldview. Mammals are cool. Reptiles not so much. Native references must be Indian Poetic, very bland. Nothing scientific. No John Quark-Dust or Jane Quantum-Leap; no John Gravitational-Lens. Maybe Jane Schrodinger's-Cat. Maybe.

The Pretend Indian is a formula. A phantom entity in the community, just as real as their story. The Pretend Indian is a zero multiplied by everything.

Imagine two Pretend Indians seated across from one another. Is it an identity doppelganger fairytale, mirrored motions and phrases? How do two Pretend Indians greet each other? Would they become feral and claw at each other? Or spontaneously combust at any Indian utterance? Do they just nod at each other, knowing they are both Pretend Indians?

What Indian accoutrement does the Pretend Indian pocket? Stone, bone, feather, leather, or made-in-China relics. How Pretend Intertribal is the Pretend Indian? Do they think collecting Indian names is like collecting Magic or Pokémon cards? Collect and trade or sell.

To begin with, poetry is a hard sell. Very few invest in it unless they are craft practitioners. In an anthology collection, to have the Pretend Indian's work next to your work—it cheapens the experience. If I were to explore seemingly cultural themes then read the Pretend Indian's similar work, there is the cultural mockery.

Can an Indian Pretend Indian? Can they racially be of the group and ethically not, but be a Pretend Indian Indian-hobbyist? Can they be intertribal, but not of the infatuated ethnic target? Does coupling up with a targeted group also lend one full reign of cultural practices of said group; a mutual orgasmic cultural knowledge acquisition?

Knowing Indians don't have the same political power as settler POCS, does this make it easier to pillage Indian knowledge after having implanted themselves into the targeted group and then assuming the group is milquetoast?

Taking knowledge, labor, worldview, and intellectual and cultural property is a colonial act, but isn't this interpretation of property a colonial attribute too? Does the idea of "nothing about us without us" or "stories about us without us is not for us" ("us" being the targeted group) still apply if one has used a consultant for a project? The consultant used as a buffer and validation of the project and the scapegoat if the project is criticized.

Do accolades for the project get a pass if other Indians praise it? Does the offended group have any recourse to defend their cultural property if "they," other Indians, applaud the project? Should the offended group stay silent to the deafening praise of the project because if the project is uplifted with its creator, it benefits all?

Did the Pretend Indian become a U.S. citizen in 1924? The militant

Pretend Indian is scary but mostly confusing. The Pretend Indian is about wolves. The Pretend Indian wolf is so sacred. I can't even.

The Pretend Indian is the dreamcatcher on the rearview mirror. The Pretend Indians' ancestry tall tale gets so vast, . . . again, I can't even.

The Pretend Indian's drunk Indians are the drunkest, most tragic, but proudest Indians to shed a single tear when garbage is thrown at them.

The Pretend Indian is the error message in a universe that has error correction compensation code.

If you don't like the Pretend Indian, this validates their pretend oppression.

The Pretend Indian is a microaggression. The accumulative effect compounding on a targeted community until justified outrage strikes. As damaging as the Indian mascot issue, the Pretend Indian causes psychological distress. Their actions are a taunt waving white privilege.

The Pretend Indian author gets off on his actions. Their conflated fabricated blurs indicate a pathology hell-bent on damaging a people's spirit to gratify themself. The masturbatory nature of what he flaunts as a white male who can yell "racism"—which positions him as seemingly untouchable. He systemically uses gaslighting tactics every time. It's too easy to digitally manufacture plausible deniability or credibility.

Ethnicity is just a flavor. Anyone can identify as any ethnicity. This is the heart of my Pretend Indian, PI, series. We see the John Smelcers, the Rachel Dolezals, the Andrea Smiths, the Ward Churchhills enter targeted communities. They stir any deemed detractors, agitators, into their gaslighting web and continue to move forward with their agenda. Often positioning themselves in authority to dictate what Indians are allowed to do or what a community can achieve.

The tactics used are systemic, and if challenged the PI falls back on their white fragility to mask perceived persecution. These individuals find there really isn't a border to contain whatever identity they wish to profess their personal. They are okay not to correct someone if they are mistaken as part of the group. These PIs fluidly move in communities and hide in the complications of Indian identity. Other Indians or other folks with their agenda are quick to point out that plausible tracks for the vagueness of the assumed identity. People were adopted out, people had to hide their race on historical documentation; whatever the muddiness is on any historical record, these are dragged out and propped in the conversation. The PI shines brightest in this fogginess and in-fighting.

There is a special kind of shittiness expressed by some Pretend Indians. Usually, if they spend any amount of time with Indians, an interior Indian seeds itself in the PI and begins to wildly bloom. Next thing we see if the PI try on Cherokee, Lenape, Lakota, and so forth . . . bloodlines to aid their personal narrative. They gather information from grandmother internet. They start to incorporate "we" when around other Indians. A nation of Pretend Indians rises. And they delight in the plight-skin of their identity conquest. The PI is a bizarro-world Indian. The PI is pleather. The PI is the Great Gazoo Indian popping into one's life to remind you they are there to shit on everything, dumb-dumb.

This is why it's important I have in my bio some identification of my tribal enrollment, my citizenship to my nation, and the sovereignty it represents. Not everyone has this significant qualifier. But this might be labeled a bully tactic because the PI is triggered and will lash out (white fragility). But it's none of my business if the PI feels usurped by the Indian enemy. It's confusing, I know.

The Speaker of this piece is writing as Lakota who sometimes self-identifies as Indian, American Indian, Native American, and Indigenous. They have heard stories of Indian blood in their ancestry going back ten generations, which contributes to their current Native roots presupposition. The Speaker is an enrolled card-carrying member of a tribe and a Native Nation citizen.

Ron Querry

Dead Indians. Live Indians.
Legal Indians.

A lot of people want to know about the Indian stuff in my books. Even more people want to know about the Indian stuff on my book jackets. So here it is. And you'll note that I do not use the term "Native American," which has become the fashion. All the Indians I know—and I know a good many—refer to themselves as "Indians." We'll often refer specifically to a tribe or nation, and I might make an occasional distinction between a "Feather Indian" and "Red Dot Indian," but that's about it.

It was, I suppose, in second or third grade that I was first required to commit to memory and recite the Pledge of Allegiance, the Lord's Prayer, and the names of the Five Civilized Tribes. Only later did it occur to me that not every young scholar in the United States was so well versed in exactly which five tribes of Indians were deemed "civilized" as were my classmates and I at Andrew Johnson Elementary in suburban Oklahoma City. I assumed that fresh young people all across America pledged and prayed and chanted "Choctaw, Chickasaw, Cherokee, Creek, Seminole" just as proudly and loudly as did I.

I am very light-skinned—over the past couple of decades I have spent a good deal of time and money having skin cancer and precancerous lesions removed, mostly from my face. My hair color has transitioned from orange (when I was born, I am told), to white blond (as a kid reciting things in elementary school), to reddish brown (in high school and the Marine Corps), to raccoon-like multicolored, to its present white. (I do not mind that my hair is white. A former principal chief of the Choctaw Nation told me once that I shouldn't mind *what* my hair turned, just as long as it didn't turn *loose*.) My eyes are blue. The only observable physical characteristics I have that might be attributable to Indian blood are my cheekbones and the fact that I have very little in the way of an ass.

Folks who get all quivery and enthusiastic about claims of Indianness sometimes get choked up when they first see my white hair, blue eyes, and cancer-riddled pale face. I'm used to it and have come to expect it. Usually, it is from equally fair-skinned, blue-eyed folks.

And, yes, occasionally it is from Indians.

I say "occasionally," but of course it is from other Indians that the cocked eyebrow or the rolled eye stings most acutely.

Thomas King is a renowned mixed-blood Cherokee novelist, filmmaker, and scholar whose work I admire very much. Born in California to a Greek mother and a Cherokee father—the latter apparently absent—King migrated to Canada as an adult after earning a PhD in American Studies and Literature at the University of Utah.

I first met King years ago when Elaine and I were living in Tucson. An imposing figure, Thomas King is six and a half feet tall. Elaine and I enjoyed him very much. Later he and his partner, Helen Hoy, were among the Native writers invited to Saint-Malo, France, in 1997 for the *Étonnants Voyageurs, Festival International du Livre*, as were Elaine and I.

I bring King up because I want to call the reader's attention to his very fine book—*The Inconvenient Indian: A Curious Account of Native People in North America*, published in Canada in 2012 and in the United States the following year—that addresses the issue of Indianness in a way that I find appealing. King's take is mostly good-natured, often funny and, I believe, refreshingly accurate. He makes the point, rightly, I think, that it's not just non-Indian folks who worry about who's an Indian and who's not. "We've done a reasonably good job of injuring ourselves without the help of non-Natives," he says.

"For instance, for decades we've beaten each other up over who is the better Indian. Full-bloods versus mixed-bloods, Indians on reservations and reserves versus Indians in cities. Those who are enrolled members of a tribe versus those who are not. Those of us who look Indian versus those of us who don't. We have been and continue to be brutal about these distinctions, a muted strain of ethnocentrism."

King maintains that there are three kinds of Indians today. Dead Indians. Live Indians. And Legal Indians.

Dead Indians, he says, are everywhere. They are immediately recognizable. They're in movies and on TV. They wear feathers and beads and go to powwows and do traditional dances. Non-Native people know about Dead Indians, and they are comfortable with them.

Live Indians, King says, are all the Native people who are alive in North America right now. However, if they're not doing Dead Indian things, they're pretty much invisible to others. When I was a child, growing up in Oklahoma, there were Indians all around.

Funny, but I don't recall thinking of Oklahoma as being particularly "Indian." I guess it was because those Indians I was around in Oklahoma were not what we considered "Feather Indians." Those were the sort of Indians we saw when we went on vacation to New Mexico—*that's* where I thought we saw Indians . . . *real* Indians. Or were those brown men wearing blankets on the little Plaza at Taos Dead Indians? And the women wrapped in blankets and sitting in front of the Governor's Palace on the Plaza selling jewelry in Santa Fe . . . were they, too, Dead Indians?

And finally, there are Legal Indians. Only Live Indians can be Legal Indians, according to King. But by no stretch of the imagination should you think that all Live Indians are Legal Indians. Legal Indians are those Indians who are recognized as being Indians by the Canadian and U.S. governments.

One more quotation from Thomas King's book: "In the United States, Legal Indians are enrolled members of tribes that are federally recognized. That's the general rule. However, tribes control how their membership rolls are created and maintained, and eligibility for membership varies from nation to nation. Most base their membership on blood quantum. If you have enough Native blood in you, then you are eligible for enrollment, and, once enrolled, are a Legal Indian."

I am a Legal Indian.

I happened upon the following during the run-up to the 2018 midterm elections. Normally, I would express great disdain and disbelief at such an attitude. I would file it away as yet another example of outdated and shopworn racist attitudes toward Native peoples.

First, the example:

A New Mexico nominee to represent the state's First Congressional District suggested in an interview that her Native American opponent isn't Native American because she didn't grow up on a reservation. "Your opponent would be the first Native American woman in Congress," the host noted. "That's what they say, but she's a military brat, just like I am, and so, you know, it evokes images that she was raised on a reservation."

Deb Haaland responded by calling that "racist, an assault on military families, and wrong. For generations, Native Americans have been subjected to genocide, forced assimilation, and government-backed family separation," she said. "Even today, Native tribes suffer through attacks on tribal sovereignty. Despite all of that, Native Americans are still here, we are proud, and we matter. I am proud to be a citizen of the Pueblo of Laguna."

In a strange coincidence, this troublesome example occurred the very same day that I experienced a similar circumstance.

Some weeks before the above took place, I had come across and joined an online group devoted to "Oklahoma Choctaws"—a Facebook group.

I come from Oklahoma—I spent a good deal of my early life in that state, and I am an enrolled member of the Choctaw Nation of Oklahoma. My late maternal grandmother was an original enrollee on the 1887–1907 Dawes Commission Rolls of American Indians of the Five Civilized Tribes living in Indian Territory at the time. More than 250,000 people applied for admission, and the Dawes Commission enrolled just over 100,000.

My mother's mother, Ruth Adella Foster, is #15,137 on the Dawes Rolls as of March 26, 1904.

The Choctaw Nation of Oklahoma determines membership by lineal descent. The tribe does not have a minimum blood quantum requirement; however, this does not mean that anyone with any amount of Indian blood can enroll. Members must be direct descendants of Original Enrollees.

The Oklahoma Choctaw group I had joined stated clearly on its Facebook page that it was a group "for Choctaws and friends of Choctaws to talk about Choctaw things." At the time there were nearly 4,700 members of the group.

Things went along smoothly for several weeks. Then a single member seemed to object to something I had posted on the site and stepped beyond the norms of civility that such groups strive for and began to harass and insult me. It reached the point where I exercised the Facebook option of "blocking" that individual so he could no longer see my posts and, more importantly to me, I would no longer have to see his.

Within a day or so, I was removed from the group. I contacted two of the listed administrators to inquire about my removal. One replied that she had no idea but would check on the matter. The other administrator replied similarly.

Turns out, the individual who was harassing me claimed to be, himself, an administrator and had removed me by fiat.

A day or so later, I was informed that I had been removed because I wasn't raised in southeastern Oklahoma, on the eleven and one-half counties designated as the Choctaw Nation of Oklahoma. Understand, I was raised in central Oklahoma—shuffled between a home in suburban Oklahoma City and my grandmother's home on her allotted land near Newcastle, an hour or so south of Oklahoma City.

I was told that Choctaws from the rural communities of Panki Bok and Broken Bow were very different from those in Oklahoma City and, I assume, different from those residing in rural farming areas like Newcastle in the 1940s and 1950s.

Good Choctaw people surrendered their homelands in Mississippi and were subjected to forced relocation to Indian Territory in the 1830s and

1840s, where they were and still are, in essence, restricted by artificial boundaries to what is now southeastern Oklahoma.

The nominee who questioned Secretary Haaland's claim to be Native because she wasn't raised on a reservation is as patently ridiculous as my being challenged because the government, in a document I possess that is signed by Choctaw chief Green McCurtain, allotted my grandmother her lands on the Choctaw and Chickasaw lands in central Oklahoma.

I doubt the single rule-making decider I blocked would have been satisfied had my grandmother been able, somehow, to intuit that just a couple of generations later her family members would be refused participation on social media, and so to avoid that absurd refusal had simply abandoned her two-hundred and ten allotted acres, with its oil and gas reserves, and returned to southeastern Oklahoma.

At that festival in France where I saw Thomas King again, there were several writers whom I admired—some I knew and some I'd only read: Jim Harrison, Louis Owens, Harry Crews, and Mary Crow Dog, among others.

I recall being on a panel with Mary Crow Dog there in France when an especially pasty audience member asked her what she thought about "mixed-bloods" meaning, obviously, this white guy sitting beside her. Mary responded that it was Sitting Bull who said that if a man had one drop of Indian blood, he was full! I don't know if Sitting Bull actually said that, but it was a nice thing for her to say. Mary Crow Dog was a stand-up guy that day.

Seeing a photograph of my mother as a young girl, you would likely proclaim her to be Indian. The same applies, with increasing certainty, to my grandmother, to her father, to his father (the latter I understand to have sported braids and, when astride a horse and under the influence of strong drink, which was not unusual, would frighten women and children—and while that story may not be entirely accurate, I hope it is), and, I trust, on back to the Choctaw woman named Otemansha, peace be upon her.

I explained earlier that my grandmother is listed as an Original Enrollee of the Choctaw Nation of Oklahoma, as are her father and her two older brothers. Her mother is enrolled as an "I.W." or "Intermarried White." My grandmother had a younger brother who was born after the rolls had closed and so, to his eternal dismay, was not considered an Original Enrollee. E. A. Foster Jr. was his name—we knew him as "Uncle Manny"—and he researched exhaustively the Foster family lineage, to wit:

My four-greats-grandmother was referred to generally in documents I possess as "the Choctaw woman, wife of William Foster" in Mississippi. In a couple of documents of court proceedings, she is called O-Te-Man-Sha, which I presume to be a phonetic attempt to spell her Choctaw-language name.

Otemansha was of the "Sixtown" Tribe or Clan of Choctaw Indians. Oklahoma historian Angie Debo says that "Sixtown Indians, *Okla Hannali*, spoke a distinctive dialect, tattooed blue marks around their mouths, and were shorter and heavier in build than the other Choctaws."[1]

When Andrew Jackson determined that the Southeastern Tribes should be removed from their homelands to what is now Oklahoma, to better accommodate the white folks who wanted more land, the Choctaw Tribe was chosen to be among the first to go on what they called The Long, Sad Walk. Those upstart Cherokees with their Trail of Tears came later. I understand that the Choctaws were chosen to be the first removed because they were deemed least likely to protest—they had already begun to assimilate, and there were farmers and storekeepers and teachers among them.

There were, to be sure, different levels of assimilation. I remember one of my uncles telling me about how our Choctaw ancestor, Otemansha, had held an important position in the Sixtown Clan back in Mississippi—that she had been a "Bone Picker." At the time, I didn't know what a Bone Picker was, and I don't recall that my uncle told me. Had he done so, I feel certain that as a young boy I would have remembered, so gruesome were the duties of that high office in Choctaw culture. If Otemansha was a "Bone Picker," she was, indeed, an honored person and would have performed important duties in the funerary practices of her community at the time. She would likely have had distinctive tattoos that identified her position, and her thumb and index fingernails would have been long and thick. For when a Choctaw Indian died, he or she was wrapped securely in robes and placed upon a wooden scaffold near the house and left to rot for a number of months. When the appropriate time had passed, the "Bone Picker" came and removed what flesh remained on the deceased's bones by using his or her fingernails. The bones were then placed in boxes and stored in a "Bone House" until such time as there were enough bones from the community to bury in a mound. To be sure, I have no real evidence that I am descended from a "Bone Picker"—only a story told by a long-deceased uncle. But I hope the story was true. I like thinking of this woman without whom I would never have been born—I like thinking about her place in her community.

In preparation for Removal, in September of 1830, at a place near what is now Philadelphia, Mississippi, the making and signing of the Treaty of Dancing Rabbit Creek took place. The Choctaw Tribe ceded almost eleven million acres and agreed to remove to Indian Territory in what is now Southeastern Oklahoma. Among the nearly two-hundred signatures on that treaty are those of my ancestor's brothers William and Hugh Foster and the *X* of their brother Thomas.

Choctaws who wished to remain in Mississippi were offered 640 acres of land and Mississippi citizenship if they would sign up with Indian agent William Ward. Colonel Ward, as it turned out, was not an honest man. When the deadline came for signing on to what is known as Ward's Register, only sixty-nine heads of Indian families had done so. Otemansha was one of thirty full-blood Indians to sign. Her sons James, William, and Hugh Foster (the latter two having also signed the Dancing Rabbit Creek Treaty, you'll recall) were three of twenty-four so-called half-breeds; fifteen of the signers were white men with Choctaw wives.[2]

Possibly owing to the fact that traditional Choctaw people, when they moved or were relocated, were bound by tradition to take the bones of their ancestors with them, Otemansha refused to ever leave her Mississippi home, as did her son James, who is my three-greats-grandfather.

James died in Mississippi in 1833 at about the age of twenty-eight. Otemansha died some four years later and is buried near the Pearl River. Hugh Foster was reportedly "killed by a white man," and is buried at Skullyville, Oklahoma.

The Treaty of Dancing Rabbit Creek, which was ratified by Congress February 25, 1831, promised, among other things, autonomy of "the Choctaw Nation of Red People *and all their descendants* [emphasis mine]" to be secured from laws of U.S. states and territories forever.

I like knowing that I am a direct descendent of a woman who may have used her fingernails to scrape clean the bones of dead people.

It is significant, I think, to note that I am of the seventh generation of Otemansha's line.

NOTES

1. Angie Debo, *The Rise and Fall of the Choctaw Republic*, 20.
2. Clara Sue Kidwell, *The Choctaws in Oklahoma*.

BIBLIOGRAPHY

Debo, Angie, *The Rise and Fall of the Choctaw Republic* (Norman: University of Oklahoma Press, 1934), 20.
Kidwell, Clara Sue, *The Choctaws in Oklahoma* (Norman: University of Oklahoma Press, 2008).

Geary Hobson

The Animals' Ballgame

The Cherokee Nation of Oklahoma (CNO), together with the nearby university in the capital city of Tahlequah, is gearing up for what has long been billed as the Nation's (*Tsa-la-gi, Tsa-ra-gi, Ji-lo-gi, Chi-la-gi, Chalaque, Cholukee, Ani-yun-wiya*, or whatever variant one prefers) "First Ever Cherokee Writers' Gathering." Word has gone out far and wide for more than a year, advertising and proclaiming it and, at the same time, beseeching all who are writers to come and take part in it. Web pages have glowed about it, the blogosphere is filled with information about it, mass mailings have ensued, and word of mouth is trumpeting it all far and wide. It promises to be, so the Nation's own web page declares, the greatest get-together of Cherokee writers ever assembled. And in the magnificent auditorium in the W. W. Keeler Complex on the university campus in Tahlequah—-the town "set like a jewel among gently rolling hills" (as a noted scholar once wrote)—-the writers, would-be writers, and wannabe writers are assembling in vast hordes and precipitous multitudes.

At last, the day of assemblage dawns, and the vast entourage of Cherokeeness comes forth into the auditorium like a fleet of unleashed Achaean warships upon the besieged Trojan city and plain. First, there are the hordes of CNO-identified writers and artists surging onto the scene in all their beastly prominence, coming forward in vast accompaniments, in virtual clutters and clowders and nuisances and destructions and kindles and litters and pounces (as in cats of all sorts and varieties), in warrens and droves and buries and traces (as in rabbits), in gazes and nurseries and rafts (likewise of beavers), and bevies and romps (ditto for otters), in drays and scurries (of squirrels), and gangs and herds (the many-hoofed majesties in all their varieties). In a word, the scribblers are coming!

The symposium's preeminent discussion—long decided on and thereby duly appointed—is to be a panel in which several differing versions of the justly famous and well-known tribal story of "The Animals' Ballgame" will be presented —most prominently, that of the famed non-Cherokee and non-Indian anthropologist James Mooney, as well as later versions by the eminent Cherokee storytellers Lloyd Arneach and Kathi Smith Littlejohn. There are to be readings of these versions, as well as renditions of still other variants. Already, quite a gaggle of volunteers have advanced themselves as commentators and elucidators. The enduring question: which of the three—and possibly more?—variants is the correct one?

Once, in the long-ago time, the Cherokee Nation of Oklahoma and all other Cherokees, spread far and wide, spoke the same language and almost, at most times, thought the same thoughts, as only an extraordinarily unified people tend to do. However, with removals, expulsions, exiles, schisms, and wanderings far afield, they were all scattered like so many wind-blown leaves, mainly through the American Southland, a diaspora that occurred at the time of The Road Where the People Cried—northwestwardly out of the southwestern portion of the traditional Cherokee homeland of the Alleghenies and Appalachians, across rivers and creeks of Tennessee, then across Kentucky and over the Ohio River, and into Ohio and Indiana and Illinois, and then into Missouri, and then southwestwardly into Arkansas and on into eastern Oklahoma— leaving not only the dead and buried, but also the runaways from the caravans, and all to be counted, by the enumerators, as part of the four thousand lost.

Most visible and preeminently recognizable of the Cherokee Nation of Oklahoma is Prof. Jonah Erskine, renowned Cherokee scholar and novelist, author of nearly sixty books on Cherokee history and lore, professor emeritus (self-retired at the early age of forty-five) from the prestigious Cherokee Nation University, father of ten Cherokeelets, uncle to two dozen more, and tribal elder of seventy-one years of age now, slow-moving (but oh, so deceptively so in his comportment), a man at ease with himself and his world—the perfect Cherokee attainment—and an everyday habitué of the *tres* stylish inn of the Cherokee Nation coffee shop and restaurant located just a mere tomcat-fling from the tribal headquarters, as well as the university auditorium. Professor Erskine had been holding forth this bright, breezy October morning. He had been ensconced in his favorite booth in passive ursine fashion, his morning stint of writing completed and his habitual ham-and-eggs breakfast dispensed with in his usual leisurely manner, accompanied by endless cups of coffee in the Smoking Allowed section. (The management, even at this late date in Civilization's advancement, would never kowtow to the rising tide of political correctness, so ever insistent about no-smoking rules as to declare the entire restaurant a No Smoking Zone, not with Professor Jonah Erskine and the sheer might of the Cherokee intelligentsia that he manifestly carries within himself, while gracing the restaurant with his magnanimity.) Now that's power! The restaurant's management feels it can bear it because Professor Jonah brings in the customers, folks eager to see the writer known to all Cherokees and friends of Cherokees everywhere—all, without exception, ever hopeful of kind and pleasant words, along with signed, autographed copies of his books. In short, his fond benediction, a blessing that all seek to obtain, and in which no one ever goes away disappointed.

Slow-moving though he appears, with a slow smile accompanying his ever-present magnanimity, he moves from restaurant to auditorium with the deceptive ursine majesty of a creature fully aware of himself and his effect on all around him. One can imagine Henry the Eighth and Richard the Lionhearted moving in similar waves of supreme self-knowledge and competence.

After Professor Jonah—as, indeed, all tend to call him—comes Juley Chatsmith, sometimes called Foxy, erstwhile chief of CNO and a quasi-writer of somewhat fragile pretensions. He has futzed and foxed around while maintaining that he is writing—even, at one point, joining with another writer to "do" a book of a most redundant nature—one replete with brilliant photos in stark and glaring colors, which graces coffee tables but, nonetheless, purports to be scholarship—claiming for himself coauthorship credit when, in all likelihood, all Foxy wrote is the scant introduction and a few touched-up paragraphs here and there. Small wonder then why folks often call him "Foxy." (And Foxy writes just like this penultimate sentence, a long one-way chase through the briars and brush so as to elude the country club huntsmen.)

And after him comes Flora Deeley-Knotts—identity sniffer par excellence—and why not? Doesn't her 1/256th degree of Cherokee blood and CNO tribal membership card grant her carte blanche to do so? Her overindulgence in perfume unfortunately works to an opposite effect, of making her somewhat stinky instead of irresistible. Skunky at her best. She is the author of many interoffice memos, emails, and blog postings.

Sal Ekorre, forthwith following Skunky—uh, Flora—is a hypertensive poet of mixed blood, with very little knowledge of her Cherokee culture, but one of the most vocal to let all know that she has her enrollment number from the CNO and, of course, she will say that's what counts. Attractive, very thin and wiry, hair of a frizzy reddish brown, she moves in rapid jerks and spasms. One often has the impression she could zoom up a tree as fast as lightning, if such were ever to be necessary. She carries a worn leather satchel in which she keeps not only copies of her four published collections of poems, but also all the early drafts of them, as well as sheaves of poems-in-progress, all like a thick sediment of cracked nutshells. One can't help but wonder what else Sal-lee has squirreled away in that bag.

After her comes Attakullakulla Terrapin, a much self-published and, unfortunately, too little self-edited Cherokee writer of vast pretensions to literary excellence. Deceptively slow-moving and hard-shelled (in other words, impervious to would-be helpful critical advice of whatever ilk, and unequivocally sure of his excellence as a writer), he waddles in, constantly on the alert, as ever, for the otherworldly, the exotic, the fantastic, all to appear in his next thriller.

Then comes Sharleen Redundant Deer Prancey, author of ninety (or is it one hundred and ninety?) books and chapbooks, on delicate toes in elegant shoes that are greatly akin to the polished hoofs of the deer tribe people. Sharleen writes incredibly long sentences, for the most part quite beautiful and balanced, although at times they come so much full circle the reader ends up lost.

Coming into the hall, she exclaims, "I come as a red deer all dressed out for the Deer Dance!" and waggles the plastic set of antlers on her head.

"But Sharleen," Professor Jonah says. "Does aren't supposed to have antlers."

To which Sharleen replies, "Oh . . ." and looks nonplussed.

Then, in Ms. Prancey's footsteps (or hoof steps) and close behind, comes Dr. G. Stu Leverett, the hip-hop of Cherokee officialdom. He is a small, hypertensive individual who blinks his eyes incessantly, nervously, while wriggling his nose from side to side and up and down, all the while causing one's attention to invariably center on a faint harelip. He is highly energetic, a skilled writer of grant proposals and edicts. (He had once hoped to be a published poet or novelist, but this never came about, though he occasionally pens the essential critical article for a website with a crusade to carry.) Over the years, he has self-published a round dozen collections of his grant proposals and, like Jonah Erskine, is nationally known—that is, Cherokee Nationally known. As a writer, he writes rapidly, with very little editing, often racking up a dozen pages in an hour's work and, like Sharleen Prancy, he, too, is guilty of writing long labyrinthine sentences (although his are often very unwieldy), so that he all too often seems to become confused in his diction as he proceeds in quick spurts, which invariably double back to the beginning. He at all times bristles with a scowling demeanor, so that a local wag—Foxy Chatsmith himself, if fact be known—often refers to him as "Mr. Pissed-Off Guy." It shouldn't be surprising that Dr. Leverett is thus known far and wide throughout Cherokeedom by his Indian name of

Wretched Ailing. Some say the name is because of his having to endure a private hurt that tampers, at all times, with his goodwill. Still others say, in their probable piques of meanness and flippancy, that his name is actually Wretched Alien, the "alien" part referencing that he is half some kind of Southwestern Indian, something Pueblo or Navajo or some such. Nonetheless, he will always inform one and all that he is a dyed-in-the-wool, legitimate Cherokee, because his number tells him so. Lately, there have been many broad hints from him making the rounds that he will use the conference to announce the unveiling of a new CNO program, a trick up his sleeve, as it were, installing himself as the executor and director, that will, as he declares in his habitual stern-mouthed fashion, "settle everyone's hash, once and for all, about this identity nonsense."

Then, behind this *jistu* of all *jistus*, comes an entourage of truly staggering proportions: antelopes, bison, buffaloes, mountain lions, cougars, pumas, bobcats and bobkitties, wolves, coyotes, opossums, minks, otters, raccoons, rats, mice, moles, prairie dogs, cats, dogs, horses, mules, cows, sheep, goats, and so forth. But notable among these thusly assembled herds and herdlets, five in particular: Justin Heath Danielson, Hud Brianson, Nelson Joshua, Beauty K. Suagee, and Wave Jester. They haven't, up to now, bored down too excessively on others, or stunk up places with skunky effluvia, or disgorged, buzzard-like, their paunches' contents onto anyone's shirt-fronts. They are, relatively speaking, fresh as the October morning's sunlight.

These, then, are the vast numberings of furry, fluffy, hoofed, tusked, and tanned beasties of the vasty CNO.

Now a gander at the invading Outlanders, united and all-acknowledging in their view of themselves as no less Cherokee than any or all of the CNO assemblage. They are a virtual biblical tide of aviarity, of surprising and stupendous multifariousness. These Outsiders/Cherokee writers come in aeries and convocations of eagles, scolds of jays, exhalations of larks, richnesses of martins, coveys of quail, murders and sieges of crows, murmurations of starlings, kettles and casts of hawks, charms of hummingbirds, flocks and gaggles of geese—in short, my-oh-my, all these flocks and flights and congregations and dissimulations and valeries and piteousnesses and cotes and exhalations and murmurations—all a vast, seemingly unending tide of feathery might.

Prominent among them, and in particular, is Sully Humdinger (or Dirtmaker, as he is often called in Cherokee), a tall, bespectacled seventyish man from Kentucky, who still retains his flowing mane of dark brown hair, which is invariably covered with a multicolored native scarf. He is a renowned storyteller and the publisher of language texts, now lives in Texas, and has been publishing for more than three decades. Mr. Humdinger is also a part-time college professor and involved in Texas and Kentucky Cherokee affairs—he has been for all his adult life. Because of his quite prominent height—right at six feet four inches—he always seems to crouch as he stands, and this has the effect of making his back extraordinarily crooked. He also has a habit of waving his arms around his sides while talking, with the effect of great flapping wings. He is widely regarded as one of the most prominent writers of Cherokee identity nationwide.

Right behind him is Dr. Wally Baldon, an Arkansas Cherokee who, ironically, has been living in Okay for the past twenty years. But he never forgets that his allegiance is to the Arkansas group. Like Sully, he is a storyteller—and also a poet and novelist and literary scholar. Though nearsighted as all-get-out, he gives the impression that he is as eagle-eyed as can be. His gaze, or stare, is drilling in its intensity. He has more irons in the fire—or eggs in the nest—than any ten other writers and rarely finishes anything. Yet he has produced a half dozen books over his long career.

Then there's Waleila Tote, a lively Cherokee lady who, though enrolled with the Keetoowah Band, has spent much of her life in California, so that she is—or at least she feels she is—shunned by CNO. She is a poet who writes small haiku-like poems, which she calls "poemlets." They come at you, as you read them, like "benevolent hummingbirds, bearing good will and comfort," as Wally Baldon once wrote in a critical article. Her hand movements are similar to that—rapid, almost faster than the human eye can follow.

Also from California comes Thomas Kingfisher, novelist, film script writer, raconteur—wing-flapping in all his delightful kingfisherness. He is often criticized for spending so much of his time in Canada, but he explains, "Hey, folks, what the hay! Cut me some slack—Cherokees are everywhere."

Comes apace Gladys "BoBo" Hoot, from North Carolina by way of Montana and Washington State and Michigan, but no less Cherokee than any of the other assembled high-flyers. Her scant three books of poetry are more power-packed than those of poets with ten times the titles to their credit. Bo Bo is an intense, dedicated artist and teacher, often working entire nights on a single line of one of her poems.

Then Jeffie Honored and Ron Well-Born lead a congregation of blackbirds, crows, starlings, grackles, and an assortment of other night-colored feathered beings. They represent the ever-growing contingent of Cherokee-blooded people—growing not so much in terms of children coming into the world, but of people too handily labeled Black or African American who have become knowledgeable of their Indian heritage—a much larger group of people than 95 percent of the American populace realizes or will even acknowledge. Jeffie is a poet of strong voice and firmly held views and opinions. She does not easily suffer the presence or dodderings of fools, and she can dispense with them in an easy, humorous fashion. Ron is older than Jeffie, coming out of the Delmarva region of Tidewater and Chesapeake America, of mixed Cherokee and other tribes along with Black and white mixed blood. He has been an established poet for three decades, the author of nearly a dozen books, each one stronger than the ones preceding it.

Professor Robin Bark, a mixed-blood out of Montana by way of Nebraska, who has become, in a relatively short time, a respected scholar in literary methods of applying traditional Indian medicine and curing practices to the manner of approaching critical theories dealing with Native American literature. She is a tall and confident person who rarely reveals dissatisfaction or disgruntlement. She is always in balance.

Chiki Dee Deedeelow, from out of Texas, and Beau Thudfall, hailing from only the Apportioner knows, come dressed in chickadee and titmouse costumes, which they have been told is the correct dress for those two important totemic avians. They are known as formidable demon slayers in their critical essays and reviews, and so they do indeed be. They are widely esteemed for their roles in the old-time, long-ago story of the dreaded *Utlun-ta*, the Spear-Finger.

In addition to all the writers on hand, there are numerous other folks on hand, broods and clusters of admirers and emulators, all desirous of someday joining this remarkable parliament of established writers.

Professor Jonah comes forth, welcoming the wing-flappers as they thread their way into the auditorium and find perches for themselves.

"Welcome, welcome," says Jonah, his short arms moving in slow, beckoning fashion. He is the epitome of courtliness.

"*Wado, wado,*" responds Professor Sully Humdinger. "On behalf of my co-fliers, I return your greeting." And one by one, Jonah shakes the hand of each of the CNO writers as the Outlanders find seats for themselves.

"I assume you are all ready to discuss the topic at hand?" Jonah says.

"Yes," says Sully, to which Prof. Wally Baldon adds, "And ready, too, to introduce other variants of the Animals' Ballgame story."

"Others?" asks Juley Chatsmith, old Foxy, as he scoots up front to where the greetings are taking place.

"Yes," answers Wally. "In addition to the widely known Mooney story—now over a century old in print—and those by Mr. Arneach and Ms. Littlejohn, there are other variants by Robert J. Conley and Gayle Ross and Gregg Howard and so on. We think these bear looking into as well."

"Well, then, *osda*," says Jonah. And as he is about to speak further, Dr. G. Stu Leverett interrupts him by interjecting his small, fidgeting body in front of him.

"Yeah, well," G. Stu says (and he always insists on being called "G. Stu," rather than just "G" or even "Stu.") "That's all well and good, but I believe we have a more pressing topic to consider"—and he pauses significantly when he becomes aware that everyone's attention is on him. "I think we first need to determine once and for all *who* and *what* a Cherokee is or is not." He speaks loudly, with his eyebrows knitted into his characteristic "Mr. Pissed-Off Guy" demeanor.

There are murmurs and groans aplenty.

"I mean, just look around. Just look at yourselves!" And he fastens his attention on Jeffie Honored and Ron Well-Born in particular. "Too dark to be real Indians and sure as heck not real Cherokees!" And then to Robin and Sully. "—and too light to be real Cherokees!"

"What kind of trick have you got up your sleeve, G. Stu?" Jonah says. Behind him, Foxy Chatsmith and Sal Ekorre and Attakullakulla Terrapin chortle and literally bounce up and down.

"But we came here to discuss traditional stories," Bo Bo says, and Wally seconds her. "And not somebody's particular political agenda!"

"And most particularly, not mean politics," Sully says.

"Well, now," says G. Stu. "Let's just say that the agenda has changed." He grins delightedly, bouncing up and down on the balls of his feet. "We're gonna pledge this conference to determining who is and who is not a real Cherokee."

All around, the groans manifest themselves more loudly, particularly from the Outlanders.

Then up come two more conference attendees. They are Thelma Small and Twisty Cade.

"We're Oklahoma Cherokees, but neither of us has ever lived here," says Twisty. "I was born and raised in California, and Thelma here was born and raised in Arkansas." And Thelma nods her head. "But, to tell the truth, we both have been more interested in other fields of study—English novels, science fiction, web page designing, even Kiowa Indians—rather than in merely Cherokee matters. But we've decided we want to reconnect, to learn—"

He is interrupted by Foxy and Sal and others.

"No, you're both Wannabes. We don't think you belong here. Go back to where you came from." Various voices clamor. Then Sully and Wally come forth and speak to them.

"Well," says Sully. "You might join our side in the debate—because I guess it looks like we are going to have to debate this whole thing that Dr. Leverett has brought up."

"Yes," says Wally. "Welcome to our side. We'll catch you up. Just come this way."

And Wally and Bo Bo take the two in hand and go over to a corner.

"Now," says Wally. "We're just going to have to expand your thinking a bit."

"Yeah," says Bo Bo. "Make real *Ji-lo-gi* out of you in no time flat!"

"Aww, you can't teach them anything!" says G. Stu, who horns his way into the group. "They ain't nothing but fly-by-nights." Then he turns to the others and says to them, "And you all are a bunch of popinjays!"

And for the next fifteen minutes or so, while the main bunch of all the conference attenders are still arguing back and forth about Cherokeeness, Wally and Bo Bo give Thelma and Twisty a crash course on identity. They can, as a result and after only a few minutes, feel their minds stretching to take in all the new ideas. Crash course it really is. Sometimes, though, as teachers will often tell you, someone can come to incredible profundity in a short matter of time, whereas others will not manage for months or years, or maybe ever, to come to certain knowledge. Thelma and Twisty are quite literally molded into new beings. They are now both Okie and Outsider Cherokees, and not merely fly-by-nights, though it must be admitted that they are that too.

"Well, damn it, let's get this show on the road," shouts G. Stu. Everyone's attention is on him. "And here's the first salvo: I go back to what I said a while ago—Why do you Arkies and Kentuckians and Texans and what-not other Outlanders look so different than us Okie *Tsa-la-gi*?"

And Sully and all look around at themselves. Yet, it is true that most of them don't exhibit as much apparent "full-bloodedness" as G. Stu and Foxy and a lot of the CNO ones do.

"And, two, do any of you have CNO enrollment cards?" And before anyone is allowed to answer, he says, "I thought not." And he laughs, licking his lips and wiggling his nose, and he says, "Two points for our side!"

"But you're not being fair—" Bo Bo starts to say, but both Sully and Wally pat her arms and caution her to stay calm.

"We'll get our turn," says Sully.

"Next," G. Stu says. "Do any of you, and the communities you come from, have a formal relationship with the federal government as a tribe or tribal people?"

More groans. Truly, most of them don't have such status.

"Now, here's an easy one," G. Stu says. "If you are Cherokee, why don't you live in Oklahoma? After all, isn't this where the government long ago decided we should all be?"

Wally starts to say something about his own twenty-five-year residence in Oklahoma, but when both Sully and Bo Bo smile at him, he calms down.

"And now," G. Stu offers. "If you are really Cherokee, why don't you all come to our tribal gatherings—our stomp dances, our churches, our national holidays . . . ?"

At this, then, Sully himself gets out of sync. He stands, crying aloud, "You are being too narrow-minded, you . . ." and he leaves his statement uncompleted as he realizes he has done exactly what he has cautioned the others about.

"Aww, what do you mean—you old gut-eater!" G. Stu sniffs at him.

But before anyone can answer, if they are so inclined, G. Stu goes on.

"And now, here's the kicker. If you are really a Cherokee—if you are *really* interested, deeply interested, in being a *real* Cherokee—then I ask you to join in my new campaign to clean up the tribe—er, I mean, to straighten out the tribe! If you really want to be involved, I ask you to join my new enterprise that I call Group Empowered Specifically to Apprehend Potential Outsiders. I promise you it will clean up our tribe. We will purge—"

Finally, realizing that she can't take it anymore, and angry, too, Robin Bark, the out-from-Montana-and-then-to-Nebraska Cherokee scholar, stands up and calls aloud to G. Stu: "You pride yourself so much on your oh-so-much-more-Cherokee-than-thou stance. If that's so, then why haven't you, through universal Cherokee courtesy and good manners, allowed any of us, as the Outsiders and Outlanders you call us, to proceed first before you began to hold forth? You, sir, Mr. G. Stu, are not only an ill-mannered person, you are a cultural bully!"

Suddenly, G. Stu's face turns woodstove-red hot in such embarrassment as he has never before known. Abjectly, he sits down, totally abashed, his face still red. He knows that Robin is correct: he has violated the cardinal rule of courtesy by not inviting guests to speak first in a social situation.

And Robin, too, is blushing, though not as badly as G. Stu, since she is conscious that she has never been so outgoing, particularly in public.

It's as if the game has suddenly changed. One after the other, various Outlanders rise and address the points raised earlier by G. Stu, now ensconced in a totally uncharacteristic silence.

Bo Bo stands up. "As to how we are said 'to look', or 'not to look,' I ask you to look over at Cora—and all due respect to you, Cora, as I say this—but brothers and sisters, isn't Cora, a bona fide CNO member, only at 1/256ths Cherokee, more non-Cherokee by far than most of us, even most of us Outlanders? I am a North Carolina Cherokee, a little less than half Cherokee by blood, but even if I'm not CNO, aren't I just as much Cherokee as Cora, or any of you?" There are calls of agreement, from both the CNO writers and the Outlander ones.

Waleila Tote stands to be heard.

"I want to respond to what our brother G. Stu said about having enrollment cards being the only qualifier of whether or not one is a real Cherokee. Well, I spent most of my early years in California after our family was relocated there in the Dark Ages period of the '50s and '60s, and I know of many Cherokees who were born there who we never allowed to be put on the tribal rolls. Remember, that was a time when the government was making another one of its efforts to get rid of Indians. By not allowing, or even informing parents of the whole process, many young ones were not enrolled and were therefore disenfranchised. As I say, I know many who were victimized by that process. And many of them were Cherokees."

Everyone assents to her point. Enrollment, then, is not the be-all or end-all requirement; that seems now to be the consensus.

Chicky Dee Deedeelow now stands and, in a heavy Texas accent, seconds all that Waleila, the marvelous hummingbird, has said. "I saw the same thing in Texas, growing up there in the '70s," she says. "I've known jillions of Indians without cards." She pauses, then amends her statement with a giggle. "Well, maybe not jillions. Billions, is more like it."

Everyone laughs. The mood of things is clearly on the mend. There is a sense of airiness, of high-flown sentiment, of airborne softness, as of a dove's downy breast.

Very promptly, others stand and offer counterarguments to those that G. Stu put forth, until finally a moment of contention arises. Flora Deeley-Knotts, with blond hair and blue eyes, stands and, in a storm of indignation, assails the convention.

"Well," she says. "I, for one, am not going to apologize for my 1/256th degree of Cherokee blood. Nor my fairness of hair and complexion. Is it my fault that my ancestry—my Cherokee connection—is so far back in history? What counts is now. Is it my fault that I can prove it, and most of you others can't?"

Out of pique and with an uncharacteristic edge of anger, Sully Humdinger stands and counters her argument.

"My degree of blood quantum goes back that far, too, young lady," he says. "But the real issue is what particular individuals did with the tribal rolls at various times in our history. Now my folks didn't get on any of the Cherokee rolls. We hid out in the Kentucky and West Virginia hills during the Trail of Tears. As did hundreds of other folks. Maybe even thousands. Some even speak some of the language today. Is this dismissible, simply because they weren't assigned a 'white man's number'?"

Sully is disgruntled with himself, principally because he knows he has uncharacteristically related something in a, to him, too personal manner. It does not accord with his long-held views of how a scholar should comport himself. He feels that he has dirtied not only Ms. Deeley-Knotts, but also himself. He glances over at her and thinks that she is equally discombobulated. He determines to make amends to her afterward.

"And another thing," says Bo Bo. "Dr. Leverett, I believe you have been sailing under a questionable flag. You indict Wannabes and seek to purge them from the CNO or anything even remotely Cherokee. Well, then, how about yourself?" Bo Bo looks at him owlishly, without a single blink of the eye.

"What do you mean? I'm no damned Wannabe!" G. Stu says, getting steamed.

"Well, what about your claims to being a writer? Do self-published grant proposals make one a writer?" She smiles as she says this.

"Well, why the hell not?" G. Stu steams. "Somebody might find some good out of them someday."

"True. But you overlook one difference between yourself and most of the other writers here." Bo Bo is still smiling.

"What's that, Little Miss Know-it-all?"

"For one thing, you are almost the only self-published writer here. There's been no process of refereeing with regard to your work. Therefore, you are a Wannabe writer." She smiles, with a surprising degree of uncharacteristic meanness, and repeats, "A Wannabe!"

Several around are laughing, and among those laughing hardest is Juley Chatsmith, old Foxy himself.

"Don't laugh, Foxy. You are also a self-published writer, for the most part."

Foxy is immediately pissed. But he sits down and keeps his mouth shut.

"So what it all boils down to, ladies and gentlemen, is a continual lesson in the willingness to accept without undue judgment and harshness. Of tolerance. Of forbearance," says Jonah.

Then little Thelma Small stands and speaks.

"How do we know that all the Cherokees are represented here today? We see that there are not only Cherokees from Oklahoma, but also Arkansas and North Carolina and Texas and on and on. How can we know where all of them are? Or even *who* they are?"

She is applauded as she resumes her seat. Then Twisty gets up.

"How can we judge people by only one way—whether they have a card and such? How about, as Dr. Humdinger put it, people who haven't had cards for generations, but yet still speak the Cherokee language? Are they, then, any less real Cherokees than those with cards who don't know even a word of the language?"

Then Dr. Justin H. Danielson stands to speak.

"Yes, you are both right," and he nods toward both Thelma and Twisty. "There are language speakers who aren't real Cherokees, by Dr. Leverett's definition, and there are blond, miniscule-fractioned blood quantum

Cherokees determined to be so because of an enrollment number. Why, then, can't we agree that there isn't just one way to be Cherokee, but actually several?"

He is applauded as he sits down.

Then Wally stands. He takes off his glasses and cleans them with a small cloth as he begins to speak. He blinks his eyes continuously as he does.

"I think we ought to all recall the greatest of all Cherokees—at least for those of us who are dedicated to the notions of literacy and education and communication and so forth—none other than Sequoyah himself.

"Sequoyah, you will remember, after he set our people on the road to literacy, the ability to read and write the language, turned his attention to another matter."

He pauses. The audience is quiet. As he replaces his glasses, he continues speaking.

"He was an old man then, after coming to the western country—which to him was at first Arkansas, you'll all recall; then it was Indian Territory—and he found something missing. In fact, he found a lot of somethings missing. He was wondering where the Lost Cherokees were."

There are sounds of approval of what Wally has been saying. He continues:

"But I will let my much younger colleagues finish here, if you all don't mind," and he nods to Thelma and Twisty.

"*Wado*, Dr. Baldon," says Thelma. "Yes, for Sequoyah, the Lost Cherokees weren't just those lost in all the movings west before the Trail of Tears. Then there were literally hundreds, maybe a thousand or so, who have all along been counted as among the dead on the Trail of Tears but who, probably, because they escaped and hid out in the hills and river bottoms and stayed in areas of the march country—Tennessee and Kentucky and Ohio and Indiana and Illinois and Missouri and Arkansas—were counted as dead by the military conductors on the trek. There were also some who, according to legend, went on into what is now Colorado, the Rockies, and who knows where else?"

"Sequoyah, as you all know, went to Mexico, because he'd heard that there were Lost Cherokees there too," says Twisty, standing side by side with Thelma.

"Brothers and sisters," says Sully as he joins the two younger people standing in front of the audience, while gesturing to Wally to join them. "The Lost Cherokees, then, are literally everywhere. Why don't we, then, as the so-called educated ones of our people, make it our destiny to look for the Lost Cherokees? To find them and add them to our numbers, whether it be in Oklahoma or Kentucky or wherever."

"I agree with you all," Jonah says as he joins them standing in front of the audience. "We can respect people who say they are Cherokees by blood, or by enrollment number, or based on how they do and think and speak things—all are aspects of Cherokeeness. We just have to keep remembering good old Sequoyah."

"Yes," says Jeffie Honored. "Now that we, in the modern age, have such things as computers, the internet, blogs, television, DNA testing, and so forth, we ought to be able to find our lost ones much more easily."

"Then our job is, in all actuality, just beginning," says Bo Bo.

There is applause as people turn to one another, talking over all that has been going on.

"It looks like things are ending on a positive note, don't you think?" says Flora to Waleila as they enjoy a cup of coffee together.

"Yeah, we really racked up the points there at the end, didn't we?" Waleila says.

Suddenly there is a commotion, at the entrance to the auditorium, of many people coming in, talking and laughing. And so, maybe it isn't all over yet. It is an entourage of writers with names like Rattlesnake Romero and Culebra Jose Blackstrike and Maria Goingback and Juan Salazar Guess and Martin Kingsnake Quintana and, gosh, who knows who else?

"*Buenas Osiyo, compadres y diginotli*! We are the Mexican Cherokees," says Rattlesnake Romero. "The children of the ones that old Sequoyah found. The legend is true, amigos."

And Sully and Foxy and Wally and Bo Bo and, yes, even G. Stu himself walk down the aisle toward them, hands extended in greeting and smiles aplenty. How long before they petition for a place in the overall nationhood of Cherokee?

Afterward, in a herd of the younger scholars, discussing the day's events, they still seem nonplussed by all that has occurred. Like young elks and deer and moose and antelopes, they masticate the subject over and over again.

"Well, one thing we can come away with," says Dr. Nelson Joshua.

The others look at him, and when he doesn't say anything further, Dr. Wave Jason asks him what it is. Nelson smiles and says:

"The toleration of diversified views."

"Come again?" Suagee K. Beauty asks.

"The ability, or the willingness, to tolerate differing points of view. Something I recall in my study of Elias Boudinot. I believe we've been seeing that whole endeavor endangered—threatened in ways we hadn't even banked on before."

"Yes, you're right. It's good that old Sully and Jonah seemed to always have that in mind," Justin Danielson says. Hud Brianson agrees.

And at another table, Foxy turns to Sully as they sit enjoying late afternoon coffee. He looks as if he has something on his mind. He does, and he brings it out.

"You know, I can't help but think about the topic we all came here thinking we would be discussing—which of the variants of "The Animals' Ballgame" is the real one, the more authentic. Which do you think it is?"

Sully clears his throat, smiles a small smile, and ducks his head in his characteristic fashion.

"Oh, that's easy," he says. And he pauses and looks shrewdly at Foxy, and Foxy, waiting for the answer, knits his brow and is about to repeat his question when Sully answers:

"They all are."

"Why? Why do you say that?"

"Because everyone always tells the story in his or her own way. No matter what the minor changes, from one telling to the next, story to story, each one is always true and special. We should never forget that."

A bit later on, Sully muses that, somewhere along the line, the symposium's systematic side-tracking was all for the best, as it turned out. Instead of examinations of the various versions of "The Animals' Ballgame," we were at last confronted with that ticklish authenticity/identity within/without the CNO subject. When, and why, did that happen? The why was vague, but the when? Well, when old G. Stu Leverett shanghaied things, with his questions about how people look (and don't look); why, then, if claiming to be Cherokee, are they not living in Oklahoma; and such and such. Well, now that we've tackled that, what next in terms of topics? Sully thought for a while then recalled listening to the brown-haired, light-complexioned Sal Ekorre as she expounded on property and policy rights for particular citizens in the Nation, sounding like a right-wing Republican (which she is)—well, a possible topic might be Cherokee mixed-bloods as baronage and/or would-be (Wannabe?) royalty. That ought to raise a hackle or two.

"Now that the confab is over, I can't for the life of me recall what we were arguing about to begin with. Can you?" says Jonah.

"No, I can't say that I can either," Sully replies.

And so the game—or the conference—ends.

Linda Boyden

We Never Spoke

We never spoke about it.
It just was. No one judged,
not in our mountains,
not in our tiny town of need
where we lived in poverty
side by side
Cherokee, Irish, and
every mixed-blood
combination.

Us kids,
dark-skinned or light-haired,
tore around, busted up stuff,
got switched from time to time.
Indian or White
no one asked.
No one cared.
No one spoke of the past
though family mattered,

and work even more.
Can you wield a plow?
Harvest a field?
Cook a meal from a potato or two?
That was the measure of a man,
the strength of a woman.

We all lost family
on the Trail of Tears, the Removal.
We all suffered something fierce.
The elders who survived
seldom spoke of
a pain this deep,
with no beginning or end.

Those who did survive,
survived in pieces,
broken but alive.
They got on,
married,
had kids.
Died.

My generation,
we kids grew up quiet,
one day at a time,
one silent meal at a time.
We watched our parents'
and grandparents' fractured lives
stay patched together;
a quilt of broken dreams
never spoken aloud.

Somehow things changed.

One elder said, "You are
the Seventh Generation.
You come from people
who chose to stay silent,
but who remembered;
who whispered the stories;
who refused to dance,
but sang the songs
behind locked doors.

We kids listened.
Word by word,
bit by bit
we collected,
we studied
we asked questions,
loud and louder until
our voices refused to stay still.

Here is what I want for my children:
plant the seeds
for *your* Seventh Generation.
Teach them our stories,
use our language and
raise up strong-willed children,
children too proud to stay quiet.

Understand a history
as long as ours needs voices.
Voices need courage.
Bravery like this will
keep our People alive.

Speak up.

WHY WE MATTER

In this final section, you will find essays that examine the importance, to the tribes, of unpapered Natives with familial ties to Native communities and the impact on the continued survival of tribal nations and tribal culture of forcing these people and future undocumented generations completely out of the community. Given the rate at which current tribal members' grandchildren are being disenrolled and disenfranchised, this should be a major concern, even for the hardliners.

Craig Santos Perez

On Being Chamorro and
Belonging to Guam

As a kid, I played American football, basketball, and baseball. Posters hung in my room of Michael Jordan, Bo Jackson, and the Oakland "Bash Brothers." I rewatched *Star Wars*, *Batman*, and *Back to the Future*. MC Hammer, Mariah Carey, and Milli Vanilli repeated on the local radio station. I turned the pages of *Berenstein Bears* and Marvel's *Spiderman*. I ate at McDonald's, KFC, and Pizza Hut. I loved SPAM. I learned English and American history and literature at school.

While this sounds like an American upbringing, I actually grew up on the small western Pacific island of Guam, thousands of nautical miles east of the American continent. Guam, which is about 30 miles long and 9 miles wide, doesn't appear on most maps of the world.

"Why does the license plate on our car say 'Guam, U.S.A,'" I asked my dad after he picked me up from school.

"We're a U.S. territory," he said bluntly. He pointed to the flagpole that rose above the coconut trees: "That's why they make you pledge allegiance to the American flag at school every day."

We never learned about being a "territory" in school. We memorized and recited the names and capitals of all fifty states. But maps of the United States never included Guam.

"Is that why we say 'Guam is Where America's Day Begins?'" I asked as we pulled into the McDonald's drive thru.

"That's our slogan," he said. "Guam is a day ahead of the states. The sun rises here first."

He placed our order: Big Mac for him, Filet-o-Fish for me. Large fries. Cokes.

"And that's also why we watch the Super Bowl on Monday," he said as he paid the cashier with American dollar bills.

"Always remember the other words on the license plate," my dad said after we finished eating. "'Tano Y Chamorro.' Land of the Chamorro. We are Chamorro. Guam is our land."

Our native Chamorro culture, history, and language weren't taught in school either.

The first thing I learned about being Chamorro was the importance of genealogy. I learned this whenever we met one of our relatives. My dad would tell me their clan name, their village, and how they were related to us. "Inafa'maolek," he said. "We're all connected."

If we met a *manåmko'*, an elder, he took their hand and bowed, touching the back of their hand to his nose. He'd say *ñora* to an auntie and *ñot* to an uncle. I would do the same.

"That's *nginge'*," he said. "*Respetu.*"

I learned that's how we show respect; we breathe in the elder's spirit and wisdom.

"When *manåmko'* speak, you *ekungok*, listen. Sometimes, they'll tell *taotaomo'na* stories, spirit stories."

Taotaomo'na means "People of Before." They guard the land and dwell within the banyan trees and their roots. *Taotaomo'na* stories teach us to always ask *petmisu*, permission, when we walk in the jungle or enter someone else's land. If you don't, the *taotaomo'na* will pinch and bruise you — *or worse*, we are warned.

"If the *manåmko'* give you money," my dad said. "Say, '*Si Yu'us ma'ase.*'

Thank you. Because it's more than just money. It's *chenchule'*. And when you're older, you give *chenchule'* to others."

Inafa'maolek. All things are interconnected. Land and water, people and animals, past and present, the living and the spirits. Kinship. Relations. Always do what is *maolek*, good, for all things.

This is what it means to be Chamorro.

Every Sunday, my family dressed up and attended mass at the island's largest Catholic church, the Dulce Nombre de Maria Cathedral Basilica, in the village of Hagåtña, the capitol of Guam. We dipped our fingers into the holy water and made the sign of the cross. In the name of the father, the son, and the holy spirit. Amen. We sat at the pew, stood, knelt. Amen. We sang and prayed. Amen. We held our hands out for the Eucharist. Body of Christ. Amen. My mom gave me a dollar bill to put in the money basket. Amen.

Catholicism is not indigenous to Guam, but most Chamorros are Catholic.

I was taught in Saturday school that Spanish missionaries arrived on Guam in the seventeenth century to save the souls of the "godless" Chamorros. The famous Jesuit Diego Luis de San Vitores named our archipelago "Islas Marianas" in honor of the queen of Spain, Maria Ana of Austria, and the Blessed Virgin Mary. He established the first Catholic church on Guam in Hagatna. The "Dulce Nombre de Maria," the sweet name of Mary. Amen.

The priests taught us that Father San Vitores was martyred by a murderous Chamorro chief, Mata'pang. What the priests didn't tell us is that many Chamorros died after being baptized. They didn't tell us that Chief Mata'pang killed San Vitores because he baptized the chief's child without permission. They didn't tell us about the Spanish military conquest that followed. That 90 percent of all Chamorros were killed by war and disease. That the surviving Chamorros were forced into mission villages. That Chamorros were converted by violence and baptized by colonialism. Amen.

Today, Chamorros go to mass on Sunday. We celebrate feast days for the saints. We wear the crucifixes around our necks. We recite the rosary. We read the Bible. We light votives. We have Spanish last names. Amen.

After mass, we drive on Purple Heart Highway to return to our village. This road connects to two other thoroughfares on Guam: Marine Corps Drive and Army Drive.

The United States annexed Guam after the Spanish-American War of 1898. Guam became an "unincorporated territory," a new political status that meant Guam could be a territory of the United States without ever being fully incorporated as a state. Guam was "foreign in a domestic sense." Not all constitutional or citizenship rights extended to Guam or the Chamorro people. Congress held plenary power over Guam. The Supreme Court upheld this colonial status in a series of cases known as "The Insular Cases."

The United States established English-only schools and declared English the official language of Guam. They displaced Chamorros from our ancestral land to build military bases, firing ranges, and weapons storage facilities. They called this land theft "eminent domain." Miles and miles of barbed wire fences snaked across our island. "No trespassing" signs. They referred to our sacred island as "uss *Guam*."

In 1950 the Organic Act of Guam was passed, which created a civilian government and granted U.S. citizenship to Chamorros. Guam has a nonvoting representative in Congress, and residents of Guam are not allowed to vote for U.S. president.

This is what it means to be an unincorporated territory. A non–self-governing territory. An American colony in the twenty-first century.

I never learned this history in school. We pledged allegiance to the American flag.

In seventh grade, my social studies teacher at St. Anthony Catholic Middle School made us memorize the names of all forty-one American presidents, whose portraits stared down at us from the classroom wall in the furthest American territory from the White House.

As I recited their names at home, my parents watched Bill Clinton play saxophone on television.

"Are you voting for him?" I asked.

My dad, wearing his army T-shirt, said, "Didn't your teacher tell you that our votes don't count. It don't matter that we're citizens or veterans."

Like many other Chamorro men of his generation, my dad was drafted into the military and sent to fight in Vietnam. In the decades since, Chamorros have enlisted in the military at a higher rate per capita than any other ethnic group because it is the main economic industry on Guam.

My dad has served in the army, my grandpa in the air force, my godfather in the marines, and many of my uncles, cousins, and friends in the navy and the reserves. Chamorros wear military uniforms with pride. Yet the military stole our land. Chamorros proudly fight in American wars. Yet we don't have the right to vote for the president that sends our people to war.

In 1995 my parents decided to migrate to California. My mom was very sick at the time and felt she could receive better health care in the states. My dad had lost his job and felt he could find a better job. They both believed that my siblings and I would receive a better education. Chamorros dream American dreams.

I was fifteen years old and had just completed my freshman year in high school. I didn't want to leave my school, my friends, and the only home I'd ever known. That summer, we sold most of our belongings and bought one-way tickets on Continental, the name of the airline, the name of our destination.

The entrance of the Guam airport is designed in the shape of an outrigger canoe, the vessel upon which our ancestors navigated the Pacific thousands of years ago to find their way here. The Chamorro word for airplane is *batkon aire*, air boat.

Our friends and relatives came to the airport to say goodbye. I hugged them and pressed my elders' hands to my forehead—*ñora, ñot*. I held my blue passport as we entered the gate and boarded the twelve-hour transoceanic flight to San Francisco.

Migration flows through Chamorro blood like the aerial roots of the banyan tree.

Since the 1960s we've migrated for jobs, schools, health care, and military service—been deployed to and stationed at bases around the world. According to the 2010 census, 44,000 Chamorros live in California, 15,000 in Washington state, 10,000 in Texas, 7,000 in Hawaii, and 70,000 more throughout the country, in every other state and even Puerto Rico. We're the most geographically dispersed Pacific Islander population within the United States. Today, more Chamorros live off-island than on-island. There are now generations of Chamorros who've been born away from our home islands. There are Chamorros today who have never been to the Marianas.

"Where are you from?" the homeroom teacher asked us on the first day at my new high school in California.

"The Mariana islands," I answered when it was my turn.

"I've never heard of that place," he replied. "Prove it exists."

Yet when I stepped in front of the world map on the classroom wall, it transformed into a mirror: the Pacific Ocean, like my body, was split in two and flayed to the margins. I found Australia, the Philippines, Japan. I pointed to an empty space between and said: "I'm from this invisible archipelago."

Everyone laughed. And even though I descend from oceanic navigators, I felt so lost—shipwrecked on the coast of a strange continent.

"You speak English well," he surprisingly proclaimed, "with almost no accent."

I was silent. I didn't tell him that one of the first acts of U.S. colonialism on Guam was to declare English the official language. That American schools were established to force Chamorros to learn English. That my grandparents were shamed, punished, and beaten for speaking Chamorro in school. That if you wanted a job on Guam, you had to speak English. That they didn't pass down the language to protect us. That Chamorro language is now endangered.

"Are you a citizen?" my teacher probed.

"Yes," I answered. "My island, Guam, is a U.S. territory."

And isn't that what it means to be a diasporic Chamorro: to feel *foreign in a domestic sense*?

My favorite classes in high school and college were English courses. I was drawn to books by Native American and ethnic minority writers because I could relate to their stories of struggle, survival, migration, and hope. But I never saw myself in the curriculum. The Pacific was a blank space on the American literary map.

This feeling of invisibility and homesickness motivated me to write. Poetry became a way for me to stay connected to Guam and to tell the stories of my people. I pursued an MFA in creative writing at the University of San Francisco and completed a manuscript of poems about Chamorro identity and the political history of Guam. The preface to my thesis began: "On some maps, Guam doesn't exist; I point to an empty space in the Pacific and say, 'I'm from here.' On some maps, Guam is a small, unnamed island; I say, 'I'm from this unnamed place.' On some maps, Guam is named 'Guam, U.S.A.' I say, 'I'm from a territory of the United States.'"

Through poetry, I could write Guam into existence, navigate my own cultural identity, and confront the violence of colonialism. Poetry became my sovereign tongue.

The same year I graduated, the Department of Defense announced a plan for a military buildup on Guam. Valiant Shield, a massive military training exercise, was conducted that year on Guam and the surrounding waters. These actions were part of the U.S. geopolitical strategy, "The Pacific Pivot," to increase its military presence and power in the region.

These actions compelled me to join a California-based Chamorro activism group called Famoksaiyan, a word that translates as "the place or time of nurturing" and "the time to paddle forward and move ahead." We organized events to raise awareness about Guam and the devastating impacts of militarism. I performed my poetry as a creative way to address the issues.

This was the first time since my family migrated that I connected more deeply with Chamorros across the diaspora. I was inspired by how many of us were finding ways to maintain our culture far from home. It's true: we carry our culture in the canoes of our bodies. Our people, scattered like stars, form new constellations when we gather.

While Guam and the Marianas will always be our ancestral "homes," I learned from diasporic Chamorros that home is not simply a house, village, or island; *home is an archipelago of belonging.*

In 2008 I traveled with a delegation of Famoksaiyan members to the United Nations headquarters in New York City to testify at the meeting of the Special Committee on Decolonization, which advocates for the remaining non–self-governing territories in the world. My testimony focused on the environmental damage caused by the U.S. military on Guam and the further pollution that would be caused by the proposed military buildup. I urged the committee to support Guam in our quest for decolonization, self-determination, and political sovereignty.

When we began our testimonies, the U.S. representative walked out of the room. This, too, is what it means to be from a territory: to speak truth even when those in power refuse to listen.

My poetry manuscript was published that same year. Empowered by speaking to the international community, I traveled across the states performing poetry and giving lectures at universities, literary festivals, libraries, and high schools. For most audience members, it was the first time they had ever heard of Guam or talked with a native Pacific Islander.

In 2010 the Guam Humanities Council invited me to be a keynote speaker in a series of "community conversations" about the legacy of militarism on Guam. This trip was my first time returning home since my family migrated fifteen years earlier. I was thirty years old.

While home, I visited and performed my poetry at several of Guam's public high schools, as well as at Guam's only community college and university. After each performance, facilitators from the council engaged the audience in conversations about the military. Poetry became a bridge to discuss politics. This profound experience solidified my belief in the power of the humanities to create space for civic reflection.

One school I performed at was George Washington, the oldest American public high school on Guam. After my reading, I noticed one of the students crying.

"Are you okay?" I asked.

"I have never seen our culture in an actual book before," she said. "I just assumed we weren't worthy of literature."

Being Chamorro means genealogy and family clans. Villages and islands. *Respetu, petmisu, chenchule', nginge', ekungot,* and *inafa'maolek.* Being Chamorro means the sword and the cross, conquest and genocide, military and colony, displacement, and migration. Being Chamorro means our lands, waters, and bodies have been polluted, contaminated, and diseased. Being Chamorro means feeling invisible and erased. It means being unincorporated and territorialized. Being Chamorro means reclaiming and revitalizing our cultures and languages. It means protesting and resisting further imperialism. It means standing up and fighting to protect our sacred island. It means dreaming that someday Guam will be an independent nation. Being Chamorro means that I pledge to write poetry to inspire my people and to speak up for my homeland. I pledge to write poetry to memorialize the past, navigate the present, and imagine a sustainable and sovereign future. I pledge to write poetry that has the power to raise political awareness, inspire environmental justice, cultivate empathy, protest oppression, empower communities, and advocate for peace.

"We are worthy of literature," I told the student before I left the classroom. "We deserve to be seen and heard."

On the flight from Guam back to San Francisco, I reminded myself: *Our stories are sacred. We will always belong in our nation of stories.*

Kimberly Wieser

Aunt Ruby's Little Sister Dances

Getting involved in this conversation was the last thing I wanted to do.

I did almost everything I could to avoid it. It's such a nasty subject. It brings out venomous behavior in people. It's emotionally traumatizing on all sides. It certainly is emotionally traumatizing for me. Knowing that people's actions and reactions can hurt me, and taking into account the adage "Hurt people hurt people. Healed people heal people," I can only suppose that this subject is hurtful for others. People hurt people over this subject. People who, otherwise, are nice people and have had good relationships with other people in the past will *hurt* people over this subject.

However, I was brought up largely by my grandparents, great aunts, and uncles, and they taught me to respect my elders. I was also taught by my academic and creative mentors, Lee Francis III and Geary Hobson, and my spiritual mentor, Eugene Blackbear Sr. (my adopted Cheyenne Grandpa/ *Namšem*), that we are all related and that, to live in a balanced way, I should engage with people as relatives and treat them with respect. I have been taught to view Diane Glancy and Linda Rodriguez as "aunties," as part of the network of relations in Native literary studies and creative writing, of which I have been a part since 1996. This network grew out of Wordcraft

Circle, NWCA (Native Writers Circle of the Americas), ASAIL (the Association for Studies in American Indian Literatures), NALS (the Native American Literature Symposium), and NAISA (the Native American and Indigenous Studies Association). The caucuses that represent Native and Indigenous people at CCCC (the Conference on College Composition and Communication) and AWP (the Association of Writers & Writing Programs) have also brought people within this circle. I have tried to be a good relative to everyone with whom I have made connections throughout this web of relationships. If I have done well by you in that regard, it is due to what the elders in the family I was born into taught me, as well as what the elders in the communities in which I have worked and lived have taught me. If I have failed you in this regard, I can blame only myself.

Because of the way I was brought up and the way I view the world and try to live, though I avoided being on a panel about this book at the 2019 Native Literary Symposium, though I saw people whom I have treated as relatives angry at that panel, when Linda wrote to me about contributing to this volume, I realized that silence isn't an option and that this is work I must do.

But I'll tell you what I am *not* going to do.

I am *not* going to argue with *anyone* about this subject.

I will tell you, on the other hand, how I *feel* and *why* I feel how I feel.

So I guess you could say this essay straddles the line between "not arguing with anyone" and "speaking truth to power."

That is the space I have lived in since my daughter died. There is no aspect of my life that is not colored by that trauma. That's something you should understand when you read this.

In *Back to the Blanket*, I said:

> As a person reared with familial knowledge of distant Cherokee ancestry, I have searched for twenty years for documentation. If some genealogies are to be believed, I have documentable Cherokee ancestors, but only ones who predate the 1903 Dawes Roll—Ada-gal'kala and his wife; their daughter, along with her husband, Inoli; and Martha Sherill, born in Cherokee, North Carolina in 1766, on my mother's

father's side of the family. There are others, also on my mother's father's side, whom I suspect are of Cherokee heritage—Rainwaters, Davises, Proctors, Smiths, and Hollands. On my father's mother's side of the family, I likewise suspect Reeds, Bryants, Littlefields, and Nances of having Cherokee ancestry. (149)

I am not enrolled. I have never been enrolled. I did, however, grow up with a family oral history of Native ancestry. Aunt Ruby made sure of that. In this essay, I am going to focus on only that side of my family. Aunt Ruby's people, my paternal grandmother's ancestors and relatives, were Robbins, Reeds, Nances, Bryants, McGarieties, Littlefields, and Wrights (who were relatives of Henry Clay's). They came from Virginia, Alabama, and North and South Carolina. Before coming to Texas, they migrated to Mississippi, Arkansas, and what is now the state of Oklahoma. While, on paper, I cannot document the Cherokee heritage claimed, along with Choctaw heritage, in my grandmother's family's oral traditions, before immigrating to Texas, some of their ancestors formed a community in Mississippi in the homelands of the Chickasaw Nation in Panola County, named after the Cherokee word for cotton, *panolo*. Some of those folks then went to Chicot County, Arkansas, before coming to Texas.

My great-great-grandmother, Carolina Virginia McGariety, later married Sam Wright. This was after the Panola County community reformed in Wrightsboro, Texas. Located in the heart of the Hill Country, it was near other communities, like Cherokee, Texas, that claim a Cherokee-diasporic heritage. His sisters' complaints about his "marrying that Indian woman" carried over the generations to their granddaughters, my Mammy, Mable Robbins Wieser, and her sisters. These are the women who reared me.

I grew up with Indianisms—some distilled from American popular culture—more than Cherokeeisms, Choctawisms, or Creekisms. Mammy and Aunt Ruby, or Sister, as she had me call her, took me to Alabama Coushatta (A.C.) dances. My grandma and my aunt made me an Indian dress—a dress based on an idea of a Plains dress, rather than a Cherokee dress or a Choctaw dress.

Either way, in that very dress, at that A.C. powwow, at the young age of two or three, I suddenly became aware, for the first time in my life, of my phenotype. I was lighter than Mammy. I was far lighter than Aunt Ruby. I was the lightest person there.

I can still see my little moccasined feet digging trenches in the summer sand under the arbor, resisting as my Aunt Ruby's hands pushed gently on my bottom, urging me to dance. I steadfastly refused. I felt far too ashamed of my light skin.

I went back in June of 2016 with my partner, Rance, and our daughter Nia. I danced.

Not only that, I judged Women's Golden age, the dance category for the eldest female dancers.

At the big new Veterans' Pavilion at the ballpark, not too far from that arbor where I had refused to dance all those years ago, I visited with Keith Bullock, an A.C. friend I had met at Baylor. I had hoped to also visit with his cousin Nita Battiste, another friend of mine, but there had been a death in the family, so she had been unable to be there. I told her later, on Facebook, about my reluctance to dance when I was a child and how, forty-five years later, I finally felt comfortable enough in my own skin to feel at home.

"Because when you're here, you *are* home," Nita said.

For Mammy and her sisters, gardening and gathering wild foods—poke salad, dew berries, mustang (muscadine) grapes, pecans, rare finds of persimmons—were part of the fabric of our lives. Bringing home seafood, freshwater fish, and wild game—squirrel, deer, ducks, turkey—were things our male relatives did for us for the most part, and we processed what they brought in, but we also engaged from a very young age in attempting to procure fish, birds, and game animals. Some of my earliest memories are of fishing on a pier, tied to Mammy's waist with a rope to prevent me from falling into the gulf below. She taught me to safely trap and release birds, to entertain me. They handed me a BB gun at the age of seven. By twelve, I could pass the police range with a .357. I learned to defend myself and procure my own meat, if necessary. I won't pretend to be any good at fishing or hunting compared to my father or my son—or even my late grandmother, who "scoped herself" and blacked her own eye with her rifle when she shot her last deer, at eighty, sitting in a tree stand—but I do know enough to survive, if I have to. Neither my dad nor my son can cook cornbread, chicken and dumplings, greens, or pinto beans as well as I can, either, but they can both cook decent food if they have to, even food other people are willing and happy to eat. While this division of labor in terms of food responsibilities and this training, which crosses that very gender division in a nonbinary dualistic framework, is Cherokee, it is also common to other tribes.

I also grew up with certain beliefs. God, particularly the Baptist version, but also the Holiness version, was the most important part of Mammy's and her sisters' lives. While they were Christian, they also held to some traditional beliefs. Aunt Ruby called me her "little Indian sister," reinforcing not only identity, but the fact that she, as the oldest female in the family, was the authority who passed on knowledge and that my job as a younger female relative was to learn from her whatever she had to teach. She was most likely to organize the gathering and gardening activities and wake young relatives (sometimes my cousins, but usually just me, as she often lived with us) before dawn to get out in the fields, woods, or garden. She was also the authority, later, on things such as not reaching above my head or attending funerals while I was pregnant. Other family members had obviously internalized these ways as values. My father wouldn't even let me see a deer he was cleaning while I was expecting my son, Cody. My mother's family also respected that idea, allowing me to go to neither the wake nor the funeral when Uncle Kenny passed away, as I was expecting my middle child, Rachel. Mammy and Aunt Ruby enacted Indianisms in object making and selection, buying Indian-patterned blankets, hanging a plaque about walking a mile in someone's moccasins, sewing house shoes made like Southeastern moccasins and pillows with Indian prints, and hand-tying—what they called "tatting"—pieced quilts. I grew up in a matriarchal, matricentric, matrilineal household, despite the presence of Pappy, my German (and as we would find out later, Jewish, as well, with the Jewish Wieser surname) grandfather. My grandmother ran her house, and she and her sisters ran our larger family. I heard their stories of survival—Aunt Ruby's several-year stint, from her mid to late teens, at a women's prison farm in Nebraska, for being along for the ride with older cousins in a stolen car, and the electric shock treatments they gave her there that left her with a stutter for life; Aunt Jessie's and Aunt Anna Belle's year in a boarding school in Houston for disadvantaged girls; Mammy's year in a foster home; Uncle Leroy's many jail breaks. The women who raised me grew up poor, so poor they often went without food, and they grew up experiencing discrimination against their phenotype, being called "poor, dirty Choctaws from Oklahoma," but they were proud of their Cherokee and Choctaw ancestry, as proud as they were of also being descended from Texans and Confederates. (Apparently, they didn't know their grandpa, John Reed Robbins, switched to the Union side midway through the war.) It was important to them that I grow up with pride in being a descendant, and they gave me as much knowledge about what that meant, mostly indirectly, as they could. I treasure the memories of being with them, doing things with them, and I treasure all the stories they told of their childhood, life experiences, and family history.

I also grew up with other Indianisms that weren't so positive, that fit stereotypes that should disturb us far more than determining who is Indian enough to count. I grew up mostly without my mother, except for visits in the dysfunction that undergirded the every-other-weekend with her folks or family trips to Mississippi and Alabama. I grew up with the statistical reality of alcoholism, sexual abuse, violence, and suicide. My maternal family also had stories of Choctaw and Creek ancestry and stories here and there about ways—apparently my great-grandma Katie had some sort of tornado medicine, and polygamy was relatively recent in the family line and, in some respects, still going on.[1] Most of all, my maternal family provided access to the homeland. Mississippi dirt roads, creeks, woods, and the mighty river herself were a huge part of my childhood—

remembering nights in a beloved two-room shack at the edge of
    a watermelon field
lean-to kitchen and bath, brand new pull-chain toilet
eating boiled green peanuts sitting on the porch stoop watching
    fireflies

But the dysfunction that remains after so many deaths still haunts my mother and me. And these sorts of inheritances also haunt Mammy's side of my extended family. I am not the only child raised by a grandmother or even a great-grandmother, but that is exactly the point. Stability existed in enough pockets that maternal families—which ours was considered to be, despite my father's presence, as my grandma was rearing me—took care of our own. *We*, not *she*, were responsible for raising children. Other colonized Indianisms enact themselves whether we want them to or not: diabetes, lactose intolerance, anemia, heart attacks, strokes, blood pressure issues, and cancer . . . diseases at the interstices of biology, diet, and capitalism colonize our bodies as much as did non-Native gene pools.

My grandma and her sisters and brothers grew up poor. They suffered discrimination because of the color of their skin and their refusal to forget who they were. They weren't citizens of any tribal nation.

I would swear to this next part in a court of law, not that any court of law cares, but I would. Just saying.

The first time I met Chad Smith was at a party in Albuquerque, New Mexico. I was there at a conference, and Lee Francis III, my mentor, was dragging me along to what he termed an "all-Cherokee party," except for Lee, who was notably Laguna Pueblo. I met the chief, along with a friend of his, in the hostess's kitchen, with a beer in his hand. Turns out the friend was married to a Littlefield, one of my distant relatives. He told the chief, "Hell, Chad! She's more Cherokee than you! I know my wife's more Cherokee than you, even if she's not enrolled."

Everybody laughed.

I wanted to believe it.

My adult autistic daughter, Rachel, was not legally American Indian either. When I found she had collapsed in our garage, on April 2, 2017 (she had been taking her laundry from the washer to the dryer), my partner Rance and I immediately began CPR, while Marley, my younger daughter, grabbed her phone and called for help. When EMTs and police officers responded to her 911 call, however, they took one look at my family, our license plates, and other markers of Indianness, put that with her age and the fact that she had a psych history, and decided this was another American Indian suicide. The medical examiner called her "American Indian" and did everything he could, in the autopsy report, to suggest that was the case, but he "couldn't prove it," and the "family wouldn't accept it." Her death certificate (filled out by the same person) lists her as white, however, and lists the cause of death as "undetermined."

The EMTs never even turned on the siren, although they knew we were performing CPR.

There were other documented instances of medical personnel failing her, though without an official cause of death, I can do nothing about it.

I still have no justice.

She was Indian enough for the EMTs to slow-code her and not even try, at all. She was Indian enough for no one to give a *shit* about justice for her.

So if I am not Indian enough for you, that is *totally* your prerogative. But if you say something in this regard *to* me or *about* me that gets back to me, via our never-ending moccasin telegraph (you cannot say *any-thing* in this "tiny In'din world" that doesn't come back to someone), I am liable to tell you that you can go straight to hell.

I just want you to know where I am coming from if I do this.

If I had kept my butt in Texas, where people just say, "You're, like, part Hispanic, right?" my daughter might still be alive.

I grew up "part Indian," Heinz 57, Deutsch mixture. Mammy told me so. Aunt Anna Belle says, "We're Choctaw." Aunt Ruby called me her little Indian sister, but I'm "part Indian." Mammy said she got called a "poor, dirty Indian" and a "poor, dirty Choctaw" so many times that all three ran together in her head, and she darned sure didn't want to be poor anymore.

She didn't want me to be poor either.

When I came into the broader community, beyond my own family and my visits with them to the Alabama-Coushatta Reservation, it was through a desire to reconnect and learn more, sparked by my study of Native literature. I remember one day in Baylor's library. I was there to return an interlibrary loan book, even more important in those olden days before library databases that could be accessed from home via the internet. As any good graduate student would, I was checking the table of contents to make sure there weren't any chapters other than the one for which I had requested the book that I should photocopy before I turned the book back in. I noticed one article was written by a Daniel F. Littlefield, who was apparently Cherokee. I wondered if he were a relative. I looked in the back of the book at the bios and noticed he taught at the University of Arkansas at Little Rock, so I looked him up and emailed him there, telling him my lineage as I knew it from research done by Aunt Anna Belle's son Wayne. Dan replied, letting me know that, indeed, we were relatives. His paternal grandfather and my grandmother's maternal great-grandma were brother and sister. He said they knew that part of the family had come to Texas and that they had stayed in contact for some time. However, he also said that his Cherokee ancestry was on his mother's side of the family. So while I'd found a relative, I hadn't found an answer. While Daniel Littlefield was a founding member of the Cherokee National Honor Society, I have heard from common acquaintances he no longer claims his Cherokee heritage. I am ashamed that the atmosphere out here is so bad that this happened. He is, of course, an award-winning scholar with ten books—he's done some of the finest archival research in our field. If whoever made him feel this way about his heritage did so because of his distant relation to me, shame on them. Decent human beings don't act that way. (One of the biggest regrets I have from the last twenty years is that I haven't spent more time with Dan. I should have. I consider him a giant for many reasons, not the least of which is that he took on Arnold Krupat at MLA over that essentialism brouhaha that stirred in the field for years. I was more tired of that than some people were of mixed-blood protagonists. The things we get stuck on forever . . . GEEZ!)

While I had no answers, I soon found the Native academic and creative writing community welcoming. Keith, the A.C. friend I mentioned earlier in this essay, encouraged me to learn more about my ancestry and to join the Native American Student Association at Baylor. I met the Blackbear family, a Cheyenne family who adopted me as a relative, through that Native student association and our powwows. I was invited to ceremonies. I participated in community events. Namšem took me under his wing and decided what I was going to do in regard to ceremonies and what I should learn. He taught me a lot. The Blackbears and my other NAC relatives taught me a lot. One thing I learned quickly was there was no such thing as "part Indian."

Deputy chief and Cherokee national treasure Hastings Shade reinforced that to me at a Wordcraft Circle event, Returning the Gift, when it was held in Tahlequah in 2000. He said, "You're either Cherokee, or you're not. There is no part anything." That left me feeling kind of confused. My family's language for what I was (which is actually kind of accurate in my mind) was not acceptable. But people were accepting of me and engaged in actions that seemed to reinforce, rather than deny, my Cherokicity. I grew to have great respect for Hastings and for another member of Turtle Island's Liar's Club, Sequoyah Guess, over the years as, of course, many, many other people had. The two of them will be so greatly missed. They were both incredible human beings and every bit the national treasures they were declared.

During that visit to the Quah² in 2000 for RTG, I won an award. Chief Chad Smith posed for pictures with those of us who had won awards for *The Cherokee Phoenix*. The accompanying article says, "Eight individuals of Cherokee descent received honors and awards at the Wordcraft Circle of Native Writers Returning the Gift IX Festival in Tahlequah, Okla., August 3–6." The Cherokee Nation won Sovereign Nation of the Year and was represented by Chief Smith. Robert "Bob" Conley won Writer of the Year for Creative-Prose-Fiction for *Cherokee Dragon* (2000) and *War Woman* (1999). Wes Studi won an award for narrating *Warrior in Two Worlds: Seneca Statesman Ely Parker.* Julia Coates won an award for a paper she wrote. Dan Agent won an award for his editorial work with the *Cherokee Advocate.* Valerie Red Horse won an award for *Naturally Native* for her directing. Craig Womack won the Academic Writing award for *Red on Red: Native American Literary Separatism.* Finally, I won an award: "Academic Professional Research Paper, Kimberly Roppolo (Cherokee, & Choctaw/Muscogee), for 'Towards a Tribal-Centered Reading of Native Literature: Using Indigenous Rhetoric(s) In/Stead of Literary Analysis'" ("Wordcraft Circle Awards Eight Tribal Descendants: Native American Writing Group Honors Cherokees," copyright Cherokee Nation, January 31, 2001).

No one interviewed me about my award. No one asked me how I wanted to identify in the newspaper or on my award. That was decided by others. It felt reaffirming of my family's oral tradition and my identity. I suspect, no, I *know*, that this has happened to others in this field who aren't enrolled. We tell people we are "part Indian," "have Cherokee ancestry," "have Native ancestry," and so forth, and they say, "There's no part Indian." Other people introduce you, other people write about you, other people give awards, and then individuals get accused of claiming they are enrolled when they never claimed that.

I certainly thought the *Phoenix* article was a sort of community recognition of descent, as was Chad's posing for pictures with us. I didn't think the nation would do those things lightly. As Principal Chief Smith said in his State of the Nation address later that year, "We now have a Cherokee newspaper that is charged with printing the news and the truth whether it's good, bad, or ugly" ("State of the Nation: Embrace and Carry Forward the Great Cherokee Legacy," from *Leadership Lessons from the Cherokee Nation: Learn from All I Observe.*)

As interrelated disciplines and an overlapping community, we—American Indian literary, rhetorical, and cultural studies, along with creative writing—are highly selective about which descendants we recognize and which we don't and either shun or "throw shade" at. For instance, in the last major identity witch hunt in the academy, we let someone whom none of us knew—a grad student whose position on her Indigenous heritage is just as tenuous as that of the person about whom she re-instigated an identity controversy—effectively lead the charge in making a senior scholar largely a persona non grata in the field. I'm not saying we should, as Native Studies scholars and creative writers, *reject* the young woman who stirred this up. She's doing good work on an important issue. So, too, has the senior scholar. In fact, the only other major scholar working on that same area had routinely cited the unenrolled scholar early on and now has only herself to cite for work on that very important area. To speak plainly, we seem fickle. We seem fickle and cliquish. We recognize and even award and laud some creative writers and scholars who are descendants or who lack federal recognition while vilifying, shunning, or bad-mouthing others.

I could name names, just as I could name some in other sections of this essay, but I won't.

I wouldn't want to draw attention to anyone else. After all, we're family. Just as I love my relatives in the field and Indian Country who are enrolled, I not only like, I love, the unenrolled descendants and non—federally recognized scholars and authors who are part of this family.

No one wants anyone to draw attention to themselves or each other. No one wants to anger the people in our community whom we know are policing identity, who have taken it upon themselves, for the past decade and a half or so, to determine who is Native enough for them and who is not. We try to stay on their good sides. We want to, anyway. After all, they also are family.

Since Tahlequah had been so welcoming of me, I came back. My best friend, Chelleye Crow, and I were good road trip buddies in those days. We both worked two teaching jobs. I had a toddler, a daughter with autism in middle school, and a teenaged son. She had two teenagers herself. Over about a five-year period, Chelleye and I (and often the girls) were in Oklahoma, going to ceremonial or social events, one or two weekends a month, in addition to being active in the urban Indian community in Central Texas. (It exists—Marley took first place in Tiny Tots at the Quanah Parker Powwow in Fort Worth the first time she competed). In addition to spending a lot of time in Watonga, El Reno, and Apache, going to NAC meetings and sweats, and time going to pow-wows with the Blackbear fam, Chelleye and I went to stomp dances out at Stokes and to Cherokee Holiday with someone else who is family to us both, Lisa Tiger. Namšem adopted Lisa as a daughter at a meeting I helped my brother Jacob Wruck sponsor for her. Though Lisa is enrolled Muscogee Creek and has Cherokee ancestry, ironically, she is my Cheyenne Auntie.

Chelleye and I went to Cherokee Holiday in 2001 and had a great time visiting folks we knew from Wordcraft Circle and from the pow-wow circuit. This is, of course, the period when Crystal Gayle, Rita Coolidge, Loretta Lynn, and all kinds of other stars were celebrated by CNO (Cherokee Nation of Oklahoma). In fact, I remember walking around out at the Heritage Center that year, chatting with Tommy Wildcat and "Uncle" Murv Jacob when we got to their booth. Tommy was telling a story about the year Crystal Gayle was a host at the Native American Music Awards (NAMA), and they were comparing hair length. Tommy won. In 2002 we went with Lisa.

At some point around that time, when Chelleye and I were together and Chad was present—like one of those many mornings we ate breakfast at the Restaurant of the Cherokees with Lee and Uncle Bob (Bob Conley—my uncle, like Murv, through Wordcraft, but also because I was friends with Bob's blood nephew Jack at Baylor)—Chad said something along the lines of "We know there's a lot of people out there with Cherokee ancestry who aren't enrolled. You're not going to be. However, you are more than welcome to come home to Tahlequah to events like this and learn about Cherokee culture and history."

I was assuming that he was referring to people whose situation was different from those he referred to in his 2000 speech, "State of the Nation: 'Sga Du Di': The Community Focus":

some who claim to be Cherokee have for their own political and self-ish gain attempted to undermine the Cherokee Nation and the legacy that our ancestors paid so dearly for. There are over 218 groups who in some form or fashion claim to be a Cherokee tribe or organization. In the last few months, two such groups claimed the legal history and assets of the Cherokee Nation. Let us be ever diligent to expose these charlatans and frauds.

This is more in line with some of what I wrote about in *Back to the Blanket:*

There are also people out there claiming to be Cherokee who may have no American Indian ancestry at all, causing quite a bit of con-sternation for those clearly identifiable as Cherokee. Mark Edwin Miller explores this subject thoroughly in *Claiming Tribal Identity: The Five Tribes and the Politics of Federal Acknowledgement.* While this may seem confusing or unimportant to non-Cherokees, for a number of years, CNO and ECBI have considered this to be a seri-ous problem. Some claiming to be Cherokee have misrepresented not only themselves, but also what it means to be Cherokee or of Cherokee descent to the outside world. Some incidents of this have been so offensive that CNO and ECBI issued 'Resolution *# 08–08'*: 'BE IT FURTHER RESOLVED that any individual who is not a member of a federally recognized Cherokee tribe, in academia or otherwise, is hereby discouraged from claiming to speak as a Cherokee, or on behalf of Cherokee citizens, or using claims of Cherokee heritage to advance his or her career or credentials.' (149)[3]

About his comments regarding people like me being welcome?
I just thought he meant what he said. It fit with my other interactions with him.
By now, it's clear that he didn't, and that I was clearly confused.

Some might think the structure of this essay is fragmented and that it reflects my feeling fragmented, like many disparate parts that can't add up to a whole anything. But I see the structure of this essay as faceted, like a bright ruby. Each facet shows you something slightly different, but they are all aspects of the same stone.

I don't feel lost. I don't feel confused about who I am. I am happily a mutt who makes her Chicot-self useful in Indian Country. As a number of enrolled tribal citizens around here said—about someone else, after that last big identity witch hunt hit a little close to home—"We have never made a habit of sending away useful people." My Comanche captor finds me useful. My Cheyenne relatives found me really useful for years until those darned Comanches stole me. *I* am an *excellent* resource. I am worth stealing.

(If you think I am making too much of being a Comanche captive, you *do not* know Comanches.)

But how can I conclude when I can't make conclusions? In regard to my multiple ancestries, unlike twenty years ago or even ten, I no longer actively search. I decided a long time ago to leave that up to God, Creator, Spirit . . . whichever box anyone tries to squeeze the Holy into. They're all too small. They're too small just like racial categories are too small.

In the meantime, I am going to keep on doing what I have been doing: living in Indian Country every day, not living in the ivory tower and visiting or simply maintaining a connection in name or in law; working for Indian people, our community, our students, our relatives, our church members, our NAC members; writing, both academically and creatively based on my own experiences and on what I have been taught; not claiming identity for any advantage; experiencing the same discrimination, through microaggressions and lack of equitable pay, that my tribally enrolled colleagues and other faculty of color experience; and living with the fact that my choice to value my Indigenous heritage, the choices I have made to stand for, by, and with Indian people, became an excuse for the powers that be to deny my child's rights and overlook their role in her death. From those little trenches I dug with my feet at the A.C. powwow grounds, to my journey to learn more about my heritage while in college, my choice to make this sojourn in Indian Country, and my struggle to survive my child's death, I just keep putting one foot in front of the other, moving forward on my own path, my own journey in life.

My walk is easier in some respects than those of others, like that of my grandmother and her sisters, who had a bumpier road in terms of hunger, poverty, and open discrimination, but it is a rocky trail in other ways.

When we lost Rachel, I meant to do a memorial for her at ou's spring powwow that next spring. According ourselves the traditional year of mourning, the timing would be right.

But the timing wasn't right for me. I just wasn't ready to dance.

In August of that year, however, Rance was asked to be head gourd dancer for a fundraiser for the Jacobson House Art Center, a local favorite of our American Indian community here in Norman. I had to get ready. Our community was asking something of us. Pulling together the resources and making the many items that would be part of our giveaway actually pulled me toward a semblance of healing. As Kim Shuck taught me when she came to comfort me and big-sister me through the toughest time in my life, I am never really going to be the same. No one can be. She did teach me, though, that some good does come out of this pain, as it always does.

This loss, the one no one wants, it leaves you able to cut straight through people's bull and able to walk off from anything that isn't worth your time. It leaves you knowing most of the things that people get worked up about aren't even important at all. You really have to watch your mouth when talking to others. You have to work to avoid minimizing their feelings. You are so detached from things that seemed significant before because your loss is so great nearly everything else seems trivial.

Giving away takes the focus off the self and off one's own pain. It allows you to thank properly those who helped you through life's greatest difficulty. Rance's being head gourd dancer gave me the inspiration I needed to be happy about something. Being happy isn't an easy thing. At first, it feels wrong. Things being remotely okay makes you feel guilty. But ways are ways for a reason. There is a reason not to dance, just like there is a reason to dance. Dancing means standing up on your feet. It means moving forward in unison, in rhythm, with your community. It means that it's okay to find comfort in living, in finding small joys.

There is a circle. I am part of it. Within it, I dance.

NOTES

1. "Ways" is the phrase American Indian people use to refer to accepted cultural practices.
2. Tahlequah.
3. The first version I saw of this document was listed as "Resolution #14–08."

BIBLIOGRAPHY

Joint Council of the Cherokee Nation and the Eastern Band of Cherokee Indians, "Resolution #14–08," April 2008. No longer available. Last accessed July 29, 2012.

Miller, Mark Edwin. *Claiming Tribal Identity: The Five Tribes and the Politics of Federal Acknowledgement.* (Norman: University of Oklahoma Press, 2013).

Smith, Chad Corntassel. *Leadership Lessons from the Cherokee Nation: Learn from All I Observe.* (New York: McGraw-Hill, 2013). See also *Learning: O'Reilly,* https://learning.oreilly.com/library/view/leadership-lessons-from/9780071808835/h4_93.html.

Wieser, Kimberly G. *Back to the Blanket: Recovered Rhetorics and Literacies in Native American Studies.* (Norman: University of Oklahoma Press, 2017).

"Wordcraft Circle Awards Eight Tribal Descendants: Native American Writing Group Honors Cherokees," *Cherokee Phoenix and Indian Advocate,* January 31, 2001, 33. *ProQuest,* https://search-proquest-com.ezproxy.lib.ou.edu/docview/362534857?accountid=12964.

Denise Dotson Low

Buffalo Heads in Diners

Remnant Populations

I just finished writing a poem called "Buffalo Heads in Diners," a description of all the trophy buffalo heads found in hunting lodges, hotels, and restaurants in my home region of the southern plains—specifically, the Flint Hills of Kansas. Many of these taxidermy specimens are mementos of the wars on Native peoples, who depended on buffalo for sustenance. The U.S. government engineered the extermination of buffalo, along with Indigenous people. When I see wall-mounted buffalo heads, they recall genocide and ecocide.

Some of my family came to the plains from remnant communities of Lenape–Munsee Delawares in New Jersey and Ohio, where forest buffalo were not uncommon. These were my maternal grandfather's people, and I explain some of their complicated lives, and mine, in *The Turtle's Beating Heart: One Family's Story of Lenape Survival*. Some of my forbears came from mixed Irish-Indigenous backgrounds in Kentucky and Virginia—the Thomas Foreman lineage and William Dotsons. These were my paternal grandfather's people. Both of my grandmothers were of German–British Isles heritage. All were immigrants to the Plains and displaced many of the original inhabitants. Delawares had been travelers, traders, and guides in previous places, so they continued this strategy for survival. Some of my relatives were desperate European-American settlers who benefited from others' tragedies. I live with a mixed legacy, and that confusion, anger, and guilt.

My mother's father lived the life of an Indigenous man. He was born on the Plains and as a teen, he became connected to the Kansas City Delaware and Wyandot community (Kansas side—not Missouri, where miscegenation laws lasted until the 1960s). Grandfather and his family had black hair and brown skin, so they were targets of random attacks and the Ku Klux Klan. They moved from the plains to Kansas City, to the Turtle Hill area, the land Lenapes sold to Wyandots. This remnant community stayed in Kansas City after the main bodies of those tribes were removed to Indian Territory (now Oklahoma). In school he met my grandmother, married, and began a life of wandering. He worked the docks of Oakland in California, meat-packing houses of Kansas City, orchards of Oregon, railyards of the Santa Fe, and other odds and ends. He ended up near his birth town in central Kansas.

Kansas Delawares were not enrolled tribal members in my grandfather's time. Some Delawares remained in Kansas because they were too ill to move to Oklahoma, and some moved to Oklahoma but died before the U.S. government's 1906 roll. Some wanted to keep their Kansas River bottomland, some were married to whites, some were orphans, and none trusted the government. Delawares had been removed over six times before Oklahoma. The federal government has withdrawn recognition of the Delaware Tribe of Indians in Bartlesville twice, and they were most recently reinstated in 2009. Delawares are never sure when political movements might end their status.

Delaware tribal members I have met have been generous in recognizing my status as a Delaware descendant (from Ohio and New Jersey). People from other Nations and non-Native people do not always understand the fragmented histories of the diverse Delaware bands and nations. As the first Atlantic Coast people to treaty with a European government, in Manhattan, Delawares have struggled since the 1500s to retain land and culture. Government-recognized Delaware nations are now in Oklahoma (two), Wisconsin, and Canada. The Ramapough Lenapes of New Jersey have sued for federal recognition for decades, but casino owners oppose them.

I was chastised once by a non-Delaware for crowdsourcing a research project about Delaware culture, because of my lack of citizenship, but Delawares I know, some enrolled and some not, were encouraging. They have supported my writings about Delaware experience, especially my memoir, and they encourage me to do more. This community support is most important to me.

In southeastern Kansas, I grew up around Delawares, Choctaws, and Cherokees, some enrolled and most not. As a child, that was my normal. We were exiles among exiles, although we had no idea. Our mixed-up peer group included some Union-sympathizing Choctaws, Cherokees, and Cherokee Freedmen descendants—all of whose grandparents had fled Indian Territory during the Civil War. Benny Smith, a descendant of Ketoowah leader Redbird Smith, told me his great-grandfather is buried in Leroy, Kansas, where he died. This was a Union refugee camp for tribal people who fled Confederate compatriots, just north of the Indian Territory (Oklahoma) border. My great-great-grandfather, also a Union veteran of Cherokee heritage, was a Methodist minister in Humboldt, thirty miles away. Not many people are aware of the Indian Home Guard of Kansas and its role in keeping the Civil War from spreading west of Arkansas, Oklahoma, and Kansas. This is a complicated history, not conforming to mainstream narratives and all of it poorly documented.

I am not a person who can debate effectively. I get too emotional and sputter. Linda Hogan has written eloquently about the silencing she felt when she was young, which echoes my experience:

> As a young person coming from silences of both family and history, I had little of the language I needed to put a human life together. I was inarticulate to voice it, therefore to know it, even from within. I had an unnamed grief not only my own.

I am not enrolled yet live with historical trauma, which affects every aspect of my life, including this unshakeable muteness. I have learned to write, but I still cannot speak effectively, so this page speaks in my place.

In the current push for enrollment status as a binary affirmative for Native identity, a two-caste system, I exist in a gray, interstitial space. From this perspective, I understand how authentically Native people, through blood and upbringing, are cast off, like my Menominee husband's disenfranchised grandchildren: their father is enrolled Lakota and their mother is enrolled Menominee. Their combined blood quantum of almost half does not meet tribal citizenship's mathematical calculations. Instead of our finding a way to bring future generations into affiliation with their parent tribes, children like these are subtracted from the community. This negation of identity is repeated endlessly across the United States and keeps Indigenous census numbers low, so the political base is limited. The winners of this calculation are the U.S. government and bigots. Indian sports mascots are a national shame, but the rule-by-majority mainstream does not take 1 percent of the population seriously.

No one wants a fraudulent group replacing Indigenous citizens who have tribal values, but in some cases they already have. Some tribal governments disenroll their own people for bigger business profits and political gain. These people are as fake as New Agers with dreamcatchers on their dashboards.

Many Indigenous writers not enrolled in a specific nation have devoted their lives to advancing Native ideas in the twentieth century and into the twenty-first They include Ai, Paula Gunn Allen, Carter Revard, Jack Forbes, Maurice Kenny, Daniel David Moses, Louis Owens, Barney Bush, Ralph Salisbury, and more. Some important writers were not enrolled, and then their tribes gained federal recognition, like Greg Sarris and Karenne Wood. Some come from families that were enrolled and then dismissed for political reasons or greater per-capita profits. All these writers have done essential work during difficult times. Respect for elders is one of the most fundamental survival values of Native peoples.

When I taught at Haskell Indian Junior College, now Haskell Indian Nations University, for twenty-five years, I could spot students who had not grown up in traditional homes. They interrupted others. They disrespected quieter students and interacted with me as a dispenser of grades. They ridiculed people not like themselves. Their classroom behavior was adapted to a public space of detachment and competition, not a tribal community. Most often, by the end of the semester, they fit in better. Being Indigenous is a matter of experience, values, behavior, spirit and, yes, community.

Buffalo, or *bison bison*, may be a stereotyped Native symbol to some, but to me a relationship with this indigenous compatriot of the plains is personal. When I was tiny, I remember my family taking me to see the buffalo in the town zoo, in the 1950s, as an important part of my education. Most small towns in Kansas had such small collections of indigenous animals. In the 1970s I took my children to see the family group of bison in our town's zoo. Now I see buffalo in herds throughout my state, free ranging and not in zoo pens. My husband and I support ranchers by including buffalo regularly in our diets. We are grateful for their survival.

Buffalo teach many lessons—how to value family, how to live in a severe climate, how to protect the vulnerable, how to defend their ground. Elders have taught me how much there is to learn from all the beings who share our cosmos, like buffalo. Elders teach how everyone has a place, and mine is on the grasslands where the Milky Way spirals like spring winds. There I am close to all the grandparents who continue to live in my blood.

BUFFALO HEADS IN DINERS

A scattered herd dots the plains, detached heads,
mostly singletons, old bulls used to being alone.

White people shelter them under diner roofs
or hunting lodge trophy rooms with spot-lit niches.

Tongues cut out, they cannot speak their history
and with fake eyes they can only listen to bar stories

like the Colby cowboy who practices rodeo roping
with quick-twisting buffalos much swifter than steers.

Custer's Last Stand still gets repeated and Indian War
battles. Less and less often beer drinkers mention

huge bones left by hunters and collected for fertilizer.
Heaped piles were final remnants of the bodies.

Their descendants look more like beefalo but still
roam hills, some herded by part-Indian cowboys.

They circle when coyotes howl and turn tails
into north winds during blizzards. So they survive.

Linda Rodriguez

And Thus the Tribes Diminish

> Americans invented Indians and forced Indians to live with the consequences of this invention.
> —Richard White, *The Middle Ground*

Every time the news media presents us with the portrait of a new con artist pretending to be a citizen of a tribal nation (often equipped with fake tribal citizenship cards) to climb an institutional structure and gain power and income or to gain media coverage and fame, I cringe. I cringe because I know that this person's acts will be destructive not only to the tribe they are falsely claiming to represent and to the Native community at large but also to people like me who are not citizens of the tribe but have tribal lineage and connection.

Such Pretendians will find their worst enemies to be unpapered people like me who love the tribal nations they are connected to and hate the damage done by such people to the tribes' valid claims of sovereignty. They are despised by tribal citizens, but they are truly anathema to unpapered people like me, who often suffer in the backwash of damage that they leave behind.

I am unpapered. I am not a citizen of the Cherokee Nation of Oklahoma, even though I consider the Cherokee Nation of Oklahoma my people, even though the Cherokee Nation of Oklahoma has honored me in the past, even though a number of people in the Cherokee Nation of Oklahoma recognize me and accept me as having a familial connection with the tribe. I know there are many people who are citizens of the Cherokee Nation or of other tribes who would consider me a Pretendian, and I don't blame them for this, even though I believe it is a misperception. It doesn't matter that I have never claimed citizenship in the Cherokee Nation of Oklahoma (for the very good reason that I am not a citizen of the Cherokee Nation) or that I always try to explain about tribal sovereignty and the importance of the rights of the individual nations to determine who is and who is not a citizen of their nation. I understand all too well where these people who mistrust me are coming from.

Every time a new story hits about some white person who has no trace of Native lineage or connection, yet masquerades as a false member of a Native tribe to get money, a higher academic position, or some other kind of professional or financial success, I cringe. I know that, along with all the damage this person has done to the tribe that they lied about being a member of and to the larger Native community—academic, literary, or artistic—they will bring the wrath of the identity hardliners down upon people like me, who are connected with our tribes and involved with our tribes and trying our best to contribute what we can to our tribal communities, as well as to the larger Native communities to which we belong.

I have grown up knowing I was Cherokee, hearing the language and stories from my grandmother when I was small and trying all my life to learn all I could about my people. Since I've been an adult, however, I have been very careful about how I identify myself. What makes me pause are two concerns: my desire to never undercut the Cherokee Nation's existence as an independent, sovereign nation (so I always clarify that I am not an enrolled citizen and try to educate about the concept of "sovereignty") and the thought of the identity hardliners, who will call me "wannabe" or "Pretendian." I have made a point of never trying to use my Cherokee heritage to gain money or awards or jobs, but instead trying to give back to the community in every way that I could, as well as learning as much about my heritage as I possibly could and connecting with my tribe and my relations, so that they could have a central position in my life.

Gadugi is a Cherokee word that has several meanings, one of which is "we all work together to lift each other up." Another meaning is similar to the motto of the Three Musketeers, "one for all and all for one." A meaning that my grandmother always stressed to me was "we take care of each other" or "take care of your family or your community." John F. Kennedy would have recognized *Gadugi*, for it basically has a similar meaning to his great command to "ask not what your country can do for you but what you can do for your country." *Gadugi* is a central tenet of Cherokee culture and belief. It has been a central tenet of my life—and certainly of the way I have dealt with the Cherokee Nation.

I think, to anyone who is Cherokee, *Gadugi* becomes an important rule for living. This is critical, because more of the Pretendians who do damage claim to be Cherokee than just about any other tribe. And yet, none of them seems to be aware of this central belief of Cherokee culture. If they were, they could not do the things that they do, exploiting the nation they call their own for their own benefit as they uncaringly inflict damage on it.

There are always identity hardliners and, as I have said, I certainly don't blame them, considering the many problems that these Pretendians, or false claimants, cause or worsen. They tend to go in cycles, however. There is a small core of identity hardliners, who don't want to recognize anyone as Native unless they carry an enrollment card for a federally recognized tribe, and sometimes not even then. This core will swell in size immediately following publicity around a major Pretendian, who has caused damage to a tribe or a native community. Eventually, the core will shrink again and return to normal. Since the Elizabeth Warren debacle, we have been in a major swelling period that shows no signs of abating, however.

The problem with taking a hard line on Native identity is that eventually, if this line is followed, there will be no more Natives whatsoever.

"My so-called Membership Identification Card (CDIB) states that my total blood is ¼ in the Cheyenne/Arapaho Tribes. . . . My husband was ⅞ Cheyenne and Arapaho, making our children ¹⁵⁄₁₆. The mathematics gets a little complicated, but suffice it to say that unless my grandchildren marry an enrolled Cheyenne and Arapaho, the family line will become extinct with them."[1] —Dr. Henrietta Mann

There are no ways to talk about blood quantum in Native tribal languages, because it was not a consideration among Natives before the European invasion. Belonging mattered. Relations mattered. Who you were related to and whether you belonged or not had nothing to do with European concepts of "blood." In the past, Natives were more interested in how to take care of each other and in their responsibilities to other members of their community.

"THE GOVERNMENT IS WATCHING YOUR BLOOD"

When my cousin and I asked a fluent Blackfoot speaker if there was a way to say "blood quantum" in our language, he created a term that means "the government is watching your blood."
    —Sterling HolyWhiteMountain

Who measures the blood,
that copper-smelling carrier of oxygen
and food for the very life of the organism?
Are those with Indigenous heritage
"bred" like pedigreed poodles
that we have to have our papers?
Of course, they do use those "breed" terms
for us who are "mixed-blood"—
"half-breed," "quarter-blood."
What fraction of German,
Italian, Swedish, Czech are you?

Why is no one,
especially the U.S. government,
interested in that?

What does the blood of the tribes
look like? smell like?
How does it differ from
all that other human blood?
Or is it even human blood?
Are you trying to show how non-human we are?
Some sort of semi-close relation,
perhaps, such as orangutans,
or at least another form
of sentience, like dolphins,
which we praise and kill by the thousands "accidentally"
(or incidentally) each year?

Perhaps the focus on blood
is due to all the People's blood
poured out to fertilize
the invaders' croplands
through all the long years.
No longer do they use smallpox-tainted blankets
or dashing long-haired cavalry officers
or missionary schools
that dislocate forever
children's thumbs for running
from a place where their language
and culture are forbidden.
No longer do they openly dissolve tribes
and hand out their sacred lands
in bits and pieces to individuals,
declaring them no longer Indian,
and handing over the biggest,

most valuable parts to rich settlers.
No longer do they pack us up
and move us off to some city
in another part of the country from our land,
saying "Assimilate!
You need to become one of us."

Now,
they slowly (and sometimes not so slowly)
decimate and destroy the tribes
with their blood quantum rule.
If you are half-Cree,
you can't also be half Comanche,
and if you marry someone half-Osage,
who can't also be Potawatomie,
your child will have four tribes to choose from,
but she must choose one
and be a "quarter-blood."
Her grandchildren will not be allowed
to claim a tribe, at all,
and thus the tribes diminish
without the bad publicity of gunsmoke.

Blood quantum is a zero-sum game for the Native community. "[An "Indian" under federal law] should be one-half. . . . What we are trying to do is get rid of the Indian problem rather than add to it."[2]

This blood quantum requirement adds another layer to the thorny dilemma of Native identity. Each sovereign nation (there are 574, though most people only know the most famous names among them—Cherokee, Navajo, Sioux) sets its own tribal standards for citizenship within the nation. Most use this settler standard of blood quantum. Some use a standard of lineage that is closer to traditional Native ways of determining tribal citizenship, but government regulations require that the lineage be computed based on U.S. government lists that were put together by settlers over a century ago with varying degrees of input from the actual members of the tribe. Consequently, with both methods, each nation has members who may not qualify for official citizenship, as required by the government, but are seen by the nation itself as a familial connection to the tribe.

This paper lineage, which tribes such as the Cherokee use (designed and controlled by the federal government, not the tribes) is not as ultimately reductive as blood quantum, but the Baby Veronica case that was recently tried before the Supreme Court showed us that there are powerful contingents of people in this country and this government who want to convert the lineage requirements of such tribes to blood quantum, to erase these nations with their sovereignty and treaty rights. All these Native identity concerns and tools of pedigree are another form of warfare against the tribes, another way of wiping out the tribes and rendering them extinct, to take the last remnants of their lands and the resources within them.

It's all about the land. When it comes to the United States and Native peoples, no matter how much they talk about their appreciation of us, no matter how much they express their concern for us and their desire to help us, it's always all about the land. This is why they will not allow tribal recognition to Native Hawaiians. This is why they will not allow tribal recognition to Indigenous Pacific Islanders. This is why the Supreme Court has proclaimed that "there is no longer any Indian country in Alaska," a state that contains 220 Native sovereign nations. It's always all about the land and the way that land can be used to create profit for powerful settlers.

For centuries, the U.S. government—and the wealthy people within the United States who control it—have wanted to destroy all traces of the sovereign Native nations that were here when the Europeans first landed on this continent. They have been quite vocal about their aims in the past. I offer a tiny sampling of quotations from speeches, letters, newspaper articles, and other documents to be easily found in a search through American history. The researcher will easily find many, many more quotations from Franklin, Jefferson, Monroe, Lincoln, Theodore

Roosevelt, and many other founding fathers and presidents, as well as governors and other civic leaders, all speaking of the need to wipe out the Indigenous population of the continent.

The only good Indians I ever saw were dead.[3]

Damn any man who sympathizes with Indians. I have come to kill Indians, and believe it is right and honorable to use any means under God's heaven to kill Indians! Scalps are what we are after . . . I long to be wading in gore![4]

Civilization or death to all American savages.[5]

Discovery gave an exclusive right to extinguish the Indian title of occupancy, either by purchase or by conquest.[6]

The immediate objectives are the total destruction and devastation of their settlements and the capture of as many prisoners of every age and sex as possible. It will be essential to ruin their crops in the ground and prevent their planting more.[7]

These government officials and wealthy Americans have gotten much better, in current times, about not openly expressing their desire to make us extinct although, in recent years, among the extremist right-wing Republicans who have taken power over that party, such restraint seems to have vanished and, once again, we have people openly expressing their desire to get rid of us.

Is it any wonder that, under such circumstances, the government wants to use paperwork and red tape to wipe out the tribes? It's much quieter, draws less bad publicity, and is actually more effective than the diseases (including smallpox-infected blankets handed out as "gifts"), the burning of fields and harvests, the enslaving of entire populations, the massacres, the many Trails of Tears and Long Walks, the imprisoning in boarding schools, the seizing of children and adopting them outside of the tribes, the deliberate destruction of culture and ceremony and languages through state and federal laws, the prisoner-of-war camps called reservations, the dissolution of tribes, the relocations to urban centers, and the many other methods this country has used in its centuries of attempting to destroy the independent sovereign nations that occupied this land when the settlers' ancestors first arrived.

Now that they think they have almost wiped us out, we Indians are "exotic" to them, and the exotic is always desirable with just an enjoyable frisson of fear. But wouldn't their own ancestral culture seem exotic to them now?

In modern times, so many people never encounter a Native person in their lives that the concept of American Indian or Native American has become wrapped in a vague cloud of nostalgic mythology. Many people actually think we have died out completely. We are in the position of the passenger pigeons. The European settlers couldn't wait to kill them by the millions but now lament their disappearance. Or, more likely, we resemble the wolf in their imaginations. Settlers worked ferociously to wipe out wolves until, believing them extinct, they began to long for the imaginary wolf and reestablished them. Now, those who live near areas where they were reestablished hate the real wolves and hunt them down with the same viciousness as in past centuries. In the areas where few Native peoples are found today, settlers long for the image of the noble Indian that their ancestors cruelly drove from the land on which these descendants now live. In the areas where Native nations are still abundant and known, the settler community's attitude toward the surviving descendants leads toward the organized violence at Standing Rock and the thousands of Native women and girls who have been murdered and kidnapped without outcry or investigation.

It is not hyperbole to make these comparisons between Native people and animals when speaking of the settler imagination. In the United States, Native people are under the jurisdiction of the Bureau of Indian Affairs in the U. S. Department of the Interior, which deals with federal land, natural resources, and wildlife and game. Because of this way of thinking about and dealing with Native citizens, we are the only people in this country who must have CDIB cards issued by the federal government listing our certified degree of Indian blood—or pedigree, as with dogs and horses.

Why are the settlers and this government of settlers so obsessed with our blood and the fractions of inheritance therein? What is it that makes the content of our blood of such strong interest to them as opposed to the content of the blood of immigrants from Italy, Ireland, Germany, Poland, England, Asia, and just about every other country in the world? We know the land is the major reason for the government, but what is it that makes all the settlers who live around us so obsessed with the makeup of our "blood"? All of us have had the experience of our settler neighbors and colleagues—especially complete, absolute strangers—asking us, "how much Indian are you?", "You don't look Indian—what's your percentage of Indian blood?" What is this obsession with the percentages of our lineage? Why do they care how mixed we are when they are usually so very mixed themselves?

Mixed-blood = contaminated blood, is that it? They have to trace the amount by which we've contaminated the European blood we also contain? Why isn't a Czech-English-German-Norwegian a mixed-blood? Sounds pretty mixed to me. Maybe that's the problem—that the Anglo-European mainstream doesn't value and study its own mix of heritages. Playwright Daniel Chacon once had a Native character say, "White people don't appreciate what's good about their own culture, so how can they appreciate what's good in other people's cultures?" After many years of living embedded within their culture, I must say that this statement seems valid.

Settler culture, within which we all must live, is locked in a downward spiral that was determined by their first actions on this continent and has continued devolving ever since, until we are faced with the possibility of a human-created mass extinction event that will include all human life. Indigenous people have been at the forefront of the modern movement to oppose that mass destruction of environment and species and remain there today. That battle has become critical to the survival of human beings. As one of the great thinkers of the twentieth century, James Baldwin, once said, "The people who think of themselves as White have the choice of becoming human or irrelevant."[8]

Perhaps it's that they don't value the ancestors, don't believe in the spirits, and cut themselves off from what could be nurturing, rich, and creative for them, because they erase the past and live for the bottom line or the next quarter. That lack of care for the ancestors, the past, and the natural world around them, that willingness to cut off the real world of trees and insects and birds and dirt with headphones, cell phones, iPads, and Bluetooths is really a way of denying their humanity, that they are an integral part of the fabric of life and nature around them. To live in a world and be unaware of the hawks and golden eagles above you or the hummingbirds at the shrub outside your door or the raccoon or possum crossing your yard in the dark or the jewel-green snake living in your grass, to live so oblivious to life is a sign of deep fear and damage.

It would be a great mistake on the part of the sovereign Native nations if we allow this "blood" obsession of settler culture and government to destroy us, trying to turn us all into "people who think of themselves as White." Within the nations, we know that we are human and thus related and connected to all other humans and all other living beings on this planet and that we have an obligation to care for all these beings to whom we are related. We know that we cannot ride roughshod over the plants and animals and other humans who share this world with us without facing terrible consequences. We know that we are all connected within the Creator's web of life, and what we do to others, whether humans or other beings, reverberates throughout this web—and if our actions are at all destructive, we can wreck it.

As usual, the settler government–power structure wants to erase the tribes, so they can take the last of the land and destroy it in their constant search for ever more profit. This time, they are using blood quantum identity concerns and regulations as their tool rather than overt physical attacks and massacres, and it may well be their most successful strategy yet. Still, we must be strong and stand against these efforts as our ancestors once did. When I think of what the results will be if we don't, I think of a chilling photo exhibit at Haskell Indian Nations University, where my son teaches.

Haskell is the only four-year, degree-granting, all-Native university in the country and struggled to become that after its birth as one of the most horrendous of the Indian boarding schools, where Native children were sent after being torn from their families by soldiers and federal agents and where they were given severe physical punishments for speaking their Native languages and trying to escape. The founder of Haskell was a great believer in the saying, "Kill the Indian to save the man," which became the motto of all the boarding schools.

This exhibit, which took place in the Haskell Cultural Center in 2015, contained photos of the student body at Haskell in the 1920s, when it was still an Indian boarding school. The photos had digital stamps over the faces of the students who would not be allowed to attend Haskell if they were applying now, because of tribes not being federally recognized or blood quantum or other restrictive constraints on tribal membership. Approximately one-fourth of the photos had stamps over the faces. That many people who were actually forced into an Indian boarding school, with all its attendant horrors, would be denied the right to be called Native today—and that right would be denied to all their descendants. This is just one example of what the federally generated identity requirements of today have already done to the membership of the tribes.

It does not require an occult gift of prophecy to foresee what will happen if things continue as they are going in the matter of Native and tribal identity. The whole process is designed to erase the tribes, with their inconvenient possession of land and treaty rights, and that process is remarkably efficient and silent. Whether the tribal nations will examine this process—and what they decide to do if they do examine it—will determine whether there are any tribal nations left in this country in another 50–100 years.

NOTES

1. Dr. Henrietta Mann, "Foreword," *The Great Vanishing Act: Blood Quantum and the Future of Native Nations*, ed. Kathleen Ratteree and Norbert Hill (Wheat Ridge CO: Fulcrum Publishing, 2017)
2. Sen. Burton K. Wheeler, Chairman of the Senate Committee on Indian Affairs [*To Grant to Indians Living Under Federal Tutelage the Freedom to Organize for Purposes of Local Self-Government and Economic Enterprise:*

Hearing on S. 2755 and S. 3645 Before the S. Comm. on Indian Affairs, 73d Cong. 100 (1934)].

3. Gen. Phil Sheridan, Conference with Fifty Indian Chiefs, Fort Cobb OK, 1869.

4. Rev. John M. Chivington, cofounder of the University of Denver and leader of the Sand Creek Massacre. See Dee Brown, *Bury My Heart at Wounded Knee* (New York: Macmillan, 1970), 86–87.

5. Maj. James Norris, *Journal of Major James Norris* (Wyoming Valley PA), 1779.

6. Chief Justice John Marshall, Johnson & Graham's Lessee v. McIntosh, 21 US 543 (1823).

7. Gen. George Washington, *Orders to Major General John Sullivan* (Middlebrook CT), 1779. Those captured prisoners of every age and sex were then sold as slaves to the West Indies.

8. "Preface," *Notes of a Native Son* (Boston: Beacon Press, 1955).

SOURCE ACKNOWLEDGMENTS

Kim Shuck's essay features poetry from her book *Exile Heart*, That Painted Horse Press, 2021.

Terra Trevor's essay appears under a different title, and in a slightly different form, in *We Who Walk the Seven Ways* by Terra Trevor, University of Nebraska Press, 2023, and was originally featured in *News from Native California* 29, No. 2 (Winter 2015–16).

Kimberly Wieser's essay includes work from her book *Back to the Blanket: Recovered Rhetorics and Literacies in Native American Studies* (Norman: University of Oklahoma Press, 2017).

Geary Hobson's "The Animals' Ball Game" was first published in *Studies in American Indian Literatures* 25, No. 4 (Winter 2013).

CONTRIBUTORS

Of mixed descent, including Cherokee, **Kimberly L. Becker** is author of five poetry collections: *Words Facing East* and *The Dividings* (WordTech Editions), *The Bed Book* and *Bringing Back the Fire* (Spuyten Duyvil), and *Flight* (MadHat Press). Her poems appear widely in journals and anthologies, including *Indigenous Message on Water*; *Women Write Resistance: Poets Resist Gender Violence*; and *Tending the Fire: Native Voices and Portraits*. Her work has been nominated for a Pushcart. She has received grants from Maryland, New Jersey, and North Carolina and has been awarded residencies at Hambidge, Weymouth, and Wildacres. Kimberly has read at Busboys and Poets, The National Museum of the American Indian (Washington DC), Split This Rock, and Wordfest. She has served as mentor for PEN America's Prison Writing and AWP's Writer to Writer programs. She currently lives in North Dakota but calls the mountains of North Carolina home. www.kimberlylbecker.com

Author, illustrator, recovering teacher, poet, **Linda Boyden** has written three and illustrated two picture books. Her first teen novel, *Twitch* from Red Planet Books, will be coming out soon (https://redplanetbooksncomics .com). She belongs to the Society of Children's Book Writers and Illustrators, Wordcraft Circle of Native Writers and Storytellers, and Redding Writers Forum. "I write. I color in or outside the lines. Poetry gives voice to our silent songs." http://www.lindaboyden.com

Abigail Chabitnoy is a Koniag descendant and member of the Tangirnaq Native Village in Kodiak. She is the author of *In the Current Where Drowning Is Beautiful* (forthcoming, Wesleyan, 2022) and *How to Dress a Fish* (Wesleyan, 2019), shortlisted for the 2020 International Griffin Prize for Poetry and winner of the 2020 Colorado Book Award, and author of the

231

linocut illustrated chapbook *Converging Lines of Light* (Flower Press, 2021). She was a 2021 Peter Taylor Fellow at Kenyon Writers Workshop and the recipient of the 2020 Witter Bynner Native Poet Residency at Elsewhere Studios in Paonia, Colorado. Her poems have appeared in *Hayden's Ferry Review, Boston Review, Tin House, Gulf Coast, LitHub*, and *Red Ink*, among others. She currently teaches at the Institute of American Indian Arts and is an assistant professor at the University of Massachusetts at Amherst. Abigail holds a BA in anthropology and English from Saint Vincent College and an MFA in creative writing from Colorado State University. Find her at salmonfisherpoet.com

Diane Glancy is member #1255 of the First Families of the Cherokee Nation. She is professor emerita at Macalester College in St. Paul, Minnesota. She has taught in the low-residency MFA program at Carlow University in Pittsburgh for five years. Glancy's latest books are *Island of the Innocent: A Consideration of the Book of Job*, 2020, *A Line of Driftwood: The Ada Blackjack Story*, 2021, and *Home Is the Road: Wandering the Land, Shaping the Spirit*, 2022. Among her awards are two National Endowment for the Arts Fellowships, an American Book Award, a Minnesota Book Award, an Oklahoma Book Award, a Pablo Neruda Prize for Poetry, and a Lifetime Achievement Award from the Native Writers' Circle of the Americas. Glancy lives in north central Texas, where many tribes camped: Apache, Comanche, Wichita, Waco, Kiowa. In Kansas she lives on land of Shawnee, Pawnee, Osage, Kansa, Kickapoo, and Wyandot. Their silenced voices are part of her work. www.dianeglancy.com

Geary Hobson is a retired professor of English at the University of Oklahoma. His areas of teaching and scholarship are Native American literature, American literature and American Studies, and creative writing. He taught at the University of Oklahoma from 1988 to 2016. He is the author of a novel, *The Last of the Ofos* (2000), and a book of poetry, *Deer Hunting and Other Poems* (1990); the editor of an anthology, *The Remembered Earth: An Anthology of Contemporary Native American Literature* (1979); and the coeditor of *The People Who Stayed: Southeastern Indian Writing After Removal* (2010) and a collection of short stories, *Plain of Jars and Other Stories* (2011). He has published poems, fiction, critical essays, and book reviews in more than one hundred magazines and anthologies.

Of Cherokee and Quapaw/Chickasaw ancestry, he has been involved in Native literary studies and teaching more than forty years, as well as with several national Native American literary organizations. In 2003 he received the Lifetime Achievement Award from the Native Writers' Circle of the Americas. He lives in Norman, Oklahoma.

Michele Leonard is an enrolled citizen of the Shinnecock Nation. Leonard is an educator, historian, activist, and author published in the *Wellesley Magazine* and a contributing writer to *Native America in the 20th Century: An Encyclopedia*. Leonard received her MFA in creative nonfiction from Carlow University and her BA in political science from Wellesley College. She is currently working on her memoir. Leonard resides on Shinnecock Territory, Southampton NY.

Denise Low, Kansas Poet Laureate 2007–9, is winner of a Red Mountain Press Award for *Shadow Light*. Other recent books are a memoir, *The Turtle's Beating Heart: One Family's Story of Lenape Survival* (University of Nebraska Press), and *A Casino Bestiary: Poems* (Spartan Press). In 2020 she joined the founding board of Indigenous Nations Poets. Low has an MFA from Wichita State University and a PhD from the University of Kansas. She lives in northern California. www.deniselow.net

Carter Meland is a White Earth Anishinaabe descendant, writer, bicycle rider, bigfoot meditator, and assistant professor of American Indian studies at the University of Minnesota, Duluth. His novel *Stories for a Lost Child* was a finalist for the 2018 Minnesota Book Awards, and he is currently working on a creative nonfiction book, *Strange Spirits: A Memoir in Monsters*, which explores the power of Anishinaabe storytelling as a way to make sense of fractured family identities and our fractured relationship to our living environments.

Deborah A. Miranda is an enrolled member of the Ohlone-Costanoan Esselen Nation, with Santa Ynez Chumash ancestry. Her mixed-genre book *Bad Indians: A Tribal Memoir* received the PEN-Oakland Josephine Miles Literary Award, was awarded a Gold Medal from the Independent Publishers Association, and was shortlisted for the William Saroyan Literary Award. She is also the author of four poetry collections: *Indian Cartography, The Zen of La Llorona, Raised by Humans,* and *Altar for Broken Things*. She is coeditor of *Sovereign Erotics: A Collection of Two-Spirit Literature*.

Jeanetta Calhoun Mish's most recent books are *What I Learned at the War*, a poetry collection (West End Press, 2016) and *Oklahomeland: Essays* (Lamar University Press, 2015). Her 2009 poetry collection, *Work Is Love Made Visible* (West End Press), won an Oklahoma Book Award, a Wrangler Award, and the WILLA Award from Women Writing the West. Dr. Mish is a faculty mentor for the Red Earth Creative Writing MFA at Oklahoma City University, where she teaches criticism and theory, poetics, poetry craft, and research for writers. She served as Oklahoma State Poet Laureate from 2017 to 2020 and, in 2019, she was awarded a Poets Laureate Fellowship from the Academy of American Poets.

Craig Santos Perez is an indigenous Chamorro writer from the Pacific Island of Guam. He is the coeditor of six anthologies and the author of five poetry collections and the monograph *Navigating Chamoru Poetry: Indigeneity, Aesthetics, and Decolonization* (2022). He is a professor in the English department at the University of Hawaii at Manoa.

Trevino L. Brings Plenty, MFA, is an enrolled member of the Cheyenne River Sioux Reservation. Brings Plenty is a filmmaker, musician, and poet. His work has appeared in *Yellow Medicine Review*, *Red Ink Magazine*, *World Literature Today*, *Plume*, *Prairie Schooner*, *North American Review*, *Waxwing*, *Poetry*, and *New Poets of Native Nations*. Brings Plenty's books are *Wakpá Wanáği Ghost River* (2015) and *Real Indian Junk Jewelry* (2012).

Ron Querry is a member of the Choctaw Nation of Oklahoma. Querry served in the U.S. Marine Corps during the 1960s and earned his PhD in American Studies from the University of New Mexico in 1975. Querry has taught and lectured at colleges and universities across the United States and served as writer-in-residence at the University of Oklahoma and the Amerind Foundation in Arizona. In addition, he has taught and lectured at the Seminar in Native American Studies at Comune di Spello, Provincia di Prugia, Italy; at Étonnants Voyageurs, Festival International du Livre, Saint-Malo, France; and at a chapter of PEN International in Mexico. In addition to being an accomplished author and scholar, Querry has also served as the associate dean of education at the Penitentiary of New Mexico and as a rancher, horseshoer, and racing official for the American Quarter Horse Association.

Linda Rodriguez's novels—*Every Hidden Fear, Every Broken Trust, Every Last Secret*—books of poetry—*Skin Hunger, Heart's Migration, Dark Sister: Poems*—and multiple edited anthologies have received critical recognition and awards, such as St. Martin's Press/Malice Domestic Best First Novel, International Latino Book Award, Latina Book Club Best Book, Midwest Voices & Visions, and Ragdale and Macondo fellowships. She is past chair of AWP Indigenous Writers Caucus, a founding board member of Latino Writers Collective and The Writers Place, and a member of Native Writers' Circle of the Americas and Kansas City Cherokee Community. http://lindarodriguezwrites.blogspot.com.

Steve Russell (1947–2021), an enrolled member of the Cherokee Nation of Oklahoma, was a poet and journalist, as well as a former Oklahoma judge and Associate Professor Emeritus of criminal justice at Indiana University Bloomington. He published six books, including *Sequoyah Rising: Problems in Post-Colonial Tribal Governance* (Carolina Academic Press, 2010), and numerous journal articles and book chapters. His first book of poetry, *Wicked Dew*, won the First Book Award from the Native Writers' Circle of the Americas, and his poems were published in multiple anthologies and journals. The Native American Journalists Association twice recognized his work as the year's best op-ed.

Steve passed away while this book was in the pipeline to publication. Having written and researched in the field of Native identity for so many years, he was thrilled that this book was to be published and that he could be a part of it. We are so disappointed that he was not able to live to see the final publication, yet grateful that his insightful essay could be a part of this book.

Kim Shuck is the seventh Poet Laureate Emerita of San Francisco. Shuck is working on her ninth solo book, which is with the publisher and awaiting an ISBN, and her tenth solo book, which is more a leaf pile of poems. Judging by the piles of volumes around her desk, Kim's writing is widely anthologized and journaled and the book artifact is not yet a dead form. In 2019 she was awarded an inaugural National Laureate Fellowship by the Academy of American Poets. Shuck likes hiding in her writing fort with a pint mug of hot tea and some good yarn.

Terra Trevor is a contributor to fifteen books and the author of two memoirs, including *We Who Walk the Seven Ways* (University of Nebraska Press). Her work and portrait are featured in *Tending the Fire: Native Voices and Portraits* (University of New Mexico Press). Her work is also included in *Children of the Dragonfly: Native American Voices on Child Custody and Education* (University of Arizona Press), *The People Who Stayed: Southeastern Indian Writing After Removal* (University of Oklahoma Press), and numerous other books, anthologies, and literary journals. She lives with her family on the Central California Coast and in the mountains in Northern California.

Dr. Kimberly Wieser is associate chair and an associate professor of English at the University of Oklahoma as well as affiliated Native Studies and Environmental Studies faculty. Her book *Back to the Blanket: Recovered Rhetorics and Literacies in American Indian Studies*—winner of the NWCA First Books Award for Prose in 2004—was published by the University of Oklahoma Press in 2017. Wieser is one of the cochairs for the American Indian Caucus for NCTE/CCCC and serves as a managing editor at *Constellations: A Cultural Rhetorics Publishing Space*. She directs the activities of the Native Writers' Circle of the Americas at the University of Oklahoma.

CPSIA information can be obtained
at www.ICGtesting.com
Printed in the USA
LVHW040024100323
741067LV00004B/15